Romania

Bulgaria

●Tirana

Albania

Istanbul

Ankara

Greece

Turkey

Athens

Crete

Cypru

Mediterranean Sea

Derna

Bardia

Benghazi   Tobruk

Gulf
of Sirte

Cyrenaica

Marsa
Matruh

Alexandria

El Alamein

El Agheila

Cairo

Egypt

PRAISE FOR UNLEASH THE DOGS OF WAR

After years of working with Colonel Bernd Horn I have a profound respect for his intellectual rigour, which he brought to his writing as well as his profession as an infantry officer. He is the classic case of a soldier-scholar, excelling at both, and his latest book, Unleash the Dogs of War, is yet another example. His meticulous research and expert narrative bring an exciting and very dramatic period of the Second World War into laser focus. Anyone interested in the global conflict, the North African campaign or special forces during the conflict will find this book of immense value and interest. It is very well worth the read.

- Lieutenant-General (ret) The Honourable Roméo Dallaire

Colonel (retired) Bernd Horn, an avid scholar of special operations history, is one of the best informed and most prolific writers on the topic. His most recent work, Unleash the Dogs of War, is testimony to his expertise. The extensive research, gripping narrative and extensive insight make for an outstanding study of the special forces' contribution to the war in North Africa in World War II, specifically Operation Crusader. This is a must read for any enthusiast of special operations forces and World War II.

- Lieutenant-General (retired) D. Michael Day

Dr. Bernd Horn delivers yet again! His knowledge of Second World War special operations is unparalleled as his latest book demonstrates. As usual, the narrative is crisp, supported by considerable research, and reads like a real-life Tom Clancy novel. Unleash the Dogs of War is a must-read for those interested in World War II and special forces. I cannot recommend this book strongly enough.

- Dr. James Kiras

Unleash the Dogs of War is the latest published work from Colonel Bernd Horn, who is recognized as an expert in special operations forces. This work, focusing on the creation and utilization of special forces in the North African campaign in the Second World War, is an exemplary marriage of thorough research, military insight and a compelling narrative.

- Colonel Howard G. Coombs, OMM, CD, PhD

...Dr. Bernd Horn's latest book, Unleash the Dogs of War is a definite must! Bernd uses his award-winning academic expertise, combined with his exemplary military experience to produce a meticulously researched and well-crafted history of the contribution of special forces to the North African campaign.

- Dr. Emily Spencer

France

Italy

● Rome

Tyrrhenian Sea

Algiers

● Tunis

Sicily

Malta

Tunisia

Algeria

Tripoli ●

Sirt

**Mediterranean
Theatre of Operations**

Tripolitania

Libya

UNLEASH THE DOGS OF WAR:

SECRET MISSIONS IN SUPPORT OF OPERATION CRUSADER

DOUBLE✝DAGGER

UNLEASH THE DOGS OF WAR:

SECRET MISSIONS IN SUPPORT OF OPERATION CRUSADER

Colonel (Retired) Bernd Horn

DOUBLE‡DAGGER

Library and Archives Canada Cataloguing in Publication
Horn, Bern. author
Unleash the Dogs of War / Bernd Horn

Issued in print and electronic formats.
ISBN: 978-1-990644-33-7 (soft cover)
ISBN: 978-1-990644-34-4 (e-book)

Editor: Norm Matheis
Cover design: Battlefield Design/Paul Hewitt
Interior Design: Winston A. Prescott
Maps: Adrienne Popke

Double Dagger Books Ltd
Toronto, Ontario, Canada
www.doubledagger.ca

TABLE OF CONTENTS

GLOSSARY OF ABBREVIATIONS

AFV	Armoured Fighting Vehicle(s)
AG	Adjutant General
BBC	British Broadcasting Company
Bde	Brigade
BEF	British Expeditionary Force
BGS	Brigadier General Staff
CIGS	Chief of the Imperial General Staff
C-in-C	Commander-in-Chief
CO	Commanding Officer
COC	Combined Operations Command
COS	Chiefs of Staff Committee
DCGS	Deputy Chief of the General Staff
DCO	Director Combined Operations
DHH	Directorate of History and Heritage
DND	Department of National Defence
DOL	Director of Opposed Landing
DZ	Drop Zone
FFI	French Forces of the Interior
G(R)	British Military Intelligence
Gal	Gallon
Gdsn	Guardsman
GHQ	General Headquarters
GOC	General Officer Commanding
HM	His Majesty
HMS	His Majesty's Ship
HQ	Headquarters
LAC	Library and Archives Canada
LG	Landing Ground
LoC	Lines-of-Communication
LRDG	Long Range Desert Group
LRPU	Long Range Patrol Unit
Lt	Lieutenant

Me	Messerschmitt
ME	Middle East
MEF	Middle East Force
MoD	Ministry of Defence
MT	Motor Transport
NA	National Archives
NCO	Non-Commissioned Officer
OKH	Oberkommando des Heeres
OKW	Oberkommando der Wehrmacht
OR	Other Rank [enlisted personnel]
OSS	Office of Strategic Services
Q or QM	Quartermaster
RAF	Royal Air Force
Recce	Reconnaissance
RN	Royal Navy
RTU	Return to Unit
RV	Rendezvous
SAAF	South African Air Force
SAS	Special Air Service
SBS	Special Boat Service
SD	Sicherheitsdienst (SS Security Service or SD)
SEAC	South East Asia Command
SF	Special Forces
SHAEF	Supreme Headquarters Allied Expeditionary Force
SOE	Special Operations Executive
SS	Special Service
TTPs	Tactics, Techniques and Procedures
W/T	Wireless Telegraphy
WDF	Western Desert Force
WO	War Office
WWI	World War I
WWII	World War II

INTRODUCTION

THE CURRENT POPULARITY, if not love affair, with Special Forces (SF), also often referred to as Special Operations Forces (SOF), is a relatively recent phenomenon. Modern special forces were created during World War II (WWII) mainly as a function of weakness. Defined at the time as specially selected and trained individuals that were given special missions, special forces were actually despised by most commanders and the conventional military at large. Critics considered them an embarrassment to real soldiering; thugs and assassins who thumbed their noses at military protocol and convention.

The condemnation of special forces was legion. The fact that SF organizations seemingly exploded during the early phase of the war resulted from two realities. First, in the dark and gloomy days of WWII, Britain and her few allies had their backs against the wall. With their equipment, weapons and doctrine smoldering on the beaches of Dunkirk, and the threat of imminent invasion of England hanging over their heads, they had little capacity to strike back at Germany other than strategic bombing and naval blockade.

The second reason SF were able to exist and expand was the relentless push by the new combative prime minister, Winston Churchill. Unlike his conventional military commanders, who were content with focusing on the defence of the island and rebuilding and retraining the army, he was not. Churchill wanted an offensive capability that would allow Britain and the allies to strike back at the Nazis. He knew this would be a tonic for the public and, equally important, it would rob the Germans of the initiative.

As a result, and only possible because of the strong insistence of Churchill and a few military commanders who were willing to entertain the concept, a litany of special forces organizations sprang up who proved vital to the war effort. They sustained the offensive spirit and public morale during the early dark days of the war until the conventional military regained its strength and ability to prosecute the war. Moreover, the special forces organizations were instrumental in forcing the Allies' enemies to expend resources on defence and countermeasures Furthermore, they became instrumental in intelligence gathering, as well as destroying Axis forces, equipment and infrastructure, all of which aided the Allied cause and chipped away at the Axis war effort.

Nowhere were special forces efforts more evident than in North Africa in the early years of the war. Powerful benefactors who believed in their potential bucked convention and allowed for the creation and growth of special forces capability within the Middle East Command, a British Army Command established prior to WWII in Egypt. The Long Range Desert Group (LRDG) was the earliest of the units to be deployed and quickly proved its worth. The renowned Special Air Service (SAS) was another legendary unit born in the desert. Although not providing an immediate return on investment on its first mission, the SAS quickly matured and became a major distraction to the Germans. During this period Commandos and the Special Boat Service (SBS) also participated in operations in the North African and Mediterranean theatres of operations.

Similar to the advent of special forces overall, in North Africa their existence was also a function of the Allies' overall weakness. The summer of 1940 was a dark period for Britain and the Allied cause. The German juggernaut had swept over Western Europe and seemed poised to launch an invasion of England itself. In North Africa, the British hold on the strategically vital Suez Canal also seemed tenuous with Germany's ally Italy having a massive superiority in troops, artillery and armour in neighbouring Cyrenaica and Tripolitania (Italian Libya). Matters seemed to get worse when Italy informed Britain on 10 June 1940 that they would be at a state of war the following day, June 11, 1940. Consequently, an Italian offensive was launched in September.

The feared Italian offensive fizzled. British forces quickly counter-attacked and reversed the enemy gains, pushing the Italians out of Libya. The remarkable victory buoyed spirits in London and provided the Allies with a ray of hope. It was not to last long. The intervention of Hitler with the dispatch of Generalleutnant Erwin Rommel and his vaunted Afrika Korps in February 1941, not only prevented an Axis disaster, but quickly reversed the tables. In fact, Rommel, quickly labelled the "Desert Fox," pushed the Allied troops back to the Egyptian frontier. However, the German offensive failed to capture the key port of Tobruk, which was now under siege.

An incensed Prime Minister Churchill pressed his Commander-In-

Chief Middle East Command, General Claude Auchinleck, to raise the siege of Tobruk and push the Germans out of Cyrenaica. The directive was laden with challenge. Accordingly, Auchinleck decided to hedge his chances of success by authorizing a number of secret missions by special forces, including the surveillance of German movements, raids to destroy German air bases deep behind their own lines and an audacious attempt to kill Rommel himself. As such, he unleashed the dogs of war, hoping that they would tilt the battle in his favour.

CHAPTER 1
THE SANDS OF VICTORY

DESPITE THE LOOMING THREAT of a German invasion hanging over England in the summer of 1940, Britain's hold on the Middle East and Africa seemed secure enough. The British assessment of Italian strongman Benito Mussolini's intent at the time was that Italy would remain on the defensive on both the Libyan and Ethiopian fronts, as well as in the Aegean Sea.[1] Initially, little attention was spent on that distant theatre while the homeland was at risk.

Nonetheless, and not surprisingly, Britain's major concern in the region was Egypt and the strategic Suez Canal, which was considered a vital link in Imperial Defence. In fact, Prime Minister Winston Churchill sent a "Most Secret" directive to his War Cabinet "that all ranks recognize that the life and honour of Great Britain depends upon the successful defense of Egypt."[2] Two days later he wrote to Major-General Hastings Lionel "Pug" Ismay, his chief-of-staff, as well as to Lord Beaverbrook and senior Admiralty officials. "The failure to win the battle of Egypt," he counselled, "would be a disaster of the first magnitude in England." He was greatly concerned it would affect how the Americans viewed them as well. "It might well determine the decisions of Turkey, Spain and Vichy," he added.[3]

Although Egypt had gained independence in 1922, Britain ensured to put in place mandates that allowed it to retain a presence and influence in Egypt, as well as in the Sudan, Palestine and Transjordan. In fact, a 1936 Anglo-Egyptian Treaty gave Britain the right to garrison 10,000 troops in Egypt, as well as the ability to reinforce in time of war.[4]

To control its North African and Middle-Eastern interests, Britain had maintained three separate Army Commands, specifically Egypt, the Sudan, and Palestine-Transjordan. It also maintained army garrisons at the naval and air bases in Malta and Aden. To streamline the various command structures, British Army Headquarters (HQ) created Middle East Command in August 1939. The Commander-in-Chief (C-in-C) of Middle East Command was now accountable for all troops in Egypt, the Sudan, Palestine-Transjordan and Cyprus. The C-in-C was also responsible for preparing operational plans for those troops, as well as for forces in Iraq, Aden, British Somaliland and the Persian Gulf. The extensive responsibilities for the Commander were enormous, as was the span of control.

British Army HQ appointed Lieutenant-General Sir Archibald Wavell, a veteran of both the Boer War and the First World War, as C-in-C of the new Command. Wavell was extremely intelligent, but also very reserved. He personified strength and resiliency, and to many represented the epitome of the British professional soldier. He was daring, risk accepting and if he sensed a chance for success, despite the seemingly difficult position he found himself in, would seize the opportunity and take offensive action. Importantly, Wavell liked the unorthodox.

However, Wavell was in a very difficult position. His biggest concern was his lack of fighting troops. The war in Europe was obviously the primary focus and the British Expeditionary Force (BEF) was concentrated

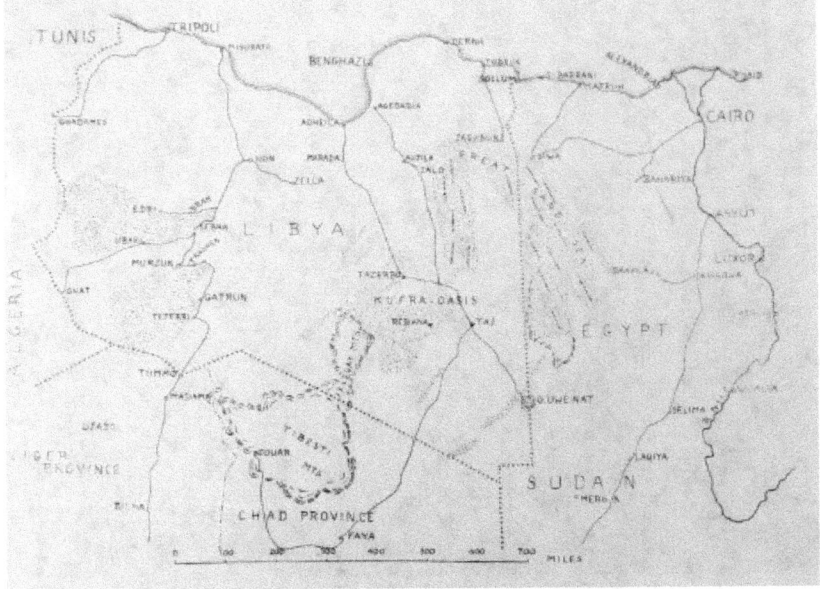

Map 1 – North African Theatre of Operations (National Archives)

in France. Nonetheless, Wavell was promised some reinforcements from throughout the Empire. He was to receive an infantry brigade from India, a British infantry battalion from the Far East, 700 men from Rhodesia, an infantry brigade and some divisional troops from Australia, as well as an infantry brigade from New Zealand.

Adding to his manpower woes, Wavell also had to contend with an extremely formidable battlespace that extended from the eastern port of Alexandria in Egypt, west 3,000 kilometres to Tripoli in Libya. To the south of the coastal belt was the immense vastness of the Sahara Desert. West of Alexandria the terrain along the coast was an unforgiving undulating rocky plain that rose sharply to a 183-metre escarpment cutting 16 kilometres inland. This escarpment stretched south to the Qattara Depression, where it fell hundreds of metres into a vast salt plain. The escarpment met the sea at the small village of Sollum on the coast at the border of Egypt and Libya. Dauntingly, there was only a single coastal road that ran through the escarpment at the vitally strategic Halfaya Pass. At this point, the escarpment ran west, virtually bordering the Mediterranean Sea, passing through the ports of Bardia and Tobruk. Further west at Derna, the ridge rose dramatically to a height of 610 metres. Here, the rugged terrain marked the beginning of the Jebel Akhdar, an immense stretch of wooded hills and

Sollum. "Destruction of an Army" (War Office (WO), Ministry of Information (MoI), 1941.)

ravines that stretched 320 kilometres to the western extreme boundary of Cyrenaica at the city of Benghazi.

Prime Minister Churchill described, "Even before the war a magnificent road had been made along the coast from the main base at Tripoli, through Tripolitania, Cyrenaica and Libya to the Egyptian frontier." He noted that the Italians created huge magazines along the route, particularly at Benghazi, Derna, Tobruk, Bardia and Sollum. "The length of this road was over a thousand miles," he observed, "and all these swarming Italian garrisons and supply depots were strung along it like beads on a string."[5]

The farthest forward British defended position was the railhead at Mersa Matruh. "There was a good road westward to Sidi Barrani," revealed Churchill, "but thence to the frontier at Sollum there was no road capable of maintaining any considerable strength for long near the frontier."[6]

In Britain's favour, the Egyptian Army's equipment was based on the British pattern. In many cases it was more plentiful and in better condition than that of most British units stationed in the Middle East. The Egyptian Army itself was responsible for patrols on the western frontier, reporting any hostile movements and contributing troops to the Mersa Matruh outpost. It was also responsible for a small mobile force that guarded the desert southwest of Cairo, as well as detachments for the protection of the railway between Alexandria and Mersa Matruh. Finally, it was also accountable for providing units for the defence of Alexandria and the provision of nine battalions for anti-sabotage duties. The duties were extensive, and the British harboured no false expectations. They realized that all of these tasks would strain the Egyptian Army to its breaking point.[7]

In spite of the focus on Europe, in February 1940, Wavell began to receive his reinforcements from the Commonwealth. The first units from the promised Australian and New Zealand divisions began to arrive. On June 8, 1940, Major-General Richard O'Connor, a veteran of the First World War, who also served under Major-General J.F.C. Fuller and his experimental brigade in the interwar years (1921-1924) and did tours of duty in India, Egypt and Palestine in the 1930s, arrived in Egypt from Palestine with the HQ of the 6th Division. He assumed command of all troops in the Western Desert and on June 17, his 6th Division HQ was re-designated HQ Western Desert Force.[8]

Importantly, in August of 1940 the British War Cabinet decided to reinforce the Middle East. By the end of 1940, Wavell was to receive 117,000 troops, including 70,000 British soldiers from England. Despite the promised infusion of troops, the reality was that Wavell had only approximately 36,000 men in Egypt and these were not well-equipped. By July 1940, not a single formation was complete. The 7th Armoured

A patrol of Gladiator fighter aircraft return to their desert airstrip. (WO, MoI, 1941.)

Division had only four tank regiments. In fact, it had only 65 Cruiser tanks instead of the war establishment of 220 (and not all of these had their proper armament). The 4th Indian Division was short a brigade and artillery. His New Zealand Division amounted to only a brigade group and was very short of equipment. Wavell had only 12 Bofors anti-aircraft guns in-country, located at Alexandria. There was a general shortage of anti-tank guns and ammunition of all kinds.[9]

In Palestine Wavell had 27,500 troops but of these only one was a British brigade and only two of the battalions were equipped and trained. These units were earmarked for duty in Iraq or for internal security in Palestine. In East Africa the British had a single brigade in the Sudan, two East African brigades in Kenya and just 1,500 local troops in British Somaliland.[10]

Adding to Wavell's woes was another major problem. At the outbreak of war there were only five permanent airfields in Egypt, three in Palestine, two in Iraq, two in Malta, one in the Sudan, two at Aden and one in Kenya. None could accommodate more than a single squadron of aircraft. With the exception of one airfield in Egypt and one in Palestine, all were unsuitable for the operation of modern bombers or fighters.[11] However that was a minor issue since Wavell had no modern fighters or long-range bombers under his control. He was also short of aircraft spares and other equipment. What he did have were 75 Gloster Gladiator biplane fighters and 96 Bristol Blenheim Mk.I and Bombay bombers.[12]

Facing Wavell was, on paper at any rate, a formidable foe. Marshal Rodolfo Graziani, known as the "Butcher of Ethiopia" because of his time as Italian governor there in 1936-37 and his ruthless counter-insurgency operations, had approximately 250,000 men in Cyrenaica and Tripolitania while His Royal Highness Prince Amedeo of Savoy, Duke of Aosta, Viceroy of Ethiopia and Supreme Commander of all armed forces in Italian East Africa (i.e. Sudan, Ethiopia) had a total of 300,000 Italian and native soldiers.[13] As of June 1940, Italy in North Africa had 84 Modern bombers (S.79 and S.81), the majority, (56) which were Ghibli bombers and 144 fighters (Fiat CR.32 or CR.42). In East Africa, the Italians held another 36 modern bombers and 114 colonial-type, 45 modern fighters and 18 others for a total of 213 aircraft.[14]

Notwithstanding the numerical Italian superiority, the British believed that the Italians would remain on the sidelines until there was a clear outcome to the war. This optimistic view however, was soon to change. On April 11, 1940, a distraught Mussolini confided to Count Galeazzo Ciano, his Foreign Minister as well as his son-in-law:

The King would like us to enter [the war] only to gather up the broken dishes. I hope that they will not break them over our heads before that. And then it is humiliating to remain with our hands folded while others write history. It matters little who wins. To make a people great it is necessary to send them to battle even if you have to kick them in the pants. This is what I shall do.[15]

Approximately a month later, on May 13, 1940, several days after the convincing German breakthrough at Sedan, France, *Il Duce*[16] proclaimed:

Some months ago, I said that the Allies had lost the victory. Today I tell you that they have lost the war. We Italians are already sufficiently dishonored. Any delay is inconceivable. We have no time to lose. Within a month I shall declare war. I shall attack France and England in the air and on the sea.[17][18]

Now assured of German victory, on June 10, 1940 the Italian Fascist dictator declared war on England. With a large military presence in North

Africa, it seemed only a matter of time before Mussolini would decide to expand his empire.

Although too weak to go onto the offensive, Wavell did not opt to relegate himself to a static defence either. Wavell had once written, "No formula or set of principles can assure success. There are no recognized openings or gambits in war, as there are in chess; each strategical problem must be dealt with on its merits as a problem in geography, in time and space calculations in organization, and, above all, in human nature."[19] This is exactly the tack that he took.

Wavell directed an aggressive patrolling and raiding policy to both gain better situational awareness with regards to the Italian disposition and intentions, as well as to attempt to keep them off-balance. He struck immediately. Wavell ordered his troops to push beyond the frontier border, which was marked by a six-foot-high, thirty-foot wide barbed-wire entanglement that ran southwards for two hundred miles from the coast along the Libyan-Egyptian border. The Italians had built the "Wire" in the 1930s as a means of controlling their disaffected native population. It now had numerous gaps that were used for sorties against Italian outposts and convoys.

Within twenty-four hours of the Italians declaring war, the 11th Hussars crossed the frontier and captured Italian prisoners that had not yet heard they were at war. The following night, on June 12, 1940, the

A British armoured car passes through the Italian wire marking the border. (WO, MoI, 1941.)

7th Hussars with a company of the 60th Rifles seized Forts Capuzzo and Maddalena, which were well inside Italian territory. Additionally, British patrols preyed on the Bardia-Tobruk highway. Italian vehicles, whether soft-skinned or armoured were taken under fire and prisoners captured. The British quickly gained the initiative and ascendency over operations.

The forays were hugely successful. Major-General H. Rowan-Robinson later wrote:

> *From the very outset of the Libyan campaigns, when Graziani was threatening Egypt with a quarter of a million invaders, small detachments from the 7th Armoured Division raided for almost incredible distances into hostile territory with the objects of obtaining information, cutting pipe-lines, intercepting convoys, laying ambushes and harassing the enemy so as to keep him constantly and unhappily on the alert. Only two days after the outbreak of war, for instance, a patrol of the 11th Hussars captured a party of two Italian officers and fifty-nine other ranks. Again, two days later small mobile detachments seized Forts Capuzzo and Maddalena with 220 prisoners. Raiders even rushed Italian advanced GHQ [General Headquarters] and caused considerable damage. In this way our light forces dominated the open country and compelled the enemy to expend an appreciable proportion of his force on protective wiring and strong escorts to convoys. They also created a legend on both sides of the frontier which sent our morale soaring and decreased that of our opponents to a like extent.*[20]

Churchill also chimed in on the success of the raids. He described the 11th Hussars as "lean, bronzed, desert-hardened and full mechanized."[21] His assessment was not wrong. The regiment had armoured cars since 1928 and they had been deployed in the Middle East since 1934. They had trained specifically in the Western desert for the previous five years and understood the hardships and nuances of desert warfare and fieldcraft as well as any other fighting force in the region.

Wavell's strategy was immensely effective. His armoured forays, as well patrols conducted by the Long Range Patrol Unit (LRPU), later renamed the Long Range Desert Group (LRDG), forced the Italians to reinforce remote outposts, which put a burden on transport and fuel consumption. They now also had to provide escorts for their supply convoys. All told, Wavell's strategy placed a major burden on the Italian logistic capability. It also created a crippling sense of doubt in the 58-year-old mind of Marshal Graziani, who now began to question the reports of Wavell's shortages of

LRDG patrol in the vast expanse of the Libyan desert. (WO, MoI,1941.)

manpower and equipment.

Up until the Italian offensive, Wavell's aggressive offensive strategy resulted in approximately 3,500 Italian casualties, 700 prisoners taken and destruction of a large number of tanks, guns and trucks at the cost of about 150 British casualties.[22] However, due to Italian numerical superiority, Wavell knew that once Graziani advanced, he would need to stop the harassing campaign. This approach was essential to conserve Allied fighting strength, which would be needed as a covering force to blunt any Italian advance on Mersa Matruh. The constant harassing attacks were also very taxing on the tracked armoured vehicles, requiring them to be maintained and ready for the defensive battles that lay ahead.

Another of Wavell's difficulties was his lack of support. Despite his offensive actions, Churchill was not a fan of his. Wavell's resistance to some of Churchill's "directives," and his inability to clearly articulate his disagreements with the Prime Minister led to a bitter relationship between the two men.[23] Churchill penned in his memoirs, "While not in full agreement with General Wavell's use of resources at his disposal, I thought it best to leave him in command."[24] And so it seemed Wavell faced a potentially difficult tenure, with a numerically impressive opponent, a harsh environment, and an unfriendly superior. However, although the comparable force numbers were discouraging, the Italian position in North Africa was largely an illusion. Count Ciano revealed in his diary, "The *Duce* is very much dissatisfied with it all [armed forces] ... He has the feeling, and he is right, that beyond appearances, which are more or less carefully put on, there is little underneath...There has been a good deal of bluffing in the military sphere."[25] Mussolini's instincts were correct. Italy was totally unprepared for war. In early April 1940, by their own admission they had only enough war stock for a few months of conflict.[26]

Even more important, their commander had no stomach for an offensive. Count Ciano confided to his diary on August 3, 1940, "Graziani, after having emptied Italy in order to supply Libya, does not feel that he is prepared to attack Egypt, mainly because of the heat. He intends to postpone the operation until spring. I do not yet know the reactions of the *Duce*, but I predict that they will be violent."[27] Five days later, Ciano recorded, "Graziani has come to see me. He talks about the attack on Egypt as a very serious undertaking, and says that our present preparations are far from perfect...he would rather not attack at all, or at any rate, not for two or three months."[28] Graziani did in fact express his opposition to the order to mount an offensive, warning, "We move towards a defeat which, in the desert, must inevitably develop into a rapid and total disaster."[29]

Regardless of Graziani's posturing and delaying, the decision was taken from his hands. On August 10, 1940, Mussolini ordered Graziani to take to the offensive. "It is not a question of aiming for Alexandria, nor even Sollum," Mussolini pleaded, "I am only asking that you attack the British forces facing you."[30]

Although the die had been cast, Marshal Graziani dragged out his order. Nonetheless, the British were expecting the worst. On August 22nd, the War Cabinet issued a general directive to the Commander-in-Chief Middle East. It warned, "a major invasion of Egypt from Libya must be expected at any time now. It is necessary, therefore, to assemble and deploy the largest possible army upon and towards the western frontier. All political and administrative considerations must be set in proper subordination to this."[31]

In addition, the War Cabinet outlined redeployments of British forces in theatre, as well as reinforcements that were being prepared to ship to North Africa.[32] With the instructions in place, the War Cabinet asserted, "by the 1st October at the latest a force of 39 Battalions together with armoured forces; a total of about 56,000 men and 212 guns [would be available]. This is exclusive of internal security troops." The War Cabinet added, "It is hoped that the armoured brigade from England of three Regiments of tanks will be passed through the Mediterranean by the Admiralty. If this is impossible their arrival round the Cape may be counted upon by the 3rd October."[33]

The concern of course was the defence of the Suez Canal. "The aim must be to destroy Italian forces in the desert," the War Cabinet stressed, "but as a last resort the line of the Delta must be held at all costs."[34] The War Cabinet delved into tactical matters giving Wavell unneeded direction. It ordered that the Mersa Matruh position be expeditiously and completely fortified; the sector held by three Egyptian battalions replaced by three British battalions; and that the road from Sollum to Mersa Matruh, and more importantly the tarmacadam road from Mersa Matruh to Alexandria, be rendered impassable and mined.

The War Cabinet seemingly was incredibly pessimistic of the chances of stopping the projected Italian offensive. They anticipated an enemy "advance of great force," led by strong armoured thrust. Its directive predicted an Italian breakthrough:

> *The final line of defence must be prepared from Alexandria along the edge of the cultivated zone and irrigation canals of the Delta. For this purpose the strongest concrete and sandbag works and pill-boxes should be built or completed from the sea to the cultivated zone and the main irrigation canal. The pipe-line forward of this front should be extended as fast as possible. The Delta zone is the most effective obstacle to tanks of all kinds, and can be lightly held by sandbag works to give protection to Egypt and form a very strong extended flank for the Alexandria front. A broad strip, four or five miles wide, should if feasible be inundated from the flood waters of the Nile, controlled at Assouan. Amid or behind this belt a series of strong posts, supported when possible by artillery, should be constructed. In this posture then the army of the Delta will finally defeat the Italian invasion.*[35]

The War Cabinet was not alone in its concern. Britain as a nation feared the Italian offensive because they so vastly outnumbered them in troops and equipment both in North Africa and in East Africa. In fact, *The Times* declared in their September 25, 1940 edition, "We are face to face in Africa with a menace almost as vital as the threat of invasion of our own country."[36] The fear was an "energetic" Italian advance from Libya to the Sudan!

Their assessment could not have been more wrong. The Italians were floundering. On September 9th, Marshal Graziani requested another month delay in mounting his offensive. Mussolini sternly replied that if he did not attack on the following Monday he would be replaced. As a result, Graziani acquiesced.

Ciano revealed to his diary, "Never, has a military operation been undertaken so much against the will of the commanders."[37]

And so, Marshal Graziani began to concentrate his forces. The hammer ominously seemed about to fall. He had approximately 215,000 men in North Africa. His 5th Army was deployed in Tripolitania (northwestern Libya) and the 10th Army, consisting of ten divisions, stationed in Cyrenaica and along the Egyptian frontier. However, the troops were poorly trained, morale was low and with the exception of three Blackshirt Divisions, there was no appetite for war.[38]

The actual advance into Egypt began on September 13, 1940, when the Italians commenced a heavy artillery bombardment and moved a strong force to the recently evacuated town of Sollum. The attack was no surprise. The British had anticipated the assault for three days as the Italian preparations were blatantly obvious. The Italian preparations had in fact triggered the British withdrawal from the frontier in conjunction with General Wavell's plan. To hinder the enemy, British engineers had mined roads, salted water supplies and torn up the coastal road, which would be a vital supply link for the Italians.[39]

The attack prompted jubilation in Rome. On September 17, 1940, Ciano recorded in his diary, "Mussolini is radiant with joy. He has taken the entire responsibility of the offensive on his shoulders, and he is proud that he was right."[40] By end month, the elation had not diminished. Ciano revealed, "I find him [*Duce*] in good humour and very happy that Italy could score in Egypt a success which affords her the glory she has sought in vain for three centuries."[41]

The opening of the Italian offensive, however, foreshadowed a dismal forecast for success. Once the dust and smoke from the bombardment had settled, the front-line British troops witnessed a remarkable spectacle. The attacking Italian forces were arrayed in parade ground formation. As one British colonel described, "In front were motor-cyclists in precise formation from flank to flank and front to rear; behind them were light tanks and many rows of mechanical vehicles." British artillery promptly cut a swath through "the generous targets presented to them."[42]

Churchill described:

Our forces fell back before these great numbers taking every opportunity to harass the enemy, whose movements seemed erratic and indecisive. Graziani afterwards explained that at the last moment he decided to change his plan of an enveloping desert movement and "concentrate all my forces on the left to make a lightning movement along the coast to Sidi Barrani." Accordingly, the great Italian mass moved slowly forward along the coast road by two parallel tracks. They attacked in waves of infantry carried in lorries, sent forward in fifties. The Coldstream Guards fell back skilfully at their convenience from Sollum to successive positions for four days, inflicting severe punishment as they went.[43]

The War Cabinet "Weekly Resume" also provided a narrative of the battle noting the slow but methodical advance. They observed, "it is evident that the Italian advance will not be allowed to over-reach the lines of communication and is being conducted with considerable caution."[44]

By the evening of 15 September, two enemy columns had reached the outskirts of Buq Buq, which prompted the British rearguard stationed there to withdraw to Sidi Barrani. By 16 September the Italians had reached Sidi Barrani. However, the cost was high. The British casualties were forty killed and wounded, while the Italian casualties were estimated at ten times that amount, as well as the loss of 150 vehicles. Once ensconced at Sidi Barani, the Italians dug in and made no further offensive moves.[45] The British assessed:

The position which had taken shape by the end of September could only appear to be an established base and not the temporary arrest of a force on the march. From these camps repeated reconnaissance raids were made. Groups of lorries with artillery and infantry would issue from their protection and would only retire when the watchful British patrols of light tanks and well-hidden artillery had shown

British Forward Observation Post watching shells falling on the Halfaya Pass. (WO, MoI, 1941.)

their teeth. The front had become static.[46]

Far from British fears, the slow and ponderous offensive fizzled. Marshal Graziani made no effort to advance beyond the line of encampments he had begun to consolidate after his three-day offensive. Quite simply, Graziani was reluctant to push forward. He believed he needed at least until November "to complete our logistic preparation which is the only real definitive guarantee of success." He added, "If our supply lines should not function well, we would have to retreat. And in the desert retreat is equivalent to a rout."[47] On October 16th, Graziani provided a reassessment asserting that he needed at least two months to prepare to renew the offensive.[48]

Significantly, Wavell's aggressive posture unnerved Graziani. British patrols of the 7th Armoured Division dominated the desert outside the Italian garrisons. The LRDG was marauding in his rear areas and the Royal Air Force (RAF) dominated the skies and prevented his air force from conducting aerial reconnaissance to try and establish British strength and dispositions. In the interim, the German Fuehrer, Adolf Hitler, met with Mussolini on October 4, 1940 to discuss North Africa. Hitler offered mechanized and specialist troops. Mussolini demurred, stating he did not require them for the move on Mersa Matruh, but he did acknowledge he would require heavy tanks, armoured cars and dive-bombers for the advance on Alexandria. Hitler's generals however resisted the urge to deploy forces to North Africa. The German High Command sent General Wilhelm Ritter von Thoma to Cyrenaica to study the issue of deploying troops to North Africa with the objective of capturing the Suez Canal. Thoma's report was anything but supportive. He found the situation unsatisfactory. In short, he assessed Libya as "a most unpromising theatre and the supply problem as very difficult."[49]

The German-proffered intervention added fuel to the fire. Mussolini was furious at Graziani's extended halt. On October 18th, Mussolini fumed, "Forty days after the capture of Sidi Barrani I ask myself the question, to whom has this long halt been any use – to us – or the enemy?"[50] Clearly the answer was the British.

Conversely, Wavell refused to wait for the Italians to rectify their indolence. Sensing that Graziani was overly cautious and not about to renew the offensive, Wavell began to formulate a plan. The Italian dispositions were poorly laid out. The garrisons were widely dispersed, incapable of mutually supporting one another and their defence had no depth. On September 24th, three additional armoured regiments had arrived at Port Said in Egypt. This reinforcement increased the British armoured forces by 152 tanks, including 48 heavily armoured Matilda II infantry support tanks. The reinforcements included 48 25-pounder artillery pieces and 500 Bren guns.[51]

Adding to the Italian troubles on October 28, 1941, Italy invaded Greece based on allegations that the Greeks had systematically violated their neutrality by allowing their territorial waters and ports to be used by the British Royal Navy (RN), by giving fuelling facilities to the RAF and by permitting a British intelligence service to be established in Greece. Greece rejected the demands for stationing Italian troops at strategic points throughout Greece as a guarantee of its neutrality.[52] This offensive only exacerbated Italy's problem. By November 8th the offensive in Greece had collapsed. More importantly, Italian forces were pushed back and thrown onto the defense.

Wavell now planned to attack the forward camps while simultaneously assaulting the Italian flanks. On November 2, 1940, when ordering his subordinates to launch an offensive in North Africa, despite the fact that the British were still outnumbered, he explained in a letter:

> I realise the risks of such an operation and am fully prepared to accept them, and the possibility of considerable casualties to personnel and to AFVs [armoured fighting vehicles]. I consider that the advantages of the operation entirely justify the risks run. Nor do I consider the risks excessive. In every thing but numbers we are superior to the enemy. We are more highly trained, we have better equipment. We know the ground and are better accustomed to desert conditions. Above all we have stouter hearts and greater traditions and are fighting in a worthier cause.[53]

Churchill was totally supportive of the offensive. On November 14th, Churchill wrote to Wavell, "It is unlikely that Germany will leave her flagging ally unsupported indefinitely. Consequently, it seems that now is the time to take risks and strike the Italians by land, sea, and air."[54] Prime Minister Churchill was a constant irritant to his generals. He loathed the defensive mindset. He was an accomplished adventurer, journalist, soldier and politician. He held an incontestable belief in the offensive. From his perspective, audacity and willpower constituted the only sound approach to the conduct of war. Churchill understood that to win a war ultimately meant offensive action.[55] Only through such action could an army instill the needed confidence and battle experience in its soldiers and leaders. Furthermore, only offensive action could sustain public and military morale. Finally, offensive action represented a shift in initiative. By striking at the enemy, the opponent is forced to take defensive measures, which represents a diversion of focus and scarce resources.

Churchill's relentlessness was not welcomed by his military chiefs. General Wavell wrote, "He [Churchill] always accused commanders of organizing 'all tail and no teeth.'"[56] Similarly, General Alan Brooke recalled, "He [Churchill] is like a child that has set its mind on some forbidden toy. It is no good explaining that it will cut his fingers or burn him. The more you explain, the more fixed he becomes in his idea."[57] Another serving officer revealed:

> *One of Mr. Churchill's idiosyncrasies is known to have been a temperamental allergy to orthodox military men. He became impatient when the generals pointed out the practical aspects of any scheme on which he had set his heart. He had a strong buccaneering streak in him, which tended to favour irregulars – commandos, special forces, and their like – and was quick to assume that more orthodox commanders were unnecessarily making difficulties.*[58]

In this instance, both Churchill and Wavell agreed. Wavell's counter-offensive was given the codename Operation Compass. Central to its success was the element of surprise, which would be achieved by secrecy and deception. "One of our most powerful aids to victory will be surprise." Wavell wrote, "Every means by which we can preserve secrecy and deceive the enemy must be studied."[59] The offensive would also assist the Greeks by creating pressure on the Italian military.

The object of the attack was to capture Sidi Barrani by exploiting the gap in the Italian defences between Rabia and Nibeiwa fortified camps, which British patrols had kept open despite Italian efforts to close it. Subsequently, according to the success achieved, the objective was to continue the advance towards Buq Buq and then onto to Sollum.[60]

The plan was based on critical Italian errors in siting their defensive positions. They had made a fundamental error in their defensive deployments. They allowed a 32-kilometre gap to exist between their right flank at Sofafi and the next nearest defensive position at Nibeiwa. This glaring vulnerability was not missed by the British. Churchill explained:

> *Between the enemy's right flank at Sofafi and his next camp at Nibeiwa there was a gap of over twenty miles. The plan was to make an offensive spring through this gap, and, turning towards the sea, attack Nibeiwa camp and the Tummar group of camps in succession from the west, that is to say, from the rear. ...The plan involved a*

serious risk, but also offered a glittering prize. The risk lay in the launching of all our best troops into the heart of the enemy's position by a move of seventy miles on two successive nights over the open desert, and with the peril of being observed and attacked from the air during the intervening days. ...The prize was worthy of the hazard. Attacked by surprise from the rear, they might well be forced as a result of vigorous fighting into mass surrenders. In this case the Italian front would be irretrievably broken. With all their best troops captured or destroyed, no force would be left capable of withstanding a further onslaught, nor could any organised retreat be made to Tripoli along the hundreds of miles of coastal road.[61]

Although the plan was for a limited advance, Wavell expounded that if the Italian showed "signs of cracking, commanders and troops must be ready morally, mentally, and administratively to take advantage of the opportunity to the utmost."[62] To ease the logistic burden, a dumping program had begun in November. Fuel, ammunition and water were stockpiled and hidden in a stretch of no man's land. On December 6, 1940, the Western Desert Force, consisting of 31,000 men and 500 vehicles, began its 112-kilometre approach march to begin the offensive.[63] The move was risky as the force was required to lay-up in the desert the day prior to the attack. However, the RAF aggressively kept the Italian air force bottled up in their airfields.

Churchill thrilled with the prospect of the attack recalled:

To secure surprise, attempts were made to give the enemy the impression that our forces had been seriously weakened by the sending of reinforcements to Greece and that further withdrawals were contemplated. On December 6 our lean, bronzed, desert-hardened, and completely mechanised army of about twenty-five thousand men leaped forward more than forty miles, and all next day lay motionless on the desert sand unseen by the Italian Air Force. They swept forward again on December 8, and that evening, for the first time, the troops were told that this was no desert exercise, but the "Real thing."[64]

Operation Compass began on December 9, 1940. The surprise was total. By 0830 hours, the attack on Nibeiwa Camp was finished. Major Henry Rew, the officer commanding one of the Matilda tank squadrons, sent a radio message that summed up the affair. "I am surrounded by at least 500 Italians," he calmly reported, "all with their hands in the air. Can you please send somebody to collect them, because they are hindering my progress and are a considerable embarrassment to me."[65]

Destroyed Italian tanks at Bardia. (WO, MoI, 1941)

In three days, between December 9-11th, the Western Desert Force captured approximately 38,300 Italian and Libyan prisoners, 237 guns and 73 light and medium tanks.[66] But the advance did not stop there. Wavell quickly realized that there was an opportunity to be had. Between December 9, 1940, and February 8, 1941, during a period of 62 days, the British army in North Africa destroyed the Italian expeditionary force in Cyrenaica. Churchill went on to gloat:

> *The Desert Army had in six weeks advanced over two hundred miles of waterless and foodless space, had taken by assault two strongly fortified seaports with permanent air and marine defences, and captured 113,000 prisoners and over 700 guns. The great Italian army which had invaded and hoped to conquer Egypt scarcely existed as a military force and only the imperious difficulties of distance and supplies delayed an indefinite British advance to the west.[67]*

Generalleutnant Erwin Rommel later commented, "The British successes were obviously having an almost paralysing effect on the Italians. They withdrew to their strongholds at Bardia and Tobruk and waited to see what the enemy would do next."[68]

Employing two divisions, one of them armoured, Wavell had destroyed ten Italian divisions. He commenced with a force of 31,000 men, advanced 1,040 km and captured in excess of 130,000 prisoners, 400 tanks, 1,300 guns, as well as a huge haul of other equipment and supplies. He suffered 500 killed, 1,373 wounded and 55 missing.[69] Anthony Eden, then the British Secretary of State for War, after a visit to the Middle East wrote to Churchill, "Never before has so much been surrendered by so many to so few."[70]

Wavell's risk bore fruit. He assessed, "Although our forces were numerically inferior to those of the enemy, their morale, training and equipment was believed to be sufficiently high to compensate for this. The enemy had so far shown little enterprise or power of manoeuvre."[71] A War Office press release echoed those sentiments. It read, "The Italians were superior in number and equipment, but we were superior in the things that in the end always decides the issue – leadership and, above all, the individual courage of the men."[72]

Ciano confided to his diary on December 10th, "News of the attack on Sidi Barrani comes like a thunderbolt. At first it doesn't seem serious, but subsequent telegrams from Graziani confirm that we have had a licking."[73] Rommel, in referring to the Italian expeditionary force in Africa, observed:

> *This army fell a long way short of the standard required by modern warfare... It was designed for a colonial war against insurgent tribesmen...Its tanks and armoured vehicles were too light and their engines under-powered. Their radius of action was short. Most of the guns with which the artillery units were equipped dated from the 1914-18 war and had a short range. The army had too few anti-tank and anti-aircraft guns and even its rifles and machine-guns were of obsolete pattern or otherwise unsuitable for modern warfare.*[74]

In the end, the campaign, which finished at Beda Fomm on February 7, 1941, resulted in the total defeat of the Italian 10th Army and 5th Squadra Aerea. This defeat represented the loss of most of the Italian armour and artillery in North Africa. The feared threat to Egypt now seemed to pass.

The victory was a tonic for the Allied cause. This triumph was the first major large-scale defeat of Axis forces, albeit Italian and their regional allies. The defeat threw Marshal Graziani into a deep funk. Ciano noted that his state of depression was "from the blow he has suffered, and besides it seems that his nerves are quite shaken ... in Libya he has a shelter built in a Roman tomb at Cyrene, sixty or seventy feet deep. Now he is upset and cannot make decisions. He pins his hopes on the possible exhaustion of the adversary, and not on his own strength, which is a bad sign."[75]

Graziani's condition only worsened. He sent a message to Mussolini recommending a withdrawal all the way back to Tripoli. Moreover, he accused the *Duce* of forcing him to undertake combat against the British forces in Egypt, a struggle he complained was a war "of the flea against the elephant."[76] By mid-month, Graziani was requesting mass intervention from German aviation in Libya," claiming "one cannot break steel armor with fingernails alone."[77]

However, the British victory had a cost. The state of British equipment was now very strained. Their tanks had considerably exceeded their engine-life, as well as a myriad of other mechanical defects.[78] By the end of December, the wastage of vehicles in the Western Desert Force was approximately 40 percent. The primary cause was not surprising. The vehicles were old, driven unceasingly by exhausted drivers over rough desert terrain, choked by perpetual dust, occasionally completely engulfed in sand storms, and throughout given only sporadic maintenance.

Despite the fatigue of troops and the state of equipment, Wavell's offensive was actually halted at Benghazi by government direction. Having pushed the Italians out of Cyrenaica, Churchill now decided to focus on Greece. As early as the initial Italian attack into Greece, Churchill had promptly promised all help within Britain's power in accordance with his earlier guarantee of assistance. Britain quickly moved forces into Crete, particularly Suda Bay because of its value to the Royal Navy. Now he felt they could do more. Churchill believed that reinforcing the Greeks, currently battling the Italians in Macedonia, would create a threat to Germany's flank. Although the offer to reinforce Greece was initially rebuffed due to fear that this would simply prompt the Germans to invade, the Greek Government accepted the offer in January of 1941.

A month later, the Allied situation was still dire, but the worst seemed to be over. The threat of a German invasion of Britain had passed and the Italians had been completely defeated in both East and North Africa. Then, in March, the Royal Navy defeated the Italian Navy at the Battle of Cape Matapan, ensuring their dominance of the Mediterranean and the sea lines-of-communication.[79] Not surprisingly, on February 23, 1941, Anthony Eden returned from a trip to Greece with a proposal. He reported to Churchill that he was convinced the Greek leaders were determined to resist the German invasion with all their strength. He recommended that Britain had no alternative but to back them regardless of consequences. The Chiefs of Staff Committee, after deliberation, endorsed Eden's recommendation. The following day, the War Cabinet authorized the deployment of military forces to Greece. As a result, Churchill ordered Wavell to halt his advance and send the largest possible force to Greece and simply use a token force to hold North Africa. The Italians posed little threat to the British after all, after their humiliating defeat.

With East and North Africa locked down, the British Chiefs of Staff ordered Wavell to strip his forces in North Africa to reinforce Greece where the threat of German invasion loomed large, wanting to assist their beleaguered Italian ally and their ill-fated attempt at occupying the country. By the end of March, over 31,000 British troops had been deployed to Greece.[80]

Wavell took the risk of stripping his African Command of his best formations and commanders because he believed the Italians in Tripolitania could be disregarded as a threat and "the Germans were unlikely to accept the risk of sending large bodies of armoured troops to Africa in view of the inefficiency of the Italian Navy."[81] The British War Cabinet agreed:

> Now that the whole of northern Cyrenaica is in our hands, nothing remains between our forces and the fertile regions of northern Tripolitania except the long, waterless and inhospitable tracts of the Sirte desert. This in itself, however, is such a formidable obstacle as to represent a very good defence for the remainder of Marshal Graziani's army, now estimated at 70,000.[82]

The Germans invaded Greece a month later, on April 6, 1941. The British venture proved disastrous. By the end of April, the Germans pushed them off the continent once again. The following month they had thrown them off the island of Crete in yet another resounding defeat.

Significantly, this misadventure cost the British the opportunity to eject the Italians, and thereby the Axis, from North Africa. Major-General O'Connor, the architect behind the successful campaign to push the Italians from Cyrenaica, believed he could have easily pushed on from Benghazi to Tripoli. Most of the other commanders in theatre agreed, as did their opponent Rommel. "When a commander has won a decisive victory," Rommel expounded, "and Wavell's victory over the Italians was devastating – it is generally wrong for him to be satisfied with too narrow a strategic aim." He emphasized, "For that is the time to exploit success. It is during the pursuit, when the beaten enemy is still dispirited and disorganised, that most prisoners are made and most booty captured. Troops who on one day are flying in a wild panic to the rear, may, unless they are continually harried by the pursuer, very soon stand in battle again, freshly organised as fully effective fighting men."[83]

The magnitude of defeat for the Italians was unquestionable. Rommel did not hesitate in laying the blame at Graziani's feet, particularly due to his ponderous advance and hesitation at Sidi Barrani. Rommel asserted, "The British, who commonly possess a good combination of brains and initiative, were given time to prepare themselves to meet a further Italian advance and to organise the defence of Egypt."[84] He added, "The gravest results of the Italian defeat were to their morale. The Italian troops had, with good reason, lost all confidence in their arms and acquired a very serious inferiority complex, which was to remain with them throughout the whole of the war."[85] Not surprisingly, Mussolini replaced Graziani with General Italo Gariboldi on March 25, 1941. He would later, on November 17, 1943, order an enquiry into Graziano's conduct.[86]

Although, arguably unforgivably caught off guard at the beginning of the war, it seemed that the Allies began to claw their way back. By the end of January 1941, it appeared that Egypt and Cyrenaica were safely back in British hands. Effort could now be focused elsewhere. Or at least that was the hope and belief.

CHAPTER 2
THE STING OF THE SCORPION

THE BRITISH POSITION IN NORTH AFRICA at the start of the war was initially tenuous. At the outbreak of war, the Italians controlled a vast amount of territory in North Africa. Their widespread bases and control of key oases provided suitable staging posts for raids or attacks into British or Allied territory. As a result, as a War Office document recorded, it was critical to ascertain what was transpiring in the inner desert west of the Nile and behind the huge protective arc of the Sand Sea. Therefore the British required situational awareness to "give warning of, and to delay, any enemy thrust from Kufra."[87]

Initially, Wavell was deeply concerned about the risk of Italian mechanized raiding parties operating deep in the interior of Libya across to the upper Nile, and potentially interfering with British lines of communication between Cairo and Khartoum in the Sudan. After all, to the east the Italians controlled a chain of oases and wells that spanned south-eastwards from Benghazi for almost 1,300 kilometres into the interior. A War Office report noted, "It was even possible that enterprising enemy parties might manage, as did the Senussi in the last war [World War I], to get across the barrier of sand dunes and occupy the Egyptian oases of Dakhla and Bahariya."[88] And so, although in hindsight this apprehension was needless due to lethargic Italian operations, at the start of the war Wavell had no way of knowing the Italian intent or ability. Therefore, he sought a means to mitigate this potential hazard. After all, the Italians had developed the Auto-Saharan Companies who operated deep in the desert in the 1930s.

Fortunately for Wavell, the British also had a talented group of adventurers in their midst. During the interwar period there were Englishmen who had made desert travel their hobby. From the late 1920s to 1938, individuals such as Ralph Bagnold, William Boyd Kennedy Shaw,

Guy Lenox Prendergast and Patrick Andrew Clayton had gained great experience in traveling in the inner desert by vehicle.[89] Some had even crossed the Egyptian Sand Sea. Importantly, they had learned to navigate in the desert, discern all types of desert surfaces, master the art of driving a vehicle up and across huge sand dunes and equally significant, how to recover a vehicle that was stuck in the sand through innovative methods such as the sand channel. Major-General Lloyd Owen, who became the last commanding officer of the LRDG, describing the small group that spent their time and money exploring the remote wilderness, explained:

> *They had learned to live hard, carrying the minimum amount of food and water, and to navigate their small parties across miles of unforgiving and featureless sand, they had learned to extract their cars from the ever-shifting dunes and from the soft patches which were salt marshes, and to calculate the amount of petrol that would be needed to cover a given distance in various conditions of 'going.' They had also found the way to fix their position by the stars at night, and to conserve water from their radiators by fitting a condenser.*[90]

Digging out a stuck vehicle. (IWM, 03532944)

The dominant figure in the intrepid group was Major Ralph Bagnold, who was well acquainted with the North African desert, as well as the Italian presence. In September 1932, on his third expedition into the desert wilderness, he ran into the Italian Auto-Saharans. Bagnold's party had travelled approximately 1,100 km south of Cairo to an area that was hitherto largely unknown, yet both Britain and Italy claimed possession of this hinterland. The meeting with the Italians in the middle of nowhere was amicable, but the Italian major observed that should the two nations ever go to war, how easy it would for the elite Auto-Saharans to raid the whole Nile Valley through the "long unguarded [desert] flank." The Italian major argued that British territory would be completely vulnerable to raids staged out of the unoccupied areas south of the great Sand Sea's dunes.[91] Ironically, his prophecy was correct. However, he got his target wrong.

Importantly, Bagnold recognized the merit in the major's observation. He had the expertise and vision to bring the concept to life. His only problem was the conservative military bureaucracy. When the war started, Bagnold, who was now 43 and had retired after 20 years of service, was recalled to duty in the fall of 1939. Bagnold immediately submitted a number of proposals to British headquarters in Egypt recommending the creation of a cadre of men for experimental long-range patrolling by vehicle, through the great sand seas to the inner depth of the Libyan Desert. His proposals were consistently shot down. The lack of foresight was as incredible as it was frustrating. At the time, the British Army in Egypt had a single map of Libya that was printed in 1915, representing information that dated from 1873.[92]

Rather than utilize Bagnold's expertise, the War Office assigned him to take up a staff position in East Africa. Fortunately, his ship was involved in a collision at sea and the vessel was subsequently taken to Alexandria for repairs. Once in port, Bagnold wasted no time in heading to Cairo. General Wavell, reading of the renowned desert explorer's presence in the city in a local newspaper, quickly summoned Bagnold for a meeting. He then offered Bagnold the opportunity to stay in the Middle East and he was subsequently posted to the 7th Armoured Division as a signals officer, under the inventive and innovative Major-General Percy Hobart. Bagnold was quickly able to convince the like-minded Hobart of the value in creating a small force capable of acting as a reconnaissance unit that could provide General Headquarters (GHQ) in Cairo with information as to what was transpiring deep in Libya. He also proposed that this force could harass the Italian outposts and garrisons. His latest pitch, submitted in November 1939, however, was once again declined by GHQ as there was little belief that the Italians would enter the war on the Axis side.[93]

Major-General Hobart was eventually replaced and sent back to England. However, Bagnold didn't give up on his idea. Fortuitously, one of Wavell's senior staff officers was an acquaintance of Bagnold. As a result, he left a copy of Bagnold's proposal for a small desert force on Wavell's desk. The Commander-in-Chief's concern for the unguarded desert flank provided the breath of life that Bagnold was waiting for. Wavell was an extremely intelligent individual, who was acknowledged as one of the best brains in the British Army. Importantly, he was not encumbered by the constraints of a conservative mind. He was completely at ease with the unorthodox and innovative. After all, he served under Field Marshal Edmund Allenby as a staff officer in the Middle East during World War I (WWI), which allowed him the opportunity to work with T.E. Lawrence in his campaign of guerrilla warfare with his Arab partners in 1917-1918. Wavell supported the Arab Revolt and later when he wrote the official history of the Palestinian campaign, he credited it with providing substantial support to the Allied cause.[94]

LRDG patrol in the desert. (National Archives (NA), E_012385)

During the interwar years Wavell commanded units that were on the forefront of innovation, undergoing experimentation with mobile operations being expounded by Major-General J.F.C. Fuller and Captain B.H. Liddell Hart. As such, he became a believer in the concept of the "motor guerrilla." Wavell fully understood and supported the concept of a small force, due to their ability to infiltrate and strike at enemy lines of communications deep in their rear, to becoming a "prominent feature of the next war."[95]

Not surprisingly then, Wavell read the report with great interest and summoned Bagnold once again so that he could provide greater detail. Bagnold relayed the story of the Italian major and the Auto-Saharans to the Commander-in-Chief and laid out his plan for a small raiding force. Already inclined to unorthodox, creative ideas, especially since his force was vastly outnumbered by the Italians, Wavell supported the concept as he intuitively realized the economy of effort effects such a force could have in buying him time, providing intelligence and tying down his opponent. After all, the absence of an adequate network of landing airstrips and fuel dumps, much less the available aircraft to patrol the vast wasteland, meant that there was a requirement for small, self-contained, self-reliant mobile vehicle patrols capable of travelling for 3,000 kms or more, on missions that could last several weeks at a time. These patrols had to be able to navigate the Great Sand Sea, traverse the great dune fields and navigate on their own over the unmapped wilderness, hundreds of kilometres behind enemy lines. In the case of the direst emergencies or crises they could expect no assistance.

Following the meeting, Wavell fully empowered Bagnold. He gave him the authority to order anything he required on a priority basis from any department in Egypt. He also had direct access to Wavell himself. The catch, Bagnold was to have the Long Range Patrol Unit (LRPU) ready to launch within six weeks.[96]

As such, the formation of the LRPU began on July 7, 1940. Despite the support from the highest level, reality came into play. Very little in the way of equipment, particularly vehicles, was available in the Middle East. Specialized equipment and vehicles just didn't exist. To add to the frustration, supply officers were not convinced that many of the items requested were actually essential. Nonetheless, with the personal intervention of the Commander-in-Chief, as well as a great deal of innovation and improvisation, not to mention support from the Egyptian Army, the patrols were eventually equipped.

LRDG patrol. (IWM, 03532945)

Major-General Owen later extolled:

> *It is extraordinary to realize how much those men did with so little. The Army had no vehicles which were suitable for the work and so Bagnold set about to find them elsewhere. He obtained a number from the Chevrolet Company in Alexandria and others borrowed from the Egyptian Army.*[97]

The LRPU organization was rudimentary at the start. It consisted of a headquarters (HQ) and three patrols ("R," "T," "W"). Each patrol had two officers and 25 other ranks (ORs) carried in ten 30-cwt Chevrolet trucks.[98] Each truck was equipped for 20 days and 2,400 kms of self-contained operation.[99] From the start Bagnold held four tenets that the LRPU would follow. These were:

- The most careful and detailed planning;
- First-class equipment;
- A sound and simple communications system; and
- A human element of rare quality.[100]

And so, from very humble beginnings the LRPU was stood up. One of the founding officers praised, "Starting from scratch, in five weeks the LRDG [LRPU at the time] had been created. I do not think that any one except Bagnold could have achieved this."[101] Brigadier Eric Shearer agreed.

"Without Bagnold," he said, "I very much doubt that anything of the kind would ever have been tried."[102]

The LRPU's main task was reconnaissance. This was its bread and butter, to determine what the enemy was doing and to confirm terrain and passable routes for the Allied forces. Wavell gave Bagnold large freedom in operating. A GHQ directive clearly stated, "Except when orders for specific operations and reconnaissances [sic] are given by this headquarters, you will act on your own initiative to supply intelligence."[103]

The LRPU however, had other tasks as well. One official report explained, "a secondary role for LRPU was a sort of mechanised highway robbery, raiding supply convoys on distant routes and attacking isolated posts. Success in this direction would compel the enemy to divert men and materials from other more important areas to combat our activities."[104] In addition, the LRPU also conducted:

- The rescue of Allied airmen and prisoners (nearly 200 men were rounded up by LRPU / LRDG in the desert;
- Provision of wireless links for other forces;
- Preparation of air strips / landing grounds for the evacuation of wounded;
- Distribution of propaganda and subversive materials;
- Reporting of meteorological conditions behind enemy lines;
- Encouragement of native levies to desert from the Axis cause;
- Planting of misleading information such as bogus maps and

Personnel from the LRDG shelter behind their vehicle during a sandstorm. (IWM, HU_024964)

operations orders; and
- Preparation of political reports.

Determining the organization structure and acquiring equipment was only part of the requirement to stand up the LRPU. Arguably, the most important factor was finding the right type of operator to man the unit. Bagnold believed that officers and ORs had to have the following qualities and attributes:

- Tact, initiative, and keen understanding of his fellow patrol members;
- Intelligence above the average;
- A sound military background;
- Courage and endurance;
- Perfect physical condition;
- A readiness to undertake any task that might be required of him;
- Some technical or language qualification; and
- Youthfulness (Few men over the age of thirty were accepted).

LRDG personnel camouflaging their vehicle. (IWM, E_012403)

One of the original officers believed that "Brains, initiative, reliability, endurance and courage were probably of equal importance."[105]

To fill his roster, Bagnold called for specific individuals to lead patrols and they were flown to him and commissioned on the spot. He had originally wanted tough Australians from the Outback for his patrols but they were unavailable. Therefore, he recruited personnel from the New Zealand forces in-country as they had a pool of manpower that was well-suited to the task and available. Bagnold felt that the Kiwis were rugged and robust and was more than pleased to accept them for his new force.

The entry standards for the LRPU were uncompromising. Every man had to be a volunteer. They also had to have a high degree of intelligence and be self-reliant. Importantly, they had to be agile in thought and action and capable of adapting to the rigors of the desert. Bagnold was firm on rejecting those who had a reputation of being "tough." He believed these individuals were often lacking in intelligence, initiative, and discipline.

For the members of the LRPU there was little distinction between officers and ORs. Major-General Owen explained, "The officers had to be just as good as the men at all the normal activities, for unless they were, they would only become a burden to the Patrol. They knew that the men would react to their leadership if they showed from the very start that they understood, and would share, all the joys and hardships of their job."[106] Medical Officer Malcolm James captured the essence of the officers' plight. He revealed, "For these men [ORs] were seldom impressed by what an officer said, or the way he spoke; it was what he did that counted with them."[107]

It was no different for the ORs; expectations were high. Even the private soldier had to undertake responsibilities that were often in the realm of the officer (e.g., navigation, planning, communications, debriefs, writing reports). The selection of personnel of character and self-discipline was particularly important due to the nature of responsibilities and unit operations. Individuals were expected to carry out tasks with little to no supervision. One member acknowledged, "Discipline was different from the Regular Army. Members of the LRDG were expected to be professional at all times; those who weren't were sent back to their original units."[108] He added, "There was hardly any saluting, no drill, no inspections. All patrol commanders were called 'Skipper,' while all other ranks were on first-name terms."[109]

Not surprisingly, there was a degree of animosity between the LRPU and GHQ, as well as other elements of the conventional British Army. Major-General Owen explained, "There is probably quite a bit of understandable jealousy that any newly formed unit should be given priority as to men and equipment; and secondly, it is only the normal reaction of any good Commanding Officer to resent having his best men attracted to such 'crackpot' outfits, when his own inherent pride in his Regiment has always led him to believe that it is the best, and second to none."[110]

Adding to the enmity was the fact that the LRPU shunned conventional uniforms. One member, Jimmy Patch, conceded "We wore whatever we liked and, more often than not, it was a mishmash of uniforms. We soon learnt what was practical for the conditions and what wasn't, and that's how we operated."[111] Despite the logic and the absence of a suitable uniform for LRPU operations, the lack of proper dress remained a sticking point for many outside the Unit.[112]

Despite the non-believers, Bagnold's determined approach had the LRPU established by late summer. He calculated that the Italians had sufficient transport to conduct operations out to a "radius of a paltry 100 miles." As such, he believed that the remainder of the desert would be his. Bagnold ruminated, "How about some piracy on the high desert?"[113] However, this was easier said than done. The vast desert was entirely uninhabited and waterless. The difficult sand dunes were alien to the British military, who had little to no experience operating in the desert.

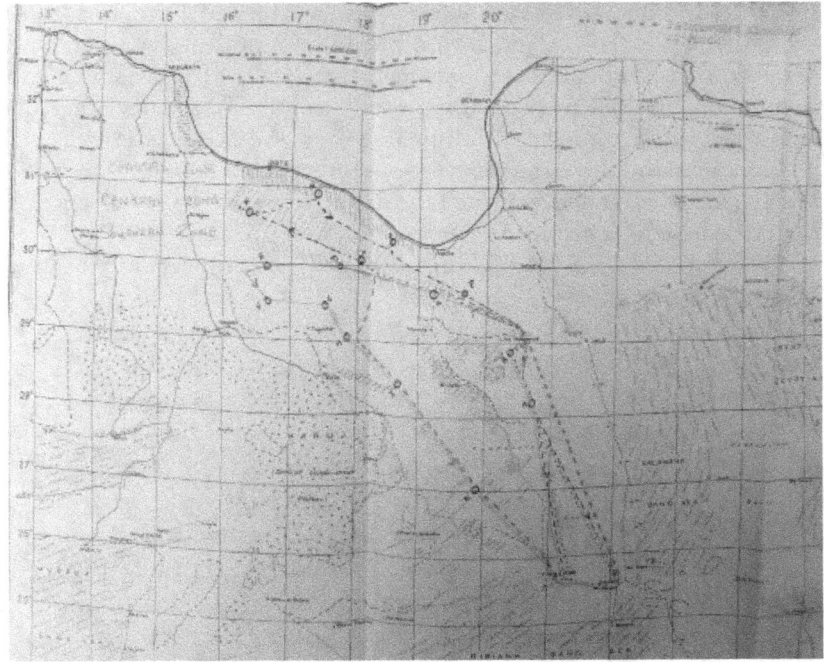

Map 2. LRDG map showing different operating zones. (National Archives)

Quite simply, the terrain they were to operate in was formidable.

In describing the topography of the theatre in question, historian D.W. Braddock noted that in the entirety of the 1,600 km between Alexandria and El Agheila, only the Jebel Akdar was not desert. Rather it was either sandy, similar to most of the coastal plain, or more commonly, it was rocky and stony, much like the desert of the Libyan Plateau. The coastal plain between El Alamein and Gazala on the eastern edge of the Jebel varies in width from 40 km to less than two km at Sollum and Maaten Baggush. The coastal plain is bordered on the south by the escarpment of the Libyan Plateau, which rises sharply to an average height of approximately 150 metres. This escarpment was of vital significance during the desert campaign because west of Sofafi it was passable by vehicles in only a few places that became vulnerable choke points. The southern boundary of the desert was marked by the oases of Siwa and Jarabub beyond which lay the impassable sand seas of Libya. North of this wasteland movement was possible in any direction subject to the occasional existence of patches of soft sand, outcrops of rock, sudden hollows and areas that became temporarily impassable after heavy rains. The Qattara Depression, which marked the eastern boundary of the desert, was a huge swath of territory in which travel was virtually impossible. It extended from within 40 km of the coast at El Alamein to the sand dunes of the Egyptian sand sea. Throughout this hostile landscape water was extremely scarce and population almost non-existent with the exception of small settlements and in the Jebel. Adding to the difficulties were the circadian extremes of temperatures and the mixed blessing of rain, which although it provided much needed water, it also turned the desert into a sea of mud restricting the movement of vehicles and rendering airfields useless.[114]

Captain Shaw, the LRPU / LRDG's intelligence officer described the operating conditions:

The sun shines on most day, shrivelling you to a cinder in summer and putting but little warmth into the winter winds. The temperature may reach 120 °F in the shade in June and fall a degree or two below freezing in the winter...There is nothing like these sand seas anywhere else in the world. Take an area the size of Ireland and cover it with sand. Go on pouring sand on to it till it is two, three or four hundred feet deep. Then with a giant's rake score the sand into ridges and valleys running north-north-west and south-south-east, and with the ridges, at their highest, five hundred feet from trough to crest.[115]

Undaunted, Bagnold used July and August of 1940 to train his personnel and test his equipment. On August 27, 1940, Wavell inspected the new unit. Subsequently he passed a message to the War Office (WO) declaring that the LRPU was operationally ready. This end-state was achieved in approximately six weeks from stand-up. Operations began in September.[116]

The first mission began on September 5, 1940. GHQ believed that the Italians were making offensive preparations, therefore, they assigned the following tasks to the LRPU:

- to form dumps of petrol, rations and water along the Libyan frontier;
- to make long distance reconnaissance; and
- to raid and destroy any enemy dumps that may exist.[117]

When the Italians at last commenced their offensive on September 13, 1940, Bagnold was ready. Captain Shaw clarified:

The Italians, after three months of hesitation, had at last shown some initiative and advanced across the Egyptian frontier to Sidi Barrani. In the inner desert they might also be on the move and so Bagnold planned a thorough examination of all the routes leading to Kufra from north and south. By watching the tracks and traffic and by taking prisoners, if possible, he hoped to learn what the Italians were doing. All three patrols were taking part.[118]

The first reconnaissance missions provided great clarity for the British. Quite simply, the threat of substantive enemy raids behind British lines was ruled out. Once that reality was confirmed, Wavell directed the LRPU to go on the offensive to attack and harass the Italians with the intent of forcing Marshal Graziani to divert forces to protect his desert outposts. A War Office missive revealed, "It had soon become clear, however, that the Italians had no offensive designs towards the south; and thereafter the Long Range Patrols grew more aggressive."[119]

The LRPU patrols in September made their presence felt. They damaged Italian airfields between Jalo and Kufra, reconnoitred approaches through the hinterlands, as well as locating airfields for the RAF, captured prisoners and enemy vehicles, as well as positioned dumps of fuel, food and water at points beyond the Libyan frontier for future use.

In October the unit set out again with a more offensive approach. By this time, it had become clear that the Italians had settled into a defensive posture and had no intention of continuing their advance. The LRPU mined roads and attacked Italian outposts, as well as supply dumps. It also worked with the RAF at developing airfields and caching stores.

The early start to operations did not go unnoticed. The War Cabinet later recorded, "Within six weeks of inception, patrols composed of picked officers and men from New Zealand forces and the Royal Armoured Corps started their activities. In conditions of indescribable hardship these patrols constantly scoured desert, shooting up convoys, destroying petrol dumps and generally harassing Italian desert garrisons. Immediate result was cessation of normal supply convoys, increase Italian garrisons and many other comings and goings."[120]

The LRPU missions continued throughout October and November 1940. Their continued success earned them a reputation for audacity and competence that they never lost. The LRPU blew up fuel dumps and pumping stations at airstrips, intercepted convoys, took prisoners and destroyed vehicles. They appeared simultaneously at locations almost 1,000 km apart.[121] Not surprisingly, radio intercepts revealed Marshal Graziani's concern for his outposts. Italian commanders were requesting more troops and additional air patrols to cover their supply convoys and far-flung outposts. Bagnold later revealed, "Only later did I begin to realize how much the C-in-C [Wavell] was gambling on a 'huge bluff.' We were to create sufficient havoc that Graziani would be forced to recalculate the real British strengths and intentions."[122]

The impact of the LRPU did not go unnoticed. By November 1940, the LRPU initial patrols provided valuable lessons. These were not lost on GHQ Middle East. Although slow to approve of the concept initially, GHQ now requested an expansion of the LRPU to double its size. GHQ desired that one large unit be created with a centralized HQ that would include a wireless telegraphy (W/T) section and a supply section, as well as two squadrons each consisting of three patrols for a total of twenty-one officers and 250 ORs. GHQ also clarified that the expansion would result in a name change. On November 9, 1940, the War Office approved the new organization, which was now called the Long Range Desert Group (LRDG).[123]

By December 1940, a Ministry of Defence report asserted, "the main purpose of the LRDG in eastern Libya had been achieved. The attention of the enemy had been appreciably distracted from the decisive battle area in the north.[124] Quite simply, the LRPU / LRDG had been instrumental in allowing Wavell to out-manoeuvre his vastly numerical enemy and secure the Egyptian frontier and Cyrenaica.

The meeting of two LRDG patrols in the desert. (IWM, E_012390)

The level of British success was fortuitous as it gave the LRDG the time it needed to complete its newly ordered expansion. The first new contingent of personnel arrived on December 5, 1940. The officers and men came from 3rd Battalion Coldstream Guards and 2nd Battalion Scots Guards. They formed the new "G" or "Guards" Patrol.

Although welcoming of the infusion of personnel, initially, Bagnold feared losing his Kiwis. When Major-General Bernard Freyberg arrived in Egypt on October 10, 1940 with the remainder of his New Zealand Division, he demanded the return of all Kiwis in the LRDG but Wavell refused, although he did agree that as replacements could be found he would release them back to the Freyberg's division. However, Freyberg eventually relented and agreed that the New Zealand personnel in the LRDG should remain with the unit. He also committed to provide replacements when required. Notwithstanding his change of heart, due to personnel constraints the three original Kiwi patrols were amalgamated into two.

On January 31, 1941, the second of the new patrols arrived, namely "S" (South Rhodesian) Patrol. Based on the differing temperaments and cultural aspects of each patrol, Bagnold maintained distinctly separate patrols, specifically, his original New Zealand patrols, "G" (Guards) Patrol consisting of his Guardsmen; "S" Patrol made up of his colonials; and later when they arrived, "Y" Patrol, which comprised individuals from British Yeomanry units.

Although, the LRDG reorganization had not been fully completed, GHQ directed new missions that ran from December 27, 1940 to February 9, 1941. Their assigned tasks were to:

- extend the "nuisance value" of the LRDG further west;
- enable the French in Chadian territory to cooperate in raids against Libya;
- spread information of British successes to the natives in Western Libya; and
- obtain geographical information for future use.[125]

With the surrender of Benghazi on February 6, 1941, it had become clear that the British now dominated the North African desert. And so, by the beginning of February 1941, the LRDG had made an outstanding impression on everybody. The key factor was the actual LRDG operator. One wartime journal described, "In truth, they [LRDG] have the best qualities of the modern soldier to a high degree - intelligence, initiative, skill and cool, calculating courage."[126] Similarly, a newspaper article described the LRDG as "the bravest, toughest and brainiest unit of Britain's great desert army."[127] Major-General Owen made no secret of how this was possible. "But I do think," he conceded, "that we were fortunate in that we were allowed to skim the cream off other units and were, therefore, bound to get men of a higher standard than the average. A higher standard of intelligence, tolerance and ability to fend for themselves. This meant that they were reliable in action and less liable to succumb to the atmosphere of strain."[128] Owen attested:

> *Every member of a Patrol not only knew his own job perfectly and was able and willing to help every other man with his: he also knew exactly what was expected of him, and what he could expect from the others. The expectations were high, and were very rarely disappointed. To fall below them might mean being RTU, or 'returned to unit.' This was a dreaded punishment. In a unit where exacting requirements had to be most precisely met, the threat of it was the only sanction ever needed.*[129]

Although a new unit, experimenting with tactics, techniques and procedures

(TTPs) at the same time as they were running operations, their value was immense. The information they gained to assist with Allied operations and the insecurity they caused in the Italian psyche had an immense impact.[130] Major-General Owen revealed:

> *The total damage inflicted by these patrols was very small but the demoralizing effect that it had on the enemy at the time was out of all proportion to the effort that we were putting into it. These few parties of ours, spread over four or five hundred miles of desert, left a trail of uncertainty all along the enemy lines of communication. Not only did they never know where or when they were likely to be attacked but it meant that they had to take appropriate measures to safeguard themselves against the possibility of it at any time and in any place.*[131]

William Kennedy Shaw, one of the original explorers and members of the LRDG agreed. "The scale of the attacks, here today and fifty miles away tomorrow, made mostly at night when accurate observation was impossible," he described, "was greatly exaggerated, especially by the fearful Italians." He added:

> *At times all traffic after dark was stopped. Transport drivers, many of them from semi-civilian contractors, were terrified, not knowing when their turn would come. Troops, armoured cars and aircraft had to be diverted from their proper use to convoy protection work.*[132]

The chaos and fear created by the LRDG patrols was reinforced by a German training bulletin on "British Commandos." "These mobile patrols [LRDG]," the training document explained, "offer a constant threat to the enemy in their power to sow confusion and disorder in his rear."[133] Both the Italians and the Germans fell victim to the marauding desert pirates.

Fitzroy Maclean, a member of the Special Air Service and post-war British member of parliament lauded, "The more I saw of the LRDG, the more impressed I was. There seemed to be nothing they did not know about the desert."[134] Similarly, General Sir John Hackett, a Middle East Force (MEF) GHQ staff officer described:

> *War is a hideous business, brutal, cruel, ruthless and unforgivably destructive. Like all human activities conducted on a grand scale at a high level of intensity, however, it is not without opportunities for elegance. The LRDG displayed this quality of elegance at every point.*[135]

Despite the unresponsive, slow uptake of the concept by the British military hierarchy at the start of the war, the LRDG quickly demonstrated its value. Wavell's leap of faith paid off in spades. The information gleaned on the enemy and terrain, as well as the raids on Italian outposts and convoys proved the LRDG to be a huge force multiplier. Importantly, the LRDG had been an instrumental factor in the lopsided victory against the Italians in Cyrenaica. By the beginning of February 1941, it seemed the worst was behind them.

CHAPTER 3
THE DAY OF THE FOX

WITH THE DEFEAT OF THE ITALIAN ARMY in Africa virtually complete, Churchill was already eyeing his African legions for other tasks. On January 6, 1941, he wrote General Ismay and directed, "the speedy destruction of the Italian armed forces in North-east Africa must be our prime major overseas objective in the opening months of 1941." He added, "Once the Italian army in Cyrenaica has been destroyed, the Army of the Nile becomes free for other tasks."[136] Four days later the prime minister sent a note to General Wavell emphasizing that "Nothing must hamper the capture of Tobruk, but thereafter all operations in Libya are subordinated to aiding Greece, and all preparations must be made from the receipt of this

Rommel giving orders in the field. (Bundesarchiv, 1011-785-0286-33)

telegram for the immediate succour of Greece up to the limits prescribed."[137]

Several weeks later, at dawn, on February 7, 1941, Lieutenant-General Annibale Bergonzoli, commanding Italian forces in Bardia and Libya, surrendered his army and the conquest of Cyrenaica was complete. In a matter of approximately two months, the British army in North Africa had advanced 800 km, destroyed an Italian army of more than nine divisions, captured 130,000 prisoners, 400 tanks and 1,290 artillery pieces.[138] In the aftermath of the stunning victory and capture of Tobruk and Benghazi, Churchill reiterated his direction to Wavell. He wrote, "Your major effort must now be to aid Greece and /or Turkey. This [requirement] rules out any serious effort against Tripoli."[139] This change in priority would come back to haunt the Allies.

In the enemy camp, changes were about to occur. Although Hitler had no real ambitions in North Africa, his intent was to ensure that Tripolitania was held by his Italian allies and that any further British advances were blocked. He had offered Mussolini support in November 1940, but the *Duce* demurred, still believing his forces could achieve a great victory and he did not want to share the glory with his ally. After an exploratory trip to North Africa, General Wilhelm Ritter von Thoma revealed, "They wanted to keep the glory of conquering Egypt for themselves."[140] However, after the debacle of Italian arms, Mussolini readily accepted the assistance. To that end, Hitler promulgated Directive No. 22, dated January 11, 1941, in which he ordered a German expeditionary force to be sent to Tripoli to ensure the recent British victory did not threaten the collapse of Axis positions in North Africa.[141]

Hitler's choice to command the German expeditionary force was General Erwin Rommel. Rommel was born in Heidenheim, Germany, on November 15, 1891. The son of a school headmaster in Württemberg, in 1910, Rommel was appointed as an officer cadet in the 124th Württemberg Infantry Regiment. Physically small but strong, he fought in the First World War in the Argonne, France, as well as in Romania and Italy. He was twice wounded and he earned the highest classes of the Iron Cross, as well as Prussia's highest honour *Pour le Mérite*, for his actions at Caporetto, Italy in 1917. Between the wars Rommel served as a regimental officer, as well as an instructor at the Infantry School at Dresden and later at Wiener-Neustadt. At the start of the war, Rommel was the commandant of the Fuehrer's personal headquarters for the Polish campaign, after which Hitler appointed him as the commander of the 7th Panzer Division of the XV Corps. He wielded his division with dash and daring and he was instrumental in the break-through over the Meuse River and the race to the French Coast. In fact his division was the first to reach the English

Rommel in a Schützenpanzer Sd.Kfz 250/3 following a Panzer III. (Bundesarchiv, Photographer Albrecht Heinrich, 1011-784-0246-22A)

Channel. The speed of his advance later earned his formation the nickname "The Phantom Division."[142]

Rommel's dynamic and aggressive leadership earned him the respect of his opponents. The great strategist B. H. Liddell Hart underscored the respect of the British soldier for the Desert Fox when he referred to the "The Rommel Legend."[143] In fact, British troops demonstrated their esteem for the German general by coining a term, to do "a Rommel," which was a synonym for a good performance.[144] Churchill himself acknowledged, "Throughout the African campaign Rommel proved himself a master in handling mobile formations, especially in regrouping rapidly after an operation and following up success. He was a military gambler, dominating the problems of supply and scornful of opposition."[145]

Within his own camp, although some of his superiors had issues with the maverick commander, most appreciated his dynamic and uncompromising spirit. Field Marshal Albert Kesselring, Commander-in-Chief South, responsible for the North African theatre and relations with the Italian allies as part of his responsibilities, assessed Rommel as "an incomparable leader of armoured formations and daring raids."[146] Major-General Friedrich von Mellenthin, one of Rommel's subordinates in North Africa, confided:

> *In planning an operation he [Rommel] was thoughtful and thorough;*
> *in taking a decision in the field he was swift and audacious – shrewdly*

assessing the chances of some daring stroke in the ebb and flow of battle. What I admired most were his courage and resourcefulness, and his invincible determination under the most adverse circumstances.[147]

Not surprisingly then, the arrival of Rommel would change everything. The British, particularly Wavell, now faced a more dynamic, determined and talented opponent. The reticent and risk-averse Italians were no longer the threat. Rommel and his African legions were.

The first inkling of trouble for the Allies was the arrival of the *Fliegerkorps X* (10th Air Corps), which Hitler dispatched to Sicily in late December of 1940. This deployment led Churchill to warn the Chiefs of Staff Committee that "the arrival of German aviation in Sicily may be the beginning of evil developments in the Central Mediterranean."[148] By February 27, 1941, the British Chiefs of Staff also began to voice concern. In view of the arrival of German armoured formations and aircraft they requested an appreciation of the situation from Wavell, who felt somewhat confident since, as he reported, "Tripoli to Agheila is 471 miles and to Benghazi 646 miles. There is only one road, and water is inadequate over 410 miles of the distance; these factors, together with lack of transport, limit the present enemy threat."[149]

He would soon regret his confidence. The German presence would represent an existential threat to British efforts in North Africa. Originally, Hitler intended to send only a brigade-size formation to undertake defensive tasks. The *Oberkommando der Wehrmacht* (*OKW*, High Command of the Armed Forces), felt that the eventual single light division that was created could act as a blocking formation to stymie any further British offensive. However, Hitler and the *Oberkommando des Heeres* (*OKH*, High Command of the Army), which was subordinate to the OKW, quickly deduced that this would be of little help to the Italians so a special corps, the Afrika Korps, consisting of two divisions, was created.[150] As part of this deployment, the Italian Ariete Armoured Division and the Trento Motorized Division were also to be sent to Tripoli in January and February 1941.

The timing for Rommel however, was inopportune. Hitler and the Wehrmacht were busy preparing and equipping forces for Operation Barbarossa, the invasion of the Soviet Union, which was to occur in the summer of 1941. As such, the OKH specifically stated that the German intervention in North Africa was to be exclusively defensive in nature. The commander-in-chief of the German Army, Field Marshal Walther von Brauchitsch, briefed the forty-nine-year-old Lieutenant-General Rommel of his new task on the morning of February 6, 1941.[151] That afternoon

Rommel had a personal audience with Hitler himself. Their direction would fall on deaf ears.

Rommel seemed almost ambivalent towards the formidable challenges facing his expeditionary force. Significantly, they had no practical experience with desert warfare. A German Lessons Learned report conceded, "German units that were transferred to Africa during the course of the campaign there received no specialized training owing to the fact that the orders for their transfer came so unexpectedly that there was no time for this purpose."[152] Moreover, they had little success extracting information or assistance from their Italian allies. As such, their organization and equipment were all based on theoretical deductions. This approach, predictably, led to trial and error. For example, they deployed their tanks without the proper air or oil filters and as a result, were forced to overhaul their engines after 1,000 to 1,500 kilometres instead of double the distance. In addition, they equipped some of their vehicles with twin tires, which tended to dig in on soft ground. They also failed to account for the importance of fresh food and vegetables, greatly underestimated water requirements and issued unsuitable clothing.[153]

Inexperience aside, the German expeditionary force did what it could. Concurrently, on February 11, 1941, Rommel reported to the *Comando Supremo* (High Command) in Rome. He briefed the Italians on the new plan to shift the defence of Tripolitania into the Gulf of Sirte, a decision that attained the reluctant agreement of the Italian High Command. Of his meeting, Rommel wrote:

It has probably never happened before in modern warfare that an operation of this type was undertaken with so little preparation. On 11 February, I reported to General Gariboldi, the commander in chief of the Italian forces and informed him of my mission. Initially, he showed no enthusiasm for my plan to organize defense positions in the region of the Bay of Sirte as a first measure. Using the poor and inaccurate Italian map material, I then proceeded to explain to General Gariboldi my ideas as to approximately how the war in Tripolitania should be conducted. Gariboldi, who was unable to give me any precise information about the terrain that would be involved, advised me to reconnoiter the terrain between Tripoli and the Bay of Sirte personally, and said that I could not possibly have any idea of the enormous difficulties this theater of war presented. Around midday I took off aboard a type HE iii plane [Heinkel He 111] to reconnoiter the combat area. We saw the field-type fortifications and the deep attack antitank ditch east of Tripoli and then flew over a wide belt of dunes which presented a good natural barrier before the fortifications of Tripoli and would prove difficult to cross with wheeled or track vehicles. Then we flew across the mountainous country between Taruna and Homs, which appeared hardly suitable for operations by armored units in contrast to the patches of level terrain between Homs and Misurate.

Like a black band the Via Balbia road could be seen extending through the desolate country, in which no tree or shrub was visible as far as the eye could reach. We passed over Buerat, a small desert fort on the coast with barracks and a landing stage, and finally circled above the white houses of Sirte. Southeast and south of this locality we saw Italian troops in their positions. With the exception of the salty swamps between Buerat and Sirte, which extended only a few kilometers southward, we found no features in any sector that would favour a defense, such as, for instance, a deep valley. This reconnaissance flight supported me in my plan to fortify Sirte and the terrain on either side of the coastal road and to concentrate the mobile units for mobile operations within the area of the defense sector in order to counterattack as soon as the enemy started an enveloping attack.[154]

As Rommel stated, General Gariboldi demonstrated little enthusiasm for a plan to develop a defensive position in Sirte. However, Rommel explained that he was concerned if the British detected little movement or opposition from the Italians they would continue their advance, not realizing at that time that the British had stripped their best forces to send to Greece. Nonetheless, Rommel deduced that if the British detected the Axis forces were prepared to defend and give battle they would be forced to build up supplies prior to continuing the advance. This requirement in turn would provide Rommel with time to build up his own strength.

Rommel attributed Gariboldi's reluctance to the fact he felt the Italian was still "extremely discouraged" from their earlier defeat. As such, he remained dubious and unsupportive of Rommel's concept. However, Rommel, based on the gravity of the situation and "the sluggishness of the Italian command," had already decided to ignore his instructions to confine himself to reconnaissance and defence and to "take command at the front into my own hands as soon as possible, at the latest after the arrival of the first German troops."[155] Kesselring later revealed that Rommel and his Italian chain-of-command "were continually at loggerheads, and Rommel was unwilling to budge an inch to avoid treading on the corns of the susceptible Italians."[156]

Destroyed Matilda tank. (WO, MoI, 1941.)

The following day, on February 12th, Rommel arrived in Tripoli two days ahead of his main body. And, true to his word, Rommel began planning offensive action immediately. His first action was to request General Hans Ferdinand Geisler, Commander of *Fliegerkorps X*, to attack the British port of Benghazi at night and then send bombers the next morning to attack British columns outside of town. Geisler refused. The Italians had asked him not to bomb the city because many of the Italian officers and civil officials owned houses there. Rommel, not to be denied his aggressive foray against the British, sought and received authority to proceed from Hitler's HQ.[157]

On February 14, 1941, the first of the German units, 3rd Reconnaissance (Recce) Battalion and an anti-tank battalion (armed with the heavy and extremely effective 88mm anti-tank guns), arrived in Tripoli Harbour. Rommel deemed the situation so dangerous that he ordered the unloading to continue into the night by lamplight despite the danger of air attack. Twenty-six hours later the Recce troops were at the frontline.

The arrival of these troops represented the vanguard of the German 5th Light Motorized Division, which comprised of 9,300 men, 130 tanks, 111 guns and 2,000 vehicles.[158] Unfortunately, due to the pressing need to equip forces for Operation Barbarossa, the 5th Light Motorized Division had only three-quarters of its allocated motor transport and it was short 50 of its war establishment of tanks.[159] In addition, the Italian Ariete Armoured Division (with half its tanks and four Italian infantry divisions, a total of some 50,000 men) also started to arrive in theatre.[160]

Still concerned of a possible British attack before he was ready, Rommel ordered his workshops to produce large numbers of dummy tanks, frames that were mounted on Volkswagen vehicles giving them the appearance of tanks, in an effort to exhibit strength. Despite his incomplete order of battle, Rommel pushed his Recce troops, along with a detachment of Italian tanks, to Sirte on February 16, 1941 and to Nofilia three days later.

The inevitable enemy encounter was not long in coming. On February 24th, a British armoured car reconnaissance patrol from the 1st King's Dragoon Guards engaged German armoured reconnaissance elements between El Agheila and Brega. By March 1st, Rommel concluded that British forces in the forward area were weak and that they were not intending any large-scale offensive operations in the short term. A little more than two weeks later on March 18th, Rommel decided that since the British had no plans for offensive action and since they were thin on the ground in the forward areas, an opportunity was ripe for the picking. The following day, Rommel briefed von Brauchitsch at OKH HQ in Berlin. The C-in-C of the German Army reiterated that there was no intention for striking a decisive blow in Africa in the near future. He reminded Rommel that he could expect no reinforcements and that he must proceed cautiously.

Subsequently, when Rommel briefed Gariboldi with regards to his planned counter-attack to reconquer Cyrenaica, the Italian commander-in-chief of the Italian forces in North Africa protested. He was against any offensive action. Major-General Alfred Toppe revealed, "Rommel felt that waiting would worsen the situation." He added, Rommel realized, "the British forces were still in a long-drawn-out column and were momentarily in a precarious condition which should be exploited immediately."[161]

The difference in opinion and approach between Rommel and his Italian chain of command was not hard to understand. Rommel's subordinates recognized his ability. Von Mellenthin asserted, "he [Rommel] was the ideal commander for desert warfare."[162] Another fellow officer described Rommel's approach to war. "His magic word is speed. Boldness is his stock in trade. He shocks the enemy, takes them unawares, overhauls them, suddenly appears far in their rear, attacks them, outflanks them, encircles them."[163] In fact, the Germans created a verb to describe an "enemy overwhelmed" - *Gerommelt* (Rommeled).[164] His soldiers shared the same respect for their commander. "Where Rommel is," they declared, "there is the front."[165]

These perspectives were entirely accurate. Rommel lived by his experience from WWI. His approach, in his own words, was:

Open fire, blanket the enemy, and use speed and shock to confound him. In an advance ignore threats to flanks or rear – march fast, march deep, throw the enemy off balance. Do not be hamstrung by convention in producing effects to distract an enemy – set his building on fire to produce smoke if you need smoke, persuade him to cease resistance by subterfuge if you can get away with it, surprise, deceive, never be afraid of the original or the unorthodox: be your own man: command from the front.[166]

Quite simply, Rommel would not brook any excuse to take to the offensive. Rommel criticized Graziani for standing fast at Sidi Barrani. He observed, "The British, who commonly possess a good combination of brains and initiative, were given time to prepare themselves to meet a further Italian advance and to organise the defence of Egypt."[167] He also critiqued Wavell. "When a commander has won a decisive victory – and Wavell's victory over the Italians was devastating," he insisted, "it is generally wrong for him to be satisfied with too narrow a strategic aim. For that is the time to exploit success." Rommel expanded, "It is during the pursuit, when the beaten enemy is still dispirited and disorganised, that most prisoners are made and most booty captured. Troops who on one day are flying in a wild panic to the rear, may, unless they are continually harried by the pursuer, very soon stand in battle again, freshly organised as fully effective fighting men."[168]

Rommel also did not allow concern over logistical issues to slow him down. In fact, he railed, "The reason for giving up the pursuit is almost always the quartermaster's growing difficulty in spanning the lengthened supply routes with his available transport...it has become the habit for quartermaster staffs to complain at every difficulty, instead of getting on with the job and using their powers of improvisation, which indeed are frequently nil."[169] Rommel wrote:

If quartermasters and civilian officials are left to take their own time over the organisations of supplies, everything is bound to be very slow. Quartermasters often tend to work by theory and base all their calculations on precedent, being satisfied if their performance comes up to the standard which this sets. This can lead to frightful disasters when there is a man on the other side who carries out his plans with greater drive and thus greater speed. In this situation the commander must be ruthless in his demands for an all-out effort.[170]

Despite Graziani's disagreement, Rommel carried on as he thought best. Although Rommel was unaware of Churchill's direction to pull troops out of North Africa to support Greece, his series of recce thrusts west of El Agheila led him to believe there was opportunity for a bold move.[171]

This action was totally unexpected by his counterpart. When the Germans occupied El Agheila on March 24, 1941, with no British reinforcements expected imminently, Wavell directed Lieutenant-General Philip Neame, General Officer Commanding and Military Governor of Cyrenaica, to delay Rommel for as long as possible. Wavell did not believe, or expect Rommel to be capable of launching a counter-attack until mid-April at the earliest. He actually hoped not before May, which would allow him to redeploy reinforcements from East Africa and allow his workshops to repair and return to service a number of his damaged tanks. As late as March 27th, Wavell reported, "No evidence yet that there are many Germans at Agheila; probably mainly Italians, with small stiffening of Germans."[172]

On March 31st, Rommel ordered an attack with limited objectives to drive back the British troops in their advanced positions at Mersa el Brega. Not that it actually mattered, but Gariboldi had finally approved such action but vehemently directed Rommel not to proceed any further without his express consent. The following day the assault went in. Rommel attacked in two columns. The 5th Panzer Regiment, with additional units followed the main coastal road while the 2nd Machine Gun Battalion and the 3rd Reconnaissance Unit began a flanking manoeuvre to the south. The British withdrawal began the following morning.

General Gariboldi cautioned Rommel not to become decisively engaged. Rommel decided to press on nonetheless and ordered his forces to seize Agedabia and the small port of Zuetina. Gariboldi then clarified that any further advance would be in direct opposition to his orders. This directive had no effect. Learning that the British were continuing to retreat, Rommel ignored Gariboldi's protests and continued to deploy forces to threaten the British southern flank. He was intent on discovering whether the British planned to defend and hold Cyrenaica. This piece of information he kept to himself. As Kesselring revealed, "Rommel had got into the habit of keeping his operations a secret from the Italians until the very last possible moment because, not to put too fine a point upon it, he did not trust them."[173]

Aerial and ground reconnaissance quickly indicated that the British were unexpectedly withdrawing to Benghazi. Without hesitation, Rommel decided to advance on Agedabia despite his orders not to undertake an aggressive offensive. The Allied house of cards quickly began to collapse. Capitalizing on the British surprise and apparent weakness, Rommel continued his offensive drive.

On April 1st, Rommel assaulted Mersa Brega in two columns. The 5th Light Motorized Division with additional units followed the main coastal road while the 2nd Machine Gun Battalion and the 3rd Reconnaissance Unit began a flanking manoeuvre to the south. The British withdrawal began the following morning.

The Allied position soon crumbled. Immediately after the capture of Agedabia on April 2nd, the British began to panic and Wavell ordered Benghazi to be abandoned. He later countermanded the order but it was too late. The withdrawal to the East quickly succumbed to chaos and confusion. The original intent of maintaining the integrity of units and formations was predictably lost as unit cohesion in a retreat often disintegrates. Bombardier Ray Ellis, rushing to the front with his artillery battery, observed:

> The deeper we got into the desert, the more alarmed we became. We began to meet columns of lorries laden with troops and equipment... all travelling at speed heading eastwards...There was more than a hint of panic in the air, and the further west we travelled the more disorderly it all became. It was soon obvious that the British Army of the Nile was in headlong retreat.[174]

Rommel deduced that the British did not intend to fight a decisive battle. He now smelled blood and so he decided to aggressively pursue the retreating Allied forces. However, rather than pursue through Cyrenaica he decided to launch an enveloping attack by driving through the desert to the south and then flanking the British and cutting off their retreat.

The British reversal quickly hit home. With regard to the loss of Benghazi, Churchill lamented, "Thus at a single stroke and almost in a day, the desert flank upon which all our decisions had depended had crumpled and the expedition to Greece, already slender, was heavily reduced."[175]

Similarly, on April 3, 1941, the British War Cabinet also took note of the sudden reversal and the build-up of German forces in theatre. An internal report assessed, "Enemy infantry estimated at two battalions, together with tanks with swastika markings, attacked some of our unarmoured troops who withdrew to a line north of Agedabia. We estimate that the number of German troops in Tripoli is still between one and two armoured divisions, but there are indications that these may shortly be reinforced."[176] That same

Rommel briefing his subordinate commanders. (Bundesarchiv, 1011-786-0327-19)

day, Wavell came to understand that the only factor stopping Rommel and his Afrika Korps from attempting to follow up their success and advance into Egypt was his ability to supply and maintain his forward troops. As such, his concern was now re-establishing a solid defensive position on the Western Desert front.

The German forces, despite their inexperience in the desert, were effectively pushing the British back to the frontier. Their Italian allies, however, were less than impressive. As the advance continued, in the Italian sector, Rommel described, "progress at first was in perfect order, but suddenly the Italians turned and fled in a wild rout to the west." As a result, Rommel dispatched an officer to determine the cause of the sudden flight. Thirty minutes later the German officer reported that an Italian infantryman stated the enemy was attacking with tanks. The German officer moved a few hundred metres when he witnessed "a British scout car herding away a company of Italians with their hands up." He at once opened fire on the British scout car in order to give the Italians an opportunity to escape. They immediately ran; however, it was towards the British lines.[177]

The unreliability was consistent. The Ariete Division, although they had not engaged in battle were down to ten out of a 100 tanks. The remainder had fallen out due to engine failure or some other mechanical malfunction. One German noted, we "can do nothing with the Italians. They either do not come forward at all, or if they do, run at the first shot. If an Englishman so much as comes in sight, their hands go up."[178] Kesselring confided:

> *As might be expected from a nation of southern temperament, the Italian armed forces were trained more for display than for action. Their barracks were ill adapted for combat training; their submarines' exhibition diving and the stunt flying of their airmen was no fit preparation for the real thing. Proper importance was not attached to combined operational training in smaller formation or indeed in the services as a whole.*[179]

Despite the shortcomings of his allies, by April 4th Rommel had decided that he had to increase the pace of his advance if he intended to bring the British forces to battle. He pushed his units from recently-seized Benghazi, to Mechili. He formed ad hoc columns as units and commanders arrived, and gave them distant objectives to secure. He knew he could depend on the German adherence to organizational flexibility and clear, well-understood doctrine to use these thrown-together columns to work effectively. This trust in German adaptability allowed him to take full advantage of the pursuit and maintain pressure on the British as they withdrew.

Rommel utilized all factors to maintain pressure – both physical and psychological. He exploited the large dust clouds to give the illusion of strength. He directed his administrative tail, the supply and baggage trains, to deploy in tank formation in order to mislead the enemy.[180]

Rommel pressed his forces hard. At one point the 5th Light Division requested a pause in the advance. As Rommel had predicted, the logistical tail demanded four days to replenish supplies. Rommel would have none of it. He ordered the division to unload all of its transport and send them back to the divisional supply dump to gather the necessary fuel, rations and ammunition for the advance through Cyrenaica. He gave them 24 hours. With the enemy in full retreat he believed he could take the risk.

Predictably, the Italian commander-in-chief, General Gariboldi was extremely unhappy with the turn of events. He pugnaciously rebuked Rommel when he returned to his headquarters. Gariboldi's concern was that the offensive was in complete contravention to explicit orders from Rome. Furthermore, Gariboldi was concerned that the Axis supply situation was far too insecure to allow for continued operations. He then, once again, ordered Rommel to halt any further advance and to take no further action without his express authority. Rommel remained unmoved and refused to be hemmed in by the hesitant Italians. The issue ceased to be a problem when the German High Command sent a message giving Rommel complete freedom of action.[181]

The situation for the British had become serious. Wavell's armoured division in Cyrenaica ceased to be an effective fighting force. This development was no real surprise since it was never up to strength in men, weapons and serviceable tanks. Moreover, it never had the necessary support in supply, transport and maintenance services to ensure it maintained its manoeuvrability. As a result, by the time the sole armoured division arrived in Cyrenaica it was already a mechanically-exhausted force.

Lieutenant-General Neame reported that he was down to 22 cruiser tanks and 25 light tanks. Worse yet, he expected to lose more to breakdowns at a rate of one tank for every 16 kilometres advanced.[182] Much of the British problem lay with mechanical failures. Wavell recounted:

I did not become aware till just before the German attack of the bad mechanical state of the cruiser regiment, on which we chiefly relied. A proportion of these tanks broke down before reaching the front, and many others became casualties from mechanical defects during the early fighting...As it was, 3d Armoured Brigade practically melted away from mechanical and administrative breakdowns during the retreat, without much fighting.[183]

Rommel's risk acceptance paid great dividends. By April 6, 1941, he had captured more than 2,000 prisoners at Mechili and Derna. On April 9th, the pursuing columns reached the Libya-Egypt border at Bardia. By April 10th, the Afrika Korps had advanced approximately 1,000 km in a little under three weeks despite blinding sandstorms, difficult roads and terrain.

Assisting Rommel's advance was the fact that the RAF was not strong enough to gain air superiority. However the Axis air forces were not in a position to take advantage of the situation either. As a result, both sides suffered only sporadic air attacks that failed to significantly impact the land battle.

For the Allies their fortunes were once again suffering. As well as the reversal in North Africa, on April 6th, German forces invaded Yugoslavia and Greece. Due to events in Cyrenaica, neither the 7th Australian Division nor the Polish Brigade could then deploy to Greece. Moreover, the forces that had been deployed were not yet fully in position. For the British commander, Lieutenant-General Henry M. Wilson, the situation looked bleak, particularly since the Greeks were near exhausted due to their fight against the Italians, and the Yugoslavs were in political turmoil and had not yet even fully mobilized for war.

The blow to the British was significant. All of the Italian territory lost to Wavell's offensive was now recaptured. Only Tobruk, which was surrounded and contained by weak forces on April 11th, was left in British hands, which now represented a salient in the German lines. A dejected Churchill wrote to

Wavell on April 7, 1941, "Tobruk, therefore, seems to be a place to be held to the death without thought of retirement."[184] The despatch was reinforced three days later. The Prime Minister and Chiefs of Staff sent a clear message to Wavell. "From here it seems unthinkable," they insisted, "that the fortress of Tobruk should be abandoned without offering the most prolonged resistance. We have a secure sea-line of communications. The enemy's line is long and should be vulnerable, provided he is not given time to organise at leisure...We are convinced you should fight it out at Tobruk."[185]

By April 10th, Rommel, convinced that the British were exhausted and on the verge of collapse, declared his objective was now the Suez Canal. He invested Tobruk to ensure the trapped Allied forces were unable to break-out.[186] It became a priority target for him as he desperately wanted to seize the strategic port for his own use. After several days of reconnaissance, the Germans attacked from the south on April 13th and 14th. The War Cabinet report of the battle explained:

> *Attacks on Tobruk from South and West on the 12th were repulsed, the R.A.F. assisting with attacks against enemy A.F.V.'s [armoured fighting vehicles], but the enemy in armoured cars succeeded in occupying Bardia. On the 13th April the enemy occupied Capuzzo, and brisk fighting commenced around Sollum. On the 14th a deliberate attack on Tobruk was attempted by infantry and tanks, the latter penetrating the perimeter, but the attack was repulsed with loss to the enemy of at least 20 tanks destroyed, 100 men killed, 263 Germans and 70 Italians captured. The prisoners' morale was low. An air attack was also repelled, 12 out of 50 bombers being shot down.*[187]

The Germans attempted yet another push from the west on April 16th and 17th. All efforts failed as the Tobruk garrison tenaciously maintained their hold on the port.

While Rommel battered at the outer perimeter of Tobruk, Mussolini urged the German OKW to halt Rommel prior to advancing into Egypt in order to ensure the attacking forces were reorganized, reinforced, and that all formations, particularly the support services had an opportunity to recover. The *Duce* was not the only one concerned with Rommel's continued offensive. General Franz Halder, Chief of the General Staff, OKH, recorded in his personal diary that "he was disturbed by the news from North Africa because he feared that Rommel was getting into difficulties from which he could only be rescued by allotting resources which ought not to be spared from more important commitments."[188] Halder fumed:

> *Rommel has not sent in a single clear report, and I have a feeling that*

things are in a mess...All day long he rushes about between his widely scattered units and stages reconnaissance raids in which he fritters away his strength...the piecemeal thrusts of weak armoured forces have been costly...His motor vehicles are in poor condition and many of the tank engines need replacing...Air transport cannot meet his senseless demands, primarily because of lack of fuel...It is essential to have the situation cleared up without delay.[189]

Halder's concerns prompted him to dispatch Lieutenant-General Friedrich Paulus, Director of Military Operations OKH to Rommel's headquarters to review the situation and send back a clear report of the situation. Halder felt that Paulus was "perhaps the only man with enough influence to head off this soldier gone stark mad."[190] The situation had not changed by early May. Halder continued to complain, "Rommel has brought about a situation for which our present supply capabilities are insufficient."[191]

Rommel, however, was not the only commander to get grief from his chain-of-command. On April 14, 1941, as if impervious to the military situation that had unravelled, Churchill continued to push Wavell to transition to the offensive. "It is important to engage the enemy even in small affairs," he pressed, "in order to make him fire off his gun ammunition, of which the supply must be very difficult."[192]

Six days later, on April 20th, Wavell sent a message to Churchill. He assessed his Western Desert Force was gravely inferior to the German's armoured strength and he believed this disparity would grow even greater by the end of the month. This warning prompted Churchill to send a convoy of ships carrying tanks, named "Tiger Convoy," across the Mediterranean. Churchill decided to take the risk of sending the fast (15 knot) merchant ships through the Straits of Gibraltar instead of the much longer, but safer, route around the Cape of Good Hope. This decision would save 40 days of sailing. On April 22, 1941, Churchill wrote Wavell, "We are sending 307 of our best tanks through the Mediterranean, hoping they will reach you around May 10. Of these, 99 are cruisers, Mark IV and Mark VI, with the necessary spare parts for the latter, and 180 'I' Tanks."[193]

The Tiger Convoy represented the first convoy to sail through the Mediterranean since January 1941, when the Luftwaffe *Fliegerkorps X* had arrived in theatre. At that time, they sunk the cruiser *Southampton* and seriously damaged the aircraft carrier *Illustrious*. The passage was not without its perils though. The *Empire Song* hit a mine, leading to a fire in the ammunition hold. Hours later she blew up and sank, taking with her 57 tanks and ten Hurricane fighter aircraft.[194]

The Prime Minister's "gift" of tanks, however, did not come without a price. "If this consignment gets through the hazards of the passage, which, of course, cannot be guaranteed," Churchill penned, "the boot will be on the other leg and no German should remain in Cyrenaica by the end of the month of June."[195] There was no nuance in Churchill's missive. Once again, he pressed for the offensive.

While the British were busy reinforcing, Rommel did not sit idle. On April 30th, he attacked the besieged port once again with a deliberate attack. By May 4th the attack stalled in the face of a British counter-attack. Nonetheless, the Germans had broken through on an approximate five-kilometre frontage with penetration up to two kilometres, thereby gaining good positions of observation, as well as possible start lines for future attacks.

With Rommel's offensive at its end, General Paulus signed off on a report on May 12, 1941. He observed that the *Deutsches Afrikakorps* (DAK) was tactically challenged due to the current dispositions throughout Cyrenaica and its supply situation was extremely tenuous. Furthermore, he counselled that strong action was necessary if a serious crisis was to be avoided. Paulus recommended proper defence of the sea routes to Tripoli and Benghazi, as well as of the harbours themselves, particularly air defences. He stressed the DAK required as a priority ammunition, petrol and rations, followed by vehicles.

The issue of resupply, from the beginning to the end of the North African Campaign, was the Achilles heel of Axis forces in North Africa. Halder explained that Axis forces required 50,000 tons of supplies a month; 30,000 for maintenance and the rest for building up stocks without which no further advance would be possible. However, the total capacity of the Axis coastal shipping was only about 29,000 tons a month.[196]

The requirement was not hard to understand. General Kesselring revealed, "the fighting was nevertheless fatally affected by our shortage of petrol, with the result that even essential operations could often not be carried through."[197] As noted earlier, the distances through the vast desert wasteland were substantial. From the port in Tripoli to Tobruk was 1,600 km and then another 160 km to the frontier.

Rommel and the DAK had achieved a major victory. They had reconquered Cyrenaica. However, the success, as Paulus had observed, forced Rommel to deploy his forces in a rather exposed manner. Tobruk represented a salient in his rear, so he had to maintain a force to keep Tobruk securely hemmed in and hold the line to prevent any break-out attempt by the garrison. "Our greatest worry," Rommel confided to his diary, "was still the difficult strategic situation caused by our dual task of having to maintain the siege of Tobruk and at the same time be ready for major British attacks from Egypt."[198] It was the potential of a British counter-attack that made the situation shaky. Rommel was forced to deploy a second force to secure the line at Sollum and, simultaneously, generate a mobile defence capable of responding to any enemy flanking manoeuvre to the south in order to prevent the enemy operating against the rear of German forces in the vicinity of Tobruk.[199]

After the second decisive defeat of the Germans at Tobruk, Wavell felt that the momentum had shifted. He realized that the Germans were now exhausted and at the end of a rather long resupply chain. As such, he wished to take advantage of their state of exhaustion before they could recover. Wavell's greatest concern was always the absence of tanks on which desert operations relied. But, on May 12th, the Royal Navy "Tiger Convoy" arrived in Alexandria carrying reinforcements and 220 tanks.

Based on the reports of his intelligence analysts, there was a fleeting opportunity that could be seized. Before the tanks could even be unloaded, Wavell decided to launch Operation Brevity. According to these analysts, Rommel was having severe supply difficulties and they expected that there was very little German armour in the frontier border region. In addition, he wanted to strike before the anticipated arrival of the 15th Panzer Division. Wavell seized on the opportunity. Mustering his available 53 tanks, he attacked with the 7th Armoured and 22nd Guards Brigades on May 15th. The gamble was initially successful. He overwhelmed the German positions on the all-important Halfaya Pass, which was a natural choke point as it provided the only route for vehicles and armour for an 80 km stretch south-east of Sollum up the desert escarpment and across to Cyrenaica (or from Cyrenaica down to Egypt). The British quickly captured Sollum and Capuzzo and then threatened Bardia.

The surprise attack, however, was no bombshell. Intercepted message traffic had warned the Germans to expect an attack. Therefore the British success was fleeting. Rommel swiftly counter-attacked with a tank battalion from the 5th Light Division, followed by another assault by a tank battalion of the 15th Panzer Division, which had arrived in theatre in April. By May 16th, the British had lost all of their gains with the exception of Halfaya Pass. However, on May 26th, Rommel renewed his assault. The following day, the Germans once again wrested control of the important choke point, capturing a vast amount of supplies in the process and driving off the British, who "fled in panic."[200] They then dug in and prepared the vital ground for the renewed British assault they knew was in the offing.

The arrival of Rommel, the "Desert Fox," and the *Deutsches Afrikakorps* changed the dynamic of the theatre. No longer could the British count on fighting timid Italian commanders and poorly trained and led Italian troops. They now had to contend with an aggressive, risk-accepting opponent who believed in audacity and bold manoeuvre. Rommel became the personification of the Axis threat in North Africa.

CHAPTER 4
RELIEVING TOBRUK

OPERATION BREVITY HAD BEEN A COLOSSAL FAILURE. Undaunted, Prime Minister Churchill pressed Wavell to return to the offensive to seize Cyrenaica and lift the siege of Tobruk. He constantly prodded Wavell to take action. The Prime Minister later wrote of his "terrible anxiety and even anger ...because the newly arrived tanks [Tiger Convoy] could only come into action so slowly."[201]

The reality was that Churchill desperately needed a victory. Defeats in North Africa, Greece and Crete, as well as the German activities in Iraq and Syria, sapped the morale of the Allies. The Prime Minister now wanted to take advantage of Rommel's strained lines of communication and supply and repeat Wavell's earlier success against the Italians. As such, he urged for an offensive to destroy the Germans in the western desert.

Although against his better judgement, Wavell relented and on May 28th gave orders for Operation Battleaxe. His intent was for the Western Desert Force (WDF) to defeat the enemy on the frontier and then beat back their forces in the Tobruk area and, finally, to exploit success and capture Derna and Mechili. This endeavour would be no easy feat. On top of a professional and very capable opponent, he also had to deal with the weather. On June 1st, for instance, it was 107 degrees. Tanks standing in the sun registered as much as 160 degrees, which was too hot to touch.[202] And yet, troops would be expected to fight.

Adding to Wavell's consternation was the fact that the Germans suspected an attack was coming. "At the beginning of June," Rommel recorded, "there were many signs that a major British attack on our Tobruk front was to be expected at about the middle of the month." This prediction was based on the fact that two British divisions were deployed opposite the positions of the 15th Panzer Division.

Wavell realized that the German supply situation was shaky and could be exploited. However, he did not fully realize to what extent. Rommel's apprehension of a British offensive was palpable. "Unfortunately, our petrol stocks were badly depleted," he confided to his diary, "and it was with some anxiety that we contemplated the coming British attack, for we knew that our moves would be decided more by the petrol gauge than by tactical requirements."[203]

Nonetheless, the decision to attack was not an easy one. Wavell was torn. He knew his troops were not fully ready but he was under great pressure from Churchill. Moreover, there was also a fleeting opportunity to take advantage of the present German position. Wavell revealed that he was "being urged to attack [by Churchill] with the least possible delay, and was myself anxious to forestall, if possible, the arrival of more German reinforcements."[204]

To take the offensive without being fully prepared, however, was a massive risk. The reconstituted 7th Division had neither the opportunity to properly train, particularly on the new Crusader tank, nor integrate as a formation. Although Wavell gave the divisional commander five extra days to train, postponing the launch of Operation Battleaxe from June 10 to 15, 1941, he fully realized that the division required far more time.

Wavell planned Operation Battleaxe as a three-phase operation:

- Defeat the enemy on the frontier;
- Advance to Tobruk and lift the siege in coordination with an attack launched by the garrison; and
- Exploit to Derna and Mechili.

On June 15, 1940, at 0400 hours, Wavell launched the assault with 25,000 men, supported by approximately 200 fighter aircraft. The British advanced in three separate formations. The 11th Indian Infantry Brigade advanced along the coast and made directly for the Halfaya Pass and Sollum. An infantry tank brigade of the 7th Armoured Division with the 22nd Guards Brigade, reinforced by strong divisional artillery assets, struck well to the south of the desert escarpment. Their intent was to avoid the enemy's prepared defensive positions, after which they planned to turn North at the appropriate time and attack the Capuzzo-Sollum defences in the flank. Finally, the third group concentrated on the Halfaya Pass from the southern flank of the escarpment.

Wavell's plan was for a converging attack to overwhelm Rommel's strong frontier defences and exploit direct to Bardia. He believed this attack would prompt Rommel to aggressively counter-attack by attempting to outflank the British forces from the wider desert. In anticipation of this move, Wavell deployed the bulk of the 7th Armoured Division to defend the left flank. This force would then meet Rommel's tanks for a decisive tank battle.

However, as mentioned, the Germans were expecting and ready for the attack. Careful monitoring and analysis of British radio traffic revealed the redistribution of forces. This information, coupled with increased rail and air activity pointed to an upcoming offensive. Moreover, of great assistance was a captured list of British codenames and call signs on the first day of battle. As a result, they could plot British movement and deduce intentions fairly accurately.[205] Major-General Toppe described:

> On 15 June after careful preparation the British launched a major offensive operation – bypassed the German border positions and pushed almost to Bardia. The situation was critical. However, on 17 June Rommel again employing the 15th Panzer Division succeeded in defeating the flank of the enemy who had advanced northwards. The enemy forces were compelled to withdraw southward to avoid the encirclement of some of their units. ...the Germans side no longer had absolute mastery of the air.[206]

Also weighing against Wavell was the fact that by the time the offensive began, the Germans had fortified the Halfaya Pass, which was the gateway between Egypt and Cyrenaica. They had deployed 900 German and Italian troops, five 88mm anti-aircraft guns in the anti-tank role, four Italian artillery pieces and a battery of 155mm captured French guns. In addition, they had captured Matilda tank turrets converted into fixed strongpoints. A game changer in the battle was the fact that the infamous and menacing German 88mm gun made their first appearance as an anti-tank weapon during the battle. It had a devastating effect. Significantly, the British had no answer to this weapon. One armoured squadron commander reported prior to his death, "They've got large calibre guns dug in and they're tearing my tanks to bits."[207]

Five separate attacks over two days failed to remove the Germans from the pass. The advance on Capuzzo, with the objective of threatening Bardia, was also a failure. A single 88mm gun brewed up three Matilda tanks in quick succession. This action prompted the other 47 tanks to cease their advance. This delaying action allowed German armoured reinforcements to arrive from Bardia. A desperate tank battle lasting several hours then ensued. The result was a British withdrawal. Attacks on June 16th faired no better. The deadly 88mm guns continued to shred the British armour, stalling all attacks.

A Matilda tank being towed up through the Halfaya Pass. (WO, MoI, 1941.)

The battle was at its tipping point on the morning of June 17, 1941, the day, Churchill later lamented, "everything went wrong."[208] Once again Rommel showed his tactical acumen. He boldly advanced towards the Halfaya Pass with both of his armoured formations in a bid to cut off the British in the Sollum -Halfaya-Capuzzo region. Badly mauled and with this latest development, Wavell directed his forces to break contact and withdraw to refit and reconstitute. By the end of day, June 17th, the British desert force was back along the Sidi Barrani-Sofafi line.

Wavell's decision to withdraw his remaining troops and armour to their start lines was prescient. Operation Battleaxe had been a costly debacle. There was little to gain by throwing away more scarce resources. As it was, the British lost 64 Matilda and 27 Cruiser tanks, as well as incurring 969 casualties. Conversely, the Germans lost just 12 panzers and suffered 1,277 casualties.[209] The deployment of the highly effective 88mm guns, as well as Rommel's foresight to concentrate and deploy his two panzer regiments at the pivotal moments on June 16th and 17th to strike the British flank, proved decisive. Major-General Mellenthin, then a member of Rommel's headquarters staff, stated, "the Afrika Korps suffered serious tank losses but under Rommel's resolute leadership turned the tables on the 7th Division and gained a notable victory."[210]

In the end, Operation Battleaxe was a monstrous failure. Wavell's misgiving about an early offensive proved accurate. He needed more time. The newly arrived tanks were not yet fitted for desert conditions and the crews were still unfamiliar with their machines. In addition, they had not yet had time to master infantry-armour combined operations. Not surprisingly, 50 percent of the newly arrived tanks were knocked out in the first 12 hours.[211]

One veteran of the battle lamented, "It was a depressing factor which weighed increasingly on all of us as the months went by. British tank design and our anti-tank guns were inadequate. The Matilda infantry tanks were heavily armoured but carried a small two-pounder gun whose shells bounced impotently off their opponents; while the cruiser tanks, although faster, seemed to break down regularly and had nothing to defend themselves with except the same small gun."[212] Wavell himself reflected, "Had tank crews had more practice with their weapons they would have destroyed a much larger number of enemy tanks; and had they all been more experienced in maintenance there would have been fewer tanks out of action through mechanical breakdowns; so that instead of being so outnumbered at the end of battle, we should have been in sufficient strength to have defeated the enemy.[213]

Although Wavell's offensive failed, Rommel's assessment of his counterpart remained high. "Wavell's strategic planning of this offensive had been excellent," Rommel gauged, "What distinguished him from other British army commanders was his great and well-balanced strategic courage, which permitted him to concentrate his forces regardless of his opponent's possible moves." Rommel added, "He [Wavell] knew very well the necessity of avoiding any operations which would enable his opponent to fight on interior lines and destroy his formations one by one with locally superior concentrations."[214]

The German success in countering the attack, however, did not mean they were out of the woods. Their position became even more precarious. From the beginning Rommel's orders were to act purely on the defensive and to build up his resources for operations later in the autumn. As a result, his latest actions and heavy losses were in direct contravention of his orders. Despite his at times dramatic success, his actions had serious consequences. Unlike the Allies, his ability to have consistent reinforcement and resupply was always in question.

Long advances in the wide-open desert allowed Rommel to utilize manoeuvre but exacerbated already difficult logistic requirements, as lengthy lines of communications were both vulnerable and difficult to sustain. Between 75,000-95,000 litres of fuel a day was required for the tanks alone during a large operation.[215] Vehicles needed frequent overhauls due to the dust, sand and difficult driving conditions. In the desert a tank engine required overhaul after 3,500 kilometres (normally they would last

Tobruk burning. (WO, MoI, 1941)

7,000-8,000 km). Volkswagen engines, for example, required change after 12,000 – 14,000 km (in other theatres of war they would normally last 50,000-70,000 km).[216] Aside from vehicles, water proved to be another major resupply burden. A battalion of approximately 600 men required daily, not including water for vehicles' radiators, about 3,000 litres. Water needed by medical units was twice that. [217]

General von Thoma had concluded early on after a visit to North Africa in October 1940, that the supply problem would be the decisive factor in theatre, not only because of the difficulties of the desert, but also due to the Royal Navy's command of the Mediterranean.[218] General Kesselring echoed those concerns. "In addition to the meagre flow of replacements conditioned by demands elsewhere," he lamented, "[resupply] was being reduced to a trickle by extraordinary losses incurred during sea transport."[219] He estimated losses running at 70 to 80 percent of those shipped.[220]

Count Ciano would later write, "There is no doubt that the task of moving supplies is most difficult, and it is that which keeps our hearts in our throats."[221] The supply dilemma made the requirement to capture Tobruk so imperative. Aside from the irritant of acting as a "sally port" from which to launch attacks into the German rear, it also represented port capacity. The Axis forces required 50,000 tons of supplies a month, or 350 tons of supplies a day to support one division. The port of Benghazi although theoretically capable of handling 50,000 tons of supplies a month, this capacity was reduced to 15,000 tons due to RAF bombing and a shortage of coastal shipping. Tripoli could manage 45,000 tons a month but a shortage of trucks created problems moving the stores to the front.[222] As a result, they required additional port facilities. Importantly, Tobruk would also decrease the distance to Cyrenaica.

Port capacity aside, Major-General Toppe also noted the impact of the losing battle at sea. "The steadily decreasing capacities for German seaborne transportation as the result of the mounting losses of ships," he conceded, "as early as July, it became evident that it would definitely not be possible for the Germans to commence any systematic attack before mid-September."[223] The only spark of hope, according to a British officer, was "the bold and skilful action of the enemy's [German] repair and maintenance services."[224] Major-General Rowan-Robinson commended, "They were as much in the forefront of the battle as any of what are ordinarily regarded as the combatant corps; and the rapidity with which they revived damaged vehicles – whether their own or captured – was one of the means by which the Germans redressed their inferiority in numbers."[225]

Rommel's supply predicament, however, only fuelled Churchill's desire to strike. The failure of Operation Battleaxe was a severe blow to the Prime Minister. Unfairly, Churchill felt that Wavell "did not convey a sense of mental vigour and the resolve to overcome obstacles." He insisted that Wavell "gave an impression of a lack of concentration upon the decisive point."[226] Both Anthony Eden and General Sir John Dill, the Chief of the Imperial General Staff (CIGS), disagreed with Churchill's assessment, however, it made no difference. Wavell had been burdened with extensive responsibilities and limited resources, and arguably had under the circumstances done a laudable job. Nonetheless, the loss of Greece and Crete, as well as the failure of Operation Battleaxe still remained. The difficult events had weighed heavily on Wavell and he was exhausted. Adding to the situation, quite simply, Churchill had never really warmed to Wavell. As a result, he sacked him, a move he had been contemplating for weeks.[227] His cable was brief and to the point. "I have come to the conclusion," Churchill wrote, "that public interest will best be served by appointment of General Auchinleck to relieve you in command of Armies of Middle East."[228]

General Sir Claude Auchinleck, whose motto was "always be bold," was now thrown into the breach. He had commanded the expedition to Norway in 1940; was general officer commanding (GOC) Southern Command in England for a period and at the time of this appointment was the Commander-in-Chief, India. He took over as C-in-C Middle East Forces on July 5, 1941.[229] On arrival, General Auchinleck paid tribute to his predecessor. "On taking over command of the Middle East Forces," he asserted, "I found the general position incomparably better than it had been a year earlier on the collapse of France. This improvement was entirely due to the energy of my predecessor, General Sir Archibald Wavell, and to his vigour in seeking out the enemy wherever he was to be found."[230]

Changes in theatre were not limited strictly to the Allied side. On the Axis front, there were a number of vicissitudes as well. On July 1, 1941, Hitler promoted Rommel to full general. A few weeks later, on July 19th, Mussolini fired General Gariboldi for his lack of cooperation with Rommel and replaced him with General Ettore Bastico.

From an equipment standpoint, the Axis situation became even more precarious. Practically no German tanks were brought into theatre between July 1941 to the end of the year. Operation Barbarossa had taken priority. As they continually emphasized, the German high command considered North Africa a subsidiary theatre. Fortunately for the Germans, by the end of July 1941, tank strength had actually increased from about 180 to 250 tanks due almost entirely to the repair of damaged tanks.[231] This small victory, however, did not make up for the lack of fuel, reinforcements and other equipment.

Organizationally, the 5th Light Motorized Division was reconstituted as the 21st Panzer Division on August 1, 1941.[232] In addition, a number of special units were regrouped and given the name 90th Light Division (also known as the "Afrika Division"). The latter was strong in firepower and mobile infantry but totally lacking in tanks. The Afrika Korps remained basically the same, an armoured corps consisting of two Panzer divisions (i.e., 15th and 21st). Alongside the German formations stood the Italian XX Motorised Corps consisting of the armoured Ariete Division and the motorised Trieste Division, as well as the XXI Army Corps that consisted of four infantry divisions. Command of the entire Axis desert force, now called *Panzergruppe Afrika*, rested with Rommel, while command of the Afrika Korps passed to Lieutenant-General Ludwig Crüwell.[233]

With changes on both sides, the summer passed relatively quietly. Predictably, upon arrival Auchinleck was immediately besieged with inquiries by Churchill on when he planned to resume the offensive. The Prime Minister was under his own pressures. For political and military reasons an offensive was important in order to attempt to relieve some pressure on his new Soviet allies, who were desperately holding on under the hammer blow of Operation Barbarossa. A desert offensive would force the Germans to fight on two fronts. In addition, the relief of Tobruk would be a tonic for the Allied public. Moreover, success could possibly encourage the Vichy French to abandon the German camp, prompt the Americans to join the Allied cause and deter Spain and Turkey from potentially joining the Axis alliance. Finally, the recapture of the Cyrenaica airfields would provide additional air cover for the fleet in the Mediterranean and take pressure off the besieged island of Malta. Churchill continually pressed the view that the desert Army should continuously engage the Germans, forcing them to use up their resources that were so difficult to replace. Clearly the stakes were high and the weight on the new C-in-C enormous.

The pressure from Britain was no surprise. British generals knew of Churchill's natural inclination to the offensive. From Churchill's perspective he believed that generals tended to be overly cautious and pedantic. He assessed:

> *Generals are often prone, if they have the chance, to choose a set-piece battle, when all is ready, at their own selected moment, rather than to wear down the enemy by continued unspectacular fighting. They naturally prefer certainty to hazard. They forget that war never stops, but burns on from day to day with ever-changing results not only in one theatre but in all.*[234]

British generals were not the only ones despondent over Churchill's constant demand for offensives and crazy schemes. The American Chiefs of Staff shared their exasperation. Former Australian war correspondent and historian Chester Wilmot eloquently captured their outlook:

> *[The Americans] fully appreciated his [Churchill] capacity to drive and inspire, but they wondered where it would lead them. They never really understood how his mind worked and they were appalled at the extravagant ideas which he would suddenly spring upon them. New plans and projects tumbled over each other in his restless and fertile brain and he kept his own Chiefs of Staff in constant anxiety about what he would propose next. They were forever placing the curb of facts upon the wild gallop of his imagination but they learned to sense when he was in earnest and when he was merely working an idea out of his system.*[235]

General Auchinleck now felt Wavell's pain. The Prime Minister demanded action. Regardless, Auchinleck held three firm prerequisites prior to launching an offensive:

- The security of his base, which included consolidating Syria;
- Strong Air and Maritime forces capable of closely cooperating and

supporting the Army; and

- Strong, properly trained armoured forces. He calculated that he would require, as a minimum, two but preferably three, armoured divisions, as well as a motorized division.[236]

Auchinleck continually pushed back, insisting that he needed a 50 percent reserve of tanks before commencing any new offensive. As such, based on projections of tanks Churchill promised, Auchinleck calculated that he should be ready to launch an offensive with 350 tanks as the strike force by end of October.[237] Fortunately, from July 1941 onwards, as a result of the Red Sea opening up to American shipping, as well as industrial output in the US, UK and the Dominions hitting war production levels, the flow of munitions and equipment from North America and the United Kingdom improved the military balance.[238] While the Germans were struggling to maintain their strength, the Allies were now consistently building up their forces. The issue of going on the offensive was one of who could reinforce and re-equip the fastest. And the battle was being lost by the Germans. In August alone, the Germans lost 35 percent of their supplies and reinforcements dispatched by sea to North Africa. In October the loss rate increased to 63 percent.[239] This scale of loss tipped the scales favourably for a British offensive.

Not wanting to let this advantage go to waste, planning for the new offensive proceeded quickly. On September 24, 1941, Auchinleck formed the Eighth Army under Lieutenant-General Sir Alan Cunningham, who he now tasked with taking the offensive in the Western Desert.[240] To assist with this difficult role, the LRDG were placed under his command. Five days later Cunningham issued clear instructions to Lieutenant-Colonel Guy Prendergast, who had taken over command of the LRDG from Bagnold. The role of the LRDG was now defined as:

- To obtain information of enemy movement on certain tracks and in certain areas; and to watch his reactions to any offensive by us;
- To provide further information as to the going;
- To try at all times to harass the enemy as far as possible, and as the Group Commander thought fit; provided the patrols did not get too deeply involved in fighting; and
- To send in tactical information as early as possible: and when doing so just before or during an operation to take the risk of W/T messages being picked up by the enemy which would not be justified in other circumstances.[241]

In addition, the LRDG moved from Kufra to Siwa to be closer to Eighth Army HQ.[242]

The LRDG, although always in the background, had made a commendable contribution to British operations. On September 29, 1941, the Commander-in-Chief Middle Eastern Forces passed on to the CO the CIGS's accolades. The CIGS wrote, "I am very impressed by the work done by your Long Range Desert Patrols. Their latest reconnaissance is a fine example of their skill and daring."[243] Even after Wavell's departure he continued to sing the praises of the LRDG to his chain-of-command:

> *I should like to take this opportunity to bring to notice a small body of men who have for a year past done inconspicuous but invaluable service, the Long Range Desert Group. It was formed under Major (now Colonel) R.A. Bagnold in July 1940, to reconnoitre the great Libyan desert on the Western borders of Egypt and the Sudan. Operating in small independent columns, the group has penetrated into nearly every part of desert Libya, an area comparable in size with that of India. Not only have the patrols brought back much information but they have attacked enemy forts, captured personnel, transport and grounded aircraft as far as 800 miles inside hostile territory. They have protected Egypt and the Sudan from any possibility of raids and have caused the enemy, in a lively apprehension of their activities, to tie up considerable forces in the defence of distant outposts. Their journeys across vast regions of unexplored desert have entailed the crossing of physical obstacles and the endurance of extreme summer temperatures, both of which would, a year ago, have been deemed impossible. Their exploits have been achieved only by careful organisation, and a very high standard of enterprise, discipline, mechanical maintenance and desert navigation.[244]*

They would also play an important role in the upcoming Operation Crusader.

The LRDG would become a critical conduit of information for Auchinleck and his strike force. By October 25, 1941, Auchinleck had the 7th Armoured Division, 4th Armoured Brigade Group, the 4th Indian Division, the New Zealand Division, and the 1st South African Division in theatre. In the Tobruk salient remained the 70th British Division (which had replaced the Australians) and the 32nd Army Tank Brigade. In Egypt the 2nd South African Division was in general reserve. Auchinleck's desert army represented the largest and best equipped force that Britain could field at the time. It consisted of 150,000 men, 532 cruiser and 204 infantry tanks.[245] In addition, at the beginning of Operation Crusader the Allies had 550 serviceable aircraft in the desert and they could depend on an additional 66 aircraft flying out of Malta. Conversely, the Axis had 342 serviceable aircraft in Cyrenaica.[246]

One issue that caused weeks of delay was the failure of British Army HQ to ensure that the tanks dispatched to the Middle East had the necessary modifications done prior to transfer. As a result, the tanks arrived in Alexandria and had to be unloaded direct from the ships to the maintenance yards to undergo the necessary refit of air and lubrication systems. This delay meant that crews had lost weeks of valuable training time to accustom themselves to the new armoured vehicles.

Lieutenant-General George Brink, the 1st South African Division commander, elaborated on the inadequacy of training time. He confided to his diary:

> *There was no time to ponder or to argue. The Army Commander was applying the acid test. I was not happy about the state of training of my Division and in my heart, I felt that it was not in a fit state, tactically, and did not possess the hitting power to engage in serious operations. We have splendid fighting material, well led and ably commanded, but the best human material in the world requires careful moulding and must have the wherewithal to engage a tough and determined enemy such as the Afrika Korps. The die was cast; however, the Division was already on the move to its concentration area and the honour of South Africa was at stake.*[247]

Adding to the mounting challenges was the issue of stockpiling water for the large offensive, which was severely disrupted. A German air attack on Fouka on October 11th damaged the water pumps. As a result, almost all the water that had been accumulated to fill the pipes and reservoirs west of Fuka for the offensive was lost. Another four weeks was required, using all available water vehicles and vessels, to replenish the water stores. This reset was achieved by November 13th.[248]

Despite all the preparations for the massive offensive, the Germans were kept completely in the dark. Surprise was achieved through a number of actions. Significantly, the RAF and South African Air Force (SAAF) kept the skies above the concentration areas clear of enemy aircraft. In addition, British intelligence scored a major coup. In July a Palestinian farm worker reported spotting a parachutist landing near Ramleh. He noted that the mysterious parachutist dug a number of holes nearby to bury something. The interloper was eventually captured. He turned out to be the Gauleiter of Mannheim,(a pseudonym for a German spy) who was dropped into Palestine by German intelligence to attempt to foment an uprising against the British among the Arabs. Buried in the ground they found Palestinian currency, a short-wave transmitter complete with codes, identification signals and specified transmission times. This information was then used to send bogus messages to the Germans. Importantly, they concocted a scheme that portrayed a picture of the preparations of the Western Desert Force being a deception to cover for the redeployment of British forces to the Caucasus to assist the Soviet Union and safeguard their own oil supplies in the Persian Gulf. Rommel, seemingly obsessed with capturing Tobruk, bought into the ruse as it supported his perception that the British would not mount an attack in the near-term, thus allowing him to focus on his own planned offensive to finally capture Tobruk.[249]

Rommel was totally duped. British operational security had been flawlessly maintained. Rommel conceded that German reconnaissance "brought back no evidence of an impending attack. No supply dumps capable of supporting a major offensive were seen in the Egyptian frontier area." He acknowledged, "The enemy's approach march and deployment passed unnoticed by our reconnaissance. His concealment of his preparations was excellent. The wireless silence which he imposed prevented our interception service detecting his approach march into the assembly areas. ...But air reconnaissance failed just as badly on the southern flank, where the British had established large supply dumps. Ground reconnaissance was equally ineffective." He concluded, "As a result the attack achieved complete tactical surprise."[250]

Discounting any British offensive intentions, Rommel focused on his assault on Tobruk. In fact, the Afrika Korps was in the process of moving into position for its attack on the enemy port, which was scheduled for November 23rd. The Germans held air superiority over the Tobruk area, therefore the British garrison had to maintain their dispositions until the last possible minute. This imposition meant that all deployments had to be done at night or on an approach march straight from the reserve positions during daylight.

Tobruk proved a vexing problem for Rommel. It denied him a port for resupply, always creating a threat to his rear area if he chose to advance, as well as tying down forces required to maintain the cordon around the salient. He required four Italian divisions and three German battalions to maintain the noose around the fortified British position. Not surprisingly then, Tobruk was a focus for him. This preoccupation however, came at a cost. Rommel's own estimate demonstrates his complete lack of awareness of the coming storm. He wrote, "My intention is to engage and destroy

Rommel speaking to a subordinate commander. (IWM, HU_016766)

the British armoured forces in the area South of Tobruk, and subsequently defeat his inf[antry] in detail, should he advance and engage my forces investing the Fortress."[251]

Rommel's decision to attack Tobruk came from a carefully crafted military appreciation. He realized that the defence of Cyrenaica was necessary until "such time as my forces are reinforced and my supply situation is sufficiently built up to enable me to prepare an offensive against the Delta."[252] He also deduced that the 7th Armoured Division was his priority "which I must engage and destroy first. Once deprived of Armoured support his Inf[antry] Div[isions]s can be dealt with in detail subsequently."[253] Rommel also recognized the threat to his lines of communication. "I must guard against a sortie against my rear from Tobruk," he wrote, "where the enemy garrison, recently reinforced by fresh troops, is still full of fight."[254]

In his calculation he also rued the lack of a credible ally. "The fighting qualities of all Italian formations are doubtful," he noted, "I must therefore rely on my Armoured Divisions to fight a successful engagement on their own; and I must, if possible, choose my ground in such a way as to enable them to do this without having to rely on support from my ally."[255]

In his deliberations Rommel didn't expect the British ready to conduct an offensive before November 1, 1941.[256] He had 220 tanks (excluding 68 Mk I and Mk II tanks, many of which were in questionable condition). He estimated British tank strength at 250-300 Cruiser tanks, in addition to some heavy tanks.[257] What concerned Rommel however, was the British increase in aircraft. "The British air forces have been greatly strengthened during the summer," he noticed, "They have unlimited petrol supplies and a large number of LGs [landing grounds] from which to operate...I must therefore prepare for a heavy scale of enemy air attack in support of his offensive."[258]

The logistical question became an ever-present anchor. "Owing to the intensity of the fighting on the Russian Front I am unlikely to obtain any substantial reinforcements in armoured or air forces for some time," he acknowledged. "Furthermore," he continued, "the ever-increasing Axis shipping losses between Italy and Africa impose a grave restriction on the flow of supplies and reinforcements generally. I must therefore conserve to the utmost these vital elements of my forces in Libya, in order that I may deploy my maximum strength at the decisive time and place, the armoured forces battle-ground."[259] Based on his limited dumping program, Rommel deduced, "I can probably safely count on being able to operate for about 3 weeks at the maximum. I must therefore force an early decision in the armoured battle, as large-scale protracted operations will place me in an increasingly precarious position."[260]

And so, by the fall of 1941, both sides were planning and preparing for a major offensive. Auchinleck was careful in his preparations and was intending to launch a surprise assault on the Axis positions. The plan for Operation Crusader, which represented the largest British armoured operation to date, called for an extremely large Allied force to cross the Egyptian frontier, which was approximately 210 kilometers from the existing railhead, and then advance another 80 to 130 kilometres to the operational battle area. Maintaining the element of surprise would be extremely difficult.

Auchinleck's plan was to engage the Afrika Korps with the 7th Armoured Division while the 1st South African Division covered their left flank. Meanwhile, on their right, XIII Corps, supported by 4th Armoured Brigade (detached from 7th Armoured Division), would make a clockwise flanking advance west of Sidi Omar and hold position, threatening the rear of the line of Axis defensive strongpoints, which ran east from Sidi Omar to the coast at Halfaya. Central to the plan was the destruction of the Axis armour by 7th Armoured Division to allow the relatively lightly armoured XIII Corps to advance north to Bardia on the coast whilst XXX Corps continued north-west to Tobruk to link-up with a breakout by the 70th Infantry Division.

The Tobruk commander felt confident of his ability to breakout and assist with the offensive. "The Italians, who represent ¾ of the investing force, have low morale," he wrote in his appreciation of the situation. "Their infantry has shown little enterprise and no offensive spirit," he observed, "The Italians are however now digging in as hard as they can and gradually closing in the available 'breathing space' between our and their positions particularly towards the right of the Eastern Sector." The Tobruk commander concluded, "Strike hard and fast and accept risk, especially against the Italians, despite their numerical superiority in number of guns and infantry."[261] His plan was "to open a corridor through the close investing forces round Tobruk and keep it open until joined by the relieving force [and] to impede any enemy withdrawal."[262]

Churchill's direction to Auchinleck was also typically sanguine. "General Auchinleck's task," The Prime Minister later wrote, "was first to recapture Cyrenaica, destroying in the process the enemy's armour, and secondly, if all went well, to capture Tripolitania."[263] His optimism would be somewhat premature.

The War Cabinet perspective of Auchinleck's intentions was more restrained. The "Weekly Resume" recorded that Auchinleck planned, "(a) to bring about a tank battle, with the particular object of destroying the German 15th and 21st Armoured Divisions; (b) at the same time, to roll up the enemy's forces in the frontier area Sollum-Bardia-Sidi Omar from the south and south-west."[264] It also noted that:

> *To provoke the tank battle, the plan was to advance on Tobruk with cruiser tank formations via Fort Maddalena and El Gobi with the object of forcing the enemy to leave his laager positions and fight in the open. The Tobruk garrison was to co-operate. The attack on the enemy in the frontier area was to be carried out primarily with unarmoured formations supported by "I" [Matilda] tanks. In addition, a third force was to advance from Jarabub on Jalo, in Western Cyrenaica, a distance of 180 miles.*[265]

Auchinleck's plan for Operation Crusader also called for a preparatory air phase that would begin five weeks prior to the commencement of the offensive. The Commander of the Western Desert Air Force, Air Vice-Marshal Arthur Coningham, had three important tasks:

- establish air superiority in Cyrenaica;
- gather situational awareness of the enemy's movements; and
- disrupt the enemy supply system.

Hurricane fighter on a desert airstrip. (WO, MoI, 1941)

All these tasks were to be executed of course, without arousing Rommel's suspicion. To achieve the desired effect, air operations were broken into two phases. In Phase One, Coningham's aircraft were to attack supply dumps, concentrations of transportation, workshops and enemy ports as well as enemy forward airfields in North Africa. In Phase Two, the Western Desert Air Force was to focus its entire efforts against enemy aircraft in theatre, as well as providing air cover for Cunningham's Eighth Army.

Starting on November 13th, despite less than favourable weather conditions and very low cloud cover, the Desert Air Force began to place immense pressure on the enemy. British aircraft bombed Axis airfields, destroying and damaging runways, buildings as well as bomber, air transport and fighter aircraft throughout Cyrenaica. Once the offensive proper started, the Desert Air Force would transition to maintaining air superiority, interfering with the enemy's supply system and providing as much reconnaissance as possible.

The LRDG also figured into the Operation Crusader plan. Initially six patrols would be used. The Eighth Army HQ directive to Lieutenant-Colonel Prendergast, the LRDG commanding officer stated, "[your] role from D-1, until modified by instructions from this HQ will be observing any enemy movement. As operations progress towards the completion of the present phase of occupying Cyrenaica, so the area of activity for LRDG will move West into Tripolitania."[266] Their main function was to observe and report on enemy movement and reactions to the Allied manoeuvre. The task of "Road Watch" was far from glamorous but it was extremely important.

To conduct road watches the LRDG patrols would erect a base camp in a wadi. Their vehicles would be dispersed and camouflaged. Then each evening at dusk, two men would find a position a few hundred metres from the road and lie up and observe until they were relieved the following night. Each two-man observation post was equipped with high powered binoculars, a notebook and recognition manuals. One person would observe while the other recorded events. It was extremely tiring and uncomfortable work. Quite often they faced almost uninterrupted flows of traffic and therefore had no chance to relax. At the end of the shift on return to the base camp on the following night, a report would be sent to HQ in Cairo.[267] Major-General Lloyd Owen described:

> It [Road Watch] was a task which was terribly boring and one which none of us liked: equally did none of us fail to realize how invaluable our reports were, for at that time so much was being landed at Tripoli in order to avoid the constant pounding that Benghazi was given by RAF bombers. It was a task we all knew we had to do sometime, but none of us were enthusiastic about it.[268]

The LRDG intelligence officer later went on to say that Road Watch was "perhaps the most useful job LRDG ever did."[269]

Auchinleck also tasked the LRDG to conduct a number of other clandestine operations in support of a number of other SOF organizations that were to participate in Operation Crusader. To expedite the success of his upcoming offensive, General Auchinleck authorized a number of secret missions, which if successful, would have a potentially dramatic effect. In an unusual show of support for "private armies" and unorthodox missions, he was about to unleash the dogs of war.

CHAPTER 5
IN SEARCH OF LEOPARDS OF THE HUNTER CLASS

THE USE OF SPECIAL FORCES by Generals Auchinleck and Wavell was somewhat atypical. Aside from Prime Minister Churchill, few senior military commanders favoured "private armies," as special forces were prone to be called. Churchill was the early champion of special organizations that piqued the tolerance of conventionally minded, traditional senior officers. Churchill's romantic image of war and freewheeling ruffians taking battle to the enemy in unorthodox ways did little to calm the anxiety of military commanders who found themselves in crisis at the beginning of World War II. Dramatic images provided by Churchill such as, "There comes from the sea a hand of steel that plucks the German sentries from their posts," may have been inspirational to some in the dark early days of the war, but the fact is, the Prime Minister's support for special forces was born from weakness, not a position of strength.[270]

The speed and violence of the German invasion of Western Europe in the spring of 1940 caught the Allies, still mired in their Great War mentality, totally by surprise. The destruction of the West took 46 days, but it was decided in only ten. With regard to the German attack on May 9th and 10th 1940, Churchill lamented, "Complete tactical surprise was achieved in nearly every case. Out of the darkness came suddenly innumerable parties of well-armed ardent storm troops, often with light artillery, and long before daybreak a hundred and fifty miles of front were aflame."[271]

The British Prime Minister went on to describe:

It was thought that on our southern flank the Ardennes were impassable for large modern armies, and south of that again began the regular fortified Maginot Line, stretching out to the Rhine and along the Rhine to Switzerland. All therefore seemed to depend upon the forward left-handed counterstroke of the Allied Northern

Armies...Marshal Petain told the Senate Army Commission, "This sector is not dangerous... Of the nine divisions deployed along this sector, only two were of the permanent regular army. The Germans broke through at every point, bridging the canals or seizing the locks and water-controls. In a single day all the outer line of the Dutch defences was mastered.[272]

France was next to fall. On the morning of May 15th, the French Premier called Churchill and stated, "We are beaten; we have lost the battle...the front is broken near Sedan; they are pouring through in great numbers with tanks and armoured cars."[273]

With their backs to the sea, the British launched Operation Dynamo using virtually any craft that could float. Aside from the Royal Navy, there were lifeboats, dockyard launches, cockle boats, fishing and pleasure craft, prime transport and commercial ships and barges. Between May 27th and June 4th, despite the German pressure, 338,226 personnel were evacuated from Dunkirk. But the cost was enormous. The losses at Dunkirk for the British Expeditionary Force (BEF) amounted to 68,111 killed, wounded, or taken prisoner. Equally significant, the British left behind 2,472 guns, 63,879 trucks, 76,000 tons of ammunition and 600,000 tons of fuel and supplies. The Royal Navy lost 243 ships (out of more than 1,000 engaged).[274]

Significantly, the desperate withdrawal resulted in the loss of virtually

German river crossing during the invasion of France. (NA, RML-000147)

all their heavy equipment, weapons and transport. The military conveyed the stark reality of the shortage of arms to the British War Cabinet. The political leadership was informed that there were fewer than 600,000 rifles and only 12,000 Bren guns in the whole of the United Kingdom.[275] Britain now braced for what seemed to be the inevitable conclusion to the German master plan - the invasion of England.

For most, the logical deduction was that Britain had no other choice but to surrender the initiative and dig-in and wait for the inevitable invasion. The British military high command, overwhelmed by the task that they faced, saw only a defensive battle in the short term. The only two viable forms of offensive action, they argued, were the traditional economic blockade utilizing the superiority of the Royal Navy on the high seas, and strategic bombing conducted by the Royal Air Force.

This unimaginative way forward, however, was not accepted by all. Importantly, on 4 June 1940, Winston Churchill was appointed prime minister. Churchill would prove to be a constant irritant to senior British commanders. He realized that only through offensive action could a nation provide its military and citizens with the necessary confidence and morale to sustain a war effort. Not surprisingly then, on the same day he was appointed prime minister he declared in the House of Commons, "we shall not be content with a defensive war."[276]

Churchill was not to be denied. That same afternoon, he penned a note to General Ismay. "We are greatly concerned," he wrote, "with the dangers of the German landing in England." He pondered rhetorically, "why should it be thought impossible for us to do anything of the same kind to them?" He then added, "We should immediately set to work to organize self-contained, thoroughly-equipped raiding units."[277] Churchill knew intuitively that winning a war meant maintaining the initiative. As such, Churchill mused, "how wonderful it would be if the Germans could be made to wonder where they were going to be struck next, instead of forcing us to try to wall in the island and roof it over!"[278]

Two days later, Churchill sent additional direction to Ismay. He explained:

Enterprises must be prepared with specially trained troops of the hunter class who can develop a reign of terror down these coasts, first of all on the "butcher and bolt" policy; but later on, or perhaps as soon as we are organized, we could surprise Calais or Boulogne, kill and capture the Hun garrison, and hold the place until all the preparations to reduce it by siege or heavy storm and been made, and then away. The passive –resistance war, in which we have acquitted ourselves so well, must come to an end. I look to the Joint Chiefs of the Staff to propose me measures for a vigorous, enterprising, a ceaseless offensive against the whole German-occupied coastline.[279]

Churchill maintained his contentious approach. Despite the constant protests of his senior military commanders, whose entire focus was seemingly on the defensive, Churchill refused to allow them to wallow in a defensive mindset.[280] Conversely, Churchill held a relentless fixation on striking back at the Germans, which drove his military commanders apoplectic. And the prime minister had no shortage of ideas. As American President Franklin Delano Roosevelt quipped, "He [Churchill] has a hundred [brilliant ideas] a day and about four of them are good."[281]

Despite widespread resistance within the military, Ismay passed Churchill's direction to the Chief of the Imperial General Staff (CIGS), General Sir John Dill. The CIGS promptly assigned the task to one of his general staff officers, Lieutenant-Colonel Dudley W. Clarke. Clarke's mission was to propose schemes by which the offensive spirit of the Army could be fostered until it was in a position to resume the offensive in the conventional manner.[282] Clarke began work immediately. He was cut from the same cloth as Churchill. He too realized that "even the lightest threats . . . must compel the Germans to turn in the midst of their feverish invasion preparations to organize defence and divert troops to guard this enormous front line [occupied Europe]."[283]

To Clarke the solution was self-evident; it had to be a focus on irregular warfare, specifically special raiding operations. He believed this solution was the optimal concept under the present conditions. Therefore, he proposed that "commandos," the term taken directly from the Boer War experience, be established, "trained in 'snatch and grab' night raiding from landing craft."[284] He believed that commandos conducting raids would disrupt the German war effort, destroy valuable resources and divert enemy personnel by requiring forces to be allocated to defend against the raids. Equally as important, the raids would restore the offensive spirit of the British Army.[285]

The CIGS briefed Churchill who took to the idea immediately. After all, it appealed to his character. He later penned a note to President Roosevelt that revealed his mindset. "[The] essence of defence," he asserted, "is to attack the enemy upon us - leap at his throat and keep the grip until the life is out of him."[286]

Despite resistance from many senior military commanders who felt that valuable resources were being frittered away for no valuable return at a time when the nation faced invasion, Churchill pressed on. For many

Commando training - scaling cliffs. (Photographer Lt. Royal. LAC, PA 213630)

officers there was a belief that "well-trained infantry could do all that was expected of the commandos, and that the formation of these special units represented a drain on infantry strength that was out of proportion to the results likely to be achieved."[287] In a remarkable display of military efficiency, by June 8th 1940 General Dill received approval for the creation of the commandos, and that same afternoon Section MO9 of the War Office was established. Four days later, Churchill appointed Lieutenant-General Sir Alan Bourne, Adjutant-General, Royal Marines as "Commander of Raiding Operations on Coasts in Enemy Occupation and Advisor to the Chiefs of Staff on Combined Operations."[288]

Clarke's concept quickly came to life. He could now establish his "picked bands of guerilla fighters who would harry the long enemy coastline in order to make him [Germans] dissipate his superior resources."[289] He proposed the creation of 12 Commando units consisting of 500 men, broken up into a headquarters and ten troops respectively. Incredibly, Lieutenant-Colonel Clarke was also directed to mount a cross channel raid "at the earliest possible moment."[290]

The next hurdle was actually raising the force. The War Office made it clear from the start that no existing units of the Army could be made available for raiding operations, nor could any personnel be diverted from the necessity of home defence. The creation of the commandos was based on the concept of stringent economy. So acute was the shortage of equipment and weaponry that commandos were "armed, equipped, organised and administered for one task and one task only – tip and run raids of not more than 48 hours from bases in England against the continent of Europe."[291] The problem was so severe that a commando unit could not draw its full complement of weapons, such as submachine guns, from a central pool until it was about to debark on a raid.[292]

Fortunately, the personnel issue was solved fairly quickly. The cadre of Nos. 1 and 2 Commandos were harvested from the ten Independent Companies that were raised earlier in the year to harass the advancing Germans in Norway. The ten Independent Companies, each consisting of approximately 20 officers and 270 men, were drawn largely from second-line Territorial Army divisions in April 1940. These units were designated exclusively for raiding, and as such were self-contained on a ship which was to be their floating base. They had no garrison and were billeted in private homes in coastal towns. However, the chaos created with the German assault on Norway forestalled any real preparation. There was practically no training for the militia soldiers or leaders of the Independent Companies before they were deployed to that beleaguered Nordic country.

Moreover, the Germans swept through Norway so quickly that the five Independent Companies that actually made it to Norway were withdrawn by early June. In the end, they conducted no raids and saw very little contact with the enemy.[293]

Nonetheless, their disbandment provided an immediate pool of manpower. However, the inexperience of the territorial troops was seen as incompatible with the intended concept and as a result, under pressure from Churchill, recruiting for the remaining commandos was done by asking for volunteers for "special service of a hazardous nature" from the regular army.[294] Prospective candidates were required to be fully trained men. Commanding Officers were picked from the volunteers and then they were given a free hand to choose their own officers, who in turn were dispatched to various units to select their own men.

The theoretical construct for selection was sound. The nature of commando operations dictated that volunteers were to be the best possible material. As such, initially, officers and men were hand-picked from volunteers. "Great care," revealed one report, "was taken in the selection of officers and men and from the outset they were specially picked units."[295] Recruiters wanted intelligent, young, exceptionally fit individuals who demonstrated courage, endurance, initiative and resourcefulness, as well as self-reliance and aggressiveness. Marksmanship and the ability to swim were also essential skills required. The selecting officers also tried to pick candidates who were mechanically inclined, able to drive motor vehicles

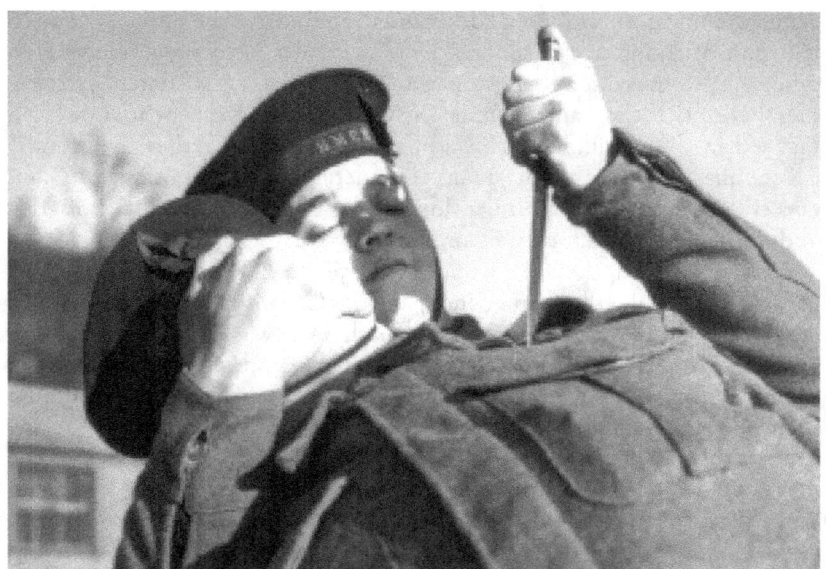

Commando training - silent killing technique. (LAC, PA 183055)

and immune to air or sea sickness.[296]

"I looked for intelligence and keenness," recalled Brigadier John Durnford-Slater, the first Commanding Officer (CO) of 3 Commando. "What I was seeking and what I obtained," he explained, "were men of character beyond normal." He added, "I intended that every soldier in the Commandos should be a potential leader; that he must be mentally and physically tough and must radiate cheerfulness, enthusiasm and confidence."[297] Importantly, they did not select a full complement of non-commissioned officers (NCOs). They preferred to promote from within once their own men proved themselves.

The men drawn to the Commando idea very quickly coalesced into the concept that was expected. Raiding was their primary role. In essence, they were to be trained to be "hard hitting assault troops" who were capable of working in cooperation with the Navy and Air Force. As such, they were expected to capture strong points, destroy enemy services, neutralize coastal batteries and wipe out any designated enemy force by surprise as detailed by higher headquarters.[298] They were also told that they would have to become accustomed to longer hours, more work and less rest than the other members of the armed forces.

Predictably, the concept of commandos attracted a like-minded group of aggressive, action-oriented individuals who quickly shaped the essence of the commando idea. "There was a sense of urgency, a striving to achieve an ideal, an individual determination to drive the physical body to the limit of endurance to support a moral resolve," explained one veteran officer. "The individual determination," he added, "was shared by every member of the force, and such heights of collective idealism are not often reached in the mundane business of soldiering."[299] Together they forged a "commando spirit" that comprised determination; enthusiasm and cheerfulness, particularly under adverse conditions; individual initiative and self-reliance; and finally, comradeship.[300]

Once selected, the next requirement was to get them organized and trained. Much like the former Independent Companies, the commandos were not put in barracks, but rather each man was given a subsistence allowance and was required to find his own accommodation and food. Commanding Officers touted this practice to be of great value because it increased a man's self-reliance, made him available for training at any time of the day or night, and eliminated the loss of manpower due to the perennial demands of administrative duties and tasks inherently associated with any garrison setting.[301] The commando troops appreciated this aspect as well. "It is the greatest job in the Army that one could possibly get, and it is a job that, if properly carried out, can be of enormous value," asserted Major Geoffrey Appleyard. He added, "no red tape, no paper work ...just pure operations, the success of which depends principally on oneself and the men one has oneself picked to do the job with you...its revolutionary."[302] Fellow commando officer Corran Purdon echoed those sentiments. "I loved the commandos more than anything," Purdon effused, "because it was so free of bullshit. The best thing I ever did as a regular officer was to be in the Commandos."[303]

The perspective of the other ranks was not different. One commando recounted, "You'd volunteered for the Commandos, they realized that you were human beings and you had a bit of sense, that you didn't need to be roared at and shouted at, screamed at all the time. Not only that, if you did anything, even in training, everything was explained to you. If you'd a different idea, even as a lowly Private, you could say 'Well, sir, don't you think if we went that way instead of this way it would be easier?' If you were right that was the method that was adopted."[304]

John Price asserted, "What I liked about the Commandos after the ordinary infantry, we were allowed to have some common sense. We were allowed to show initiative. We were briefed before we went into action, not herded like sheep."[305] Ernie Chappell, one of the original Commandos added, "Many soldiers weren't cut out for this sort of thing - those who had been schooled in regimentation rather than guerilla tactics ... we were belligerent. And, we wanted to have a go."[306]

The difference in approach to soldiering in the Commandos as compared to the regular army appealed to many and they remained desperate to stay. That is why the "RTU" (return to unit) became the CO's most powerful punishment.[307]

Initially, training was the responsibility of the individual commando unit commanding officers. However, in December 1940, the castle grounds at Achnacarry became a Holding Unit and a special training centre until December of the following year when it officially became the Commando Depot. Its purpose was to achieve a level of uniformity and concentration in the early stages of a commando recruit's training. Once a recruit completed his basic course at the Depot, he was dispatched to the Commando Holding Unit where he underwent further advanced collective and combined arms training prior to being posted to an active commando unit.[308] The standards were unrelenting. Individuals who failed to meet the requisite training requirements were immediately returned to their original units.

Whether at the Depot, Holding Unit, or at the unit, commando training was exceptionally gruelling. Long marches (up to 40 miles in a 24-hour period), strenuous assault courses, cliff climbing and exercises that focussed on arduous and exhausting activities were routinely undertaken. Blank ammunition was unheard of. The requirement for realism, as well as mental and physical challenge, necessitated the use of only live ammunition and bombs. As its foundation, the training was intended to make soldiers tough and willingly to endure and strive for mission completion regardless of the hardship or obstacles they faced.

At its core, the training was designed to achieve a number of goals. Firstly, it was devised to foster in the commando soldier the offensive spirit - an ever-present eagerness to "have a go" at the enemy. Secondly, it nurtured the belief that darkness and the night was an aid rather than a deterrent in "closing with and attacking the enemy." Equally important, it developed self-reliance and the ability of the soldier to act, whenever necessary, on his own initiative to accomplish the mission.[309] In addition, the training endowed him with a degree of physical fitness akin to that of a trained athlete.

The training program also had a very tangible practical side as well. It taught specific skills that were crucial to raiding. For instance, it developed a familiarity with the sea and with ships and small craft, as well as the ability to "live off the land" and scale cliffs and mountainous terrain. Commando soldiers also learned infiltration tactics, demolition and sabotage techniques, parachuting and the "art of bluff and low cunning."[310]

The commandos were expected to be able to conduct assault landings

Commando training exercise with small craft. (LAC, PA 113247)

before first light to seize and destroy coastal defence artillery batteries or installations, and / or landings in the dark in rough weather and on rocky coasts in areas where defences were deemed to be weaker. They were also responsible for landings under cliffs with scaling operations to strike inshore in locations where the enemy least expected attacks. Commandos were also given the task of penetrating behind enemy lines, either by infiltration in small parties or by landing on the coast from surface craft, submarines, or flying boats. Night assaults were conducted against headquarters, tank harbours, communications facilities or installations on the enemy's lines of communication, as well as ambushes of enemy forces moving forward to the battle area.

Commandos were also tasked with the ability to infiltrate airfield perimeters to destroy aircraft, as well as conducting raids to obtain identification and other information required on the enemy, or simply to create tension, disruption and anxiety with the enemy defences. Finally, they were also expected to create large scale diversionary raids, by one or two commando units, to induce the enemy to commit his reserves.[311]

Although the commandos began to attract the requisite amount and type of manpower, and despite their high-level sponsor, predictably they quickly met resistance. "As ever," lamented Brigadier Anthony Farrar-Hockley, "a new concept, a new organization tends to be resisted, even at a peak of crisis in a nation's affairs."[312] Resistance came from both the War

Office and particularly from operational commanders. Not surprisingly, many felt that the diversion of resources during the critical period of likely invasion was not sound. And even once this threat passed, many still felt that the investment in commandos and raiding was not worth the return. "Descending on the enemy, killing a few guards, blowing up the odd pillbox, and taking a handful of prisoners," critiqued Major-General Julian Thompson in later years, "was not a cost-effective use of ships, craft and highly trained soldiers."[313]

Furthermore, directors and commanding officers were upset with the prospect of losing some of their best men who invariably volunteered for the special duty. "The resistances of the War Office were obstinate," Churchill whinged, "and increased as the professional ladder was descended." He explained that "the idea that large bands of favoured 'irregulars,' with their unconventional attire and easy-and-free bearing, should throw an implied slur on the efficiency and courage of the Regular battalions was odious to men who had given all their lives to the organised and discipline of permanent units." He added, "The colonels of many of our finest regiments were aggrieved."[314] One official report acknowledged that "Home Forces have consistently used their predominating influence at the War Office to thwart the efforts of those well-disposed to us."[315]

Despite the opposition, their existence, as well as the raiding concept, were pushed forward. Much of this was due to Churchill's active interest and aggressive sponsorship. On June 18, 1940, Churchill prompted Ismay for a report. To Churchill commandos represented offensive power and were just as effective in home defence as they were for raiding. As such, he demanded to know what had been done "about storm troops." He visualized a force of "at least twenty thousand Storm Troops or "Leopards" poised to spring at the throat of any small landings or descents."[316] Weeks later, he wrote Anthony Eden, the Secretary of State for War, to stress the requirement for his unconventional but extremely offensive forces. "If we are to have any campaign in 1941," he stressed, "it must be amphibious in its character and there certainly will be many opportunities of minor operations all of which will depend on surprise landings of lightly equipped mobile forces accustomed to work like packs of hounds instead of being moved about in the ponderous manner which is appropriate to the regular formations." He emphasized that "we must develop the storm troop or commando idea."[317] Frustrated with the seemingly endless resistance from within the military, he suggested to Eden that an example should be made of "one or two" of the reluctant officers.[318]

The initial raids did little to help the fledgling commandos win support from their detractors. The first raid was conducted less than three weeks

Commando training with landing craft. (LAC, PA113245)

after Churchill authorized the creation of commandos, on the night of June 23/24, 1940, by 120 commando troops who were landed at various points on the French coast south of Boulogne. Their mission was to determine the nature of the German defences and capture prisoners. The raid, bemoaned Lieutenant-Colonel Clarke, who accompanied the expedition, "was a muddle from start to finish."[319] Immediately, two of the eight RAF high-speed crash rescue boats loaned for the mission developed engine trouble. This mishap pared the force down by 60 troops from the original 180 that were to participate.

Also complicating matters was the fact that for security reasons, the boats all left from various ports of departure; as they sailed for their rendezvous in the English Channel, they came under almost immediate scrutiny by RAF fighters and bombers who, having not been informed of the raid, showed a very deep interest in the boats. In addition, the navigation equipment in the craft were unreliable for long passages and caused endless confusion and delay. Together, these factors resulted in a failure of the raiding force to link-up. The navigational problems almost led to the loss of three of the boats that inadvertently approached Boulogne harbour. The Germans, believing them to be friendly craft, lit up their searchlights and harbour lights. The commando craft quickly turned away and amazingly proceeded up the coast without drawing any enemy fire or undue attention.

The actual action on the objective was equally disappointing. One group landed and took up positions inland amidst some unoccupied sand dunes. A chance encounter with a five-man German patrol ended with a brief firefight that resulted in Clarke almost losing an ear which was hit by a bullet. The Germans quickly retreated to gather reinforcements. The commando party used this interval to quickly withdraw, narrowly missing a German E-boat that was patrolling just off the coast.

Another party landed near a small hotel where they killed two sentries but were unable to enter the hotel because of its wire defences. They then lobbed grenades through the windows, fired at the building, and withdrew. A third group found themselves in the middle of a seaplane anchorage but before they could cause any damage, an aircraft took off, almost hitting them. Activity in the anchorage seemed to suddenly explode as more seaplanes began to arrive, so the commando craft departed as suddenly as it appeared. In all, very little was accomplished. Luckily all were unscathed. Despite the results, the commandos received a hero's welcome when they returned to Dover.[320]

The next raid was launched several weeks later, on the night of July 14/15. It too was unimpressive. "The raid was a very amateurish affair," confided Lieutenant-Colonel Durnford-Slater, the designated raiding commander, "from which we were very fortunate to return." He explained that "everything was faulty from the higher direction in London down to the landing craft and our own training."[321] The intent was to conduct a small raid on the Channel Island of Guernsey to seize some prisoners and gather as much information as possible, as well as inflict the maximum number of casualties on the Germans. However, the execution failed to meet the aim. Neither of the two groups participating achieved any real success.

The first group consisting of No. 11 Independent Company had only four boats. Two developed engine problems almost immediately, one ran into a rock and the final craft had problems with its compass and landed on the island of Sark by mistake. Fortunately, all managed to return to England safely.

The second group made up of No. 3 Commando reached their target. However, the boats could not reach the beach due to large rocks. As a result, the soldiers were forced to disembark and wade to shore in chest deep water over a bottom that was laced with boulders. Having overcome this obstacle, the raiders were now faced by a daunting steep climb to reach the target enemy barracks. But once at the top, despite a thorough search, no Germans could be found. Their objective was completely abandoned. Having run out of time, Durnford-Slater ordered his men back to the boats. However, the tide was now coming in and three-foot waves were breaking over the beach. The motor launches could come no closer than 50 metres to shore, and a small dinghy that was used to ferry troops to the boats had already capsized, irretrievably losing its precious cargo of submachine guns, as well as one soldier who went missing. There was no choice for the commando troops but to swim out to the boats. Unfortunately, three of the soldiers were non-swimmers and were left on the island. In the end, the expedition cost the commandos four individuals, as well as a number of weapons and several motor launches.[322]

"The raid was," conceded Durnford-Slater, "a ridiculous, almost a comic failure." He explained that "We captured no prisoners. We had done no serious damage. We had caused no casualties to the enemy...we had cut through three telegraph cables." He added, "A youth in his teens could have done the same."[323] He was right. The poor results provided further ammunition for their critics. They also earned the censure of those who supported the Commandos and raids. Churchill angrily directed that there be no more "silly fiascos like those perpetrated at Boulogne and Guernsey." He asserted that "The idea of working all these coasts up against us by pinprick raids is one to be strictly avoided."[324]

Nonetheless, the commandos and the raiding policy were allowed to evolve. Churchill however, wanted the commando idea and the raiding concept to be conducted properly. Overall, the commandos came under the control of the Combined Operations Command (COC) which was responsible for raiding operations to harass the enemy and cause him to disperse his forces. COC essentially was the mounting authority for all raids from northern Norway to the western limit of German-occupied France.[325] Two days after the most recent fiasco, on July 17, 1940, Churchill appointed Admiral of the Fleet Sir Roger Keyes, the hero of Gallipoli and Zeebrugge, as the Director of Combined Operations Command. "The truth of the matter," divulged Keyes to a friend, "is these irregular troops are very unpopular in certain quarters in the War Office. But, as you know, the Prime Minister is determined that five thousand shall be specially trained and available for raiding operations under my direction."[326] The change in command was also meant to mark the transition in policy from small to larger-scale raids even though, for lack of enough ships and trained men, they could not be undertaken immediately.[327]

Despite the best efforts of the 68-year-old Keyes, he could not gain the cooperation of others, namely the Chiefs of Staff of the different Services. They consistently resisted his ideas and efforts. "I have not yet acquired patience, and am tired of having to waste time and energy," Keyes wrote pleadingly to Churchill, "trying to overcome the supine objections of our own people in order to make real war on the enemy."[328]

The bureaucratic forbearance also showed itself in organizational turmoil for the Commandos. In November 1940, the War Office decided to reorganize the Commandos into five "Special Service Battalions" each consisting of a HQ and two Commandos. Each battalion was manned by 72 officers and 1,000 other ranks (ORs) divided into 20 sub-units. Very quickly this new organization proved to be unwieldy and the battalion structure was abandoned. Major-General Robert Laycock later assessed:

> *Operations in Europe were further restricted by the limitations inherent in the organization of the Commandos themselves. They had no power of endurance, possessing neither supporting weapons nor administrative personnel. They were armed only with short range raiding weapons and their training catered only for operations of an hour or two's duration...Partial re-organization was therefore undertaken but it affected neither the training nor equipment of the personnel but merely entailed a change in the method by which they were transported from their bases to the theatre of operations.*[329]

As a result of the failed reorganization, by February 1941, independent Commandos were once again reinstituted. However, the 11 Commandos which now existed were grouped in a Special Service (SS) Brigade. The SS Brigade's primary mission remained that of carrying out raids. It was also given the secondary tasks of acting as an elite or shock assault brigade to seize and hold a bridgehead to cover a landing in force, as well as providing specially trained covering forces for any operation.[330]

The War Office also decided to deploy commandos to the Middle East. This decision was premised on the fact that most military commanders saw no real purpose for them in Europe. Rather, they saw the North African and Middle East theatre as a more lucrative operational area for raiding.

One official assessment explained:

> *In the Mediterranean however the vital lines of communication in North Africa, Italy, and the Balkans lie open to sea and air-borne raids, astride of which operations could now be launched. Few important objectives were accessible to Commandos in France and Germany and such as existed were strongly defended and could have been attacked more effectively by Bomber Command...In the Mediterranean, there are many vulnerable installations about which we continually receive accurate and up-to-date information from our Photographic Reconnaissance Units and which lie within striking distance of a raiding force. They are often difficult targets for aircraft and might be more suitably engaged by Commandos which can strike with greater discrimination. It is also evident that the results of raids in the Mediterranean and especially in Italy itself would prove very detrimental to enemy morale since the Italians are obviously more susceptible in this respect than the more phlegmatic occupants of Northern France and Germany... Whereas little use has subsequently been made of Commandos operating from the United Kingdom it is submitted that there is ample scope for their employment in the Middle East provided that they are radically re-organized.*[331]

Accordingly, on February 1, 1941, the War Office dispatched Nos. 7, 8 and 11 Commandos to Egypt.[332] The three Commandos sailed in three GLEN ships (i.e. *HMS Glenroy, Glengyle* and *Glenearn*) to the Middle East with the aim of participating in amphibious operations.[333] In March 1941, Nos. 50 and 52 Middle East (ME) Commandos (consisting of locally raised volunteers (e.g. Palestinians and Spanish Foreign Legion)) were added to the Special Service force. For security reasons the Commandos were re-designated as battalions. For instance, Nos. 7, 8 and 11 Commandos were called "A," "B," and "C" Battalions respectively. 50 and 52 ME Commando were combined to create "D" Battalion.[334] The entire organization was allocated a brigade HQ and placed under the command of Colonel Laycock. It was subsequently known as "Layforce."[335]

Laycock believed that the partial reorganization fell short of what was required and the force was "still ill-equipped to meet the changing conditions of modern war."[336] The entire outlook for commandos remained tenuous. In March 1941, a staff officer at GHQ ME, wrote, "It is difficult to see at this moment what the future of Commandos will be in the Middle East, as the question of wastage and replacements is an extremely difficult one owing to the embargo on using Australian or New Zealand troops which cannot be employed on extra Regimental duties outside their Divisional Commands."[337] Other staff officers argued the Middle East Commandos should be disbanded "owing to the large percentage of first class leaders absorbed by them."[338]

The argument against the creation of special forces type units never disappeared. Historian Barrie Pitt, a veteran of the Middle-East and European theatres of operation in WWII observed:

> *The trouble was that service with them seemed so attractive, especially to the more romantically minded of the new arrivals in the theatre. They offered an escape from the regulation and discipline of battalion life, freedom for the young subaltern or private from the incessant disfavor of adjutant or regimental sergeant-major, and they were all at one time or another gilded with glamour. ...and a place in the Long Range Desert group was one for which captains would willingly drop to lieutenants and sergeants to privates; and those who failed to get into either, eagerly volunteered for any other formation which promised the same apparent freedom and cachet, however non-existent its record or doubtful its purpose. From the point of view of the Cairo Headquarters, these formations were allowed to sprout because they seemed to promise a quick return for a minimal outlay, and if they had all performed as successfully as those first ones this could have been a profitable policy; but too often these ad hoc units were set up as a result of little but enthusiasm coupled with social salesmanship, and manned by youngsters with cheerfully vague notions of "swanning around the blue," blowing up enemy dumps with loud bangs and spectacular pyrotechnics, and wearing unorthodox and somewhat flamboyant variations of uniform.*[339]

Despite the constant sniping, Layforce maintained its existence. On May 26/27, 1941, "A" and "D" Battalions were despatched to Crete to assist with the defence of the island against the relentless German airborne invasion. Upon arrival the Allied force was in full retreat and Colonel Laycock was ordered to use his commandos as a rear-guard for the withdrawal of the British and Allied defenders so they could escape from the island. The Commandos held their final position until May 31 when the Brigade HQ and the remnants of the two battalions were evacuated to Alexandria. Of the 1,200 commandos sent, only 400 returned.[340]

Additionally, Laycock ordered "C" Battalion (11 (Scottish) Commando) to conduct an independent operation in Syria, which was still controlled by the Vichy French Government. Importantly, the Germans and Italians had begun to use bases for their Air Forces. The Vichy French forces held a line of defences along the Litani River. The Commander of 7th Australian Division, to whom 11 (Scottish) Commando was attached, ordered the Commando to land by sea at the mouth of the Litani River and prevent the demolition of a key bridge across the water obstacle. On June 9, 1941, the assault against formidable defences began. Although the bridge was destroyed, elements of 11 Commando were able to cross the river in canvas boats and create a bridgehead for Australian follow-on forces. Although successful, casualties were heavy (i.e., 25) and the CO, Lieutenant-Colonel Richard Pedder, was killed.[341] Major Geoffrey Keyes was subsequently promoted and took command of 11 (Scottish) Commando.

Despite Laycock's best efforts, external considerations ran against the maintenance of the commandos. On return to Egypt on June 1, 1941, GHQ MEF informed Laycock that Layforce would be disbanded because it could not be kept up to establishment strength due to the shortage of manpower. Laycock explained, "Repeated cancellation of combined operations caused continued inactivity of the S.S. Bde [Special Service Brigade]."[342] Furthermore, the actual operations undertaken in Crete and the Litani River, resulted in the requirement for reinforcements, which were just not available in a theatre of operations that was already short-manned. As a result, on June 25, 1941, Auchinleck ordered the disbandment of Layforce.[343]

Consequently, Layforce officially disbanded on July 1, 1941. However, "C" Battalion did not disband until September 1st upon its return from Cyprus where it had been deployed for the defence of the island.[344] The War Office endorsed the disbandment decision on July 2, 1941. An official message noted, "The majority of the special service troops which were employed with the GLEN ships are being disbanded on completion of their voluntary engagement and are returning to their own units. The future policy will be to train regular units when available in combined operations."[345]

The disbandment created additional turmoil. Members of Layforce were initially told that they could return to their original units; volunteer for guerilla activities in Far East, or remain in a special service unit.[346] However, the C-in-C MEF reneged on the original War Office guarantee to officers and other ranks who joined a S.S. unit that at the end of six months of service they could return to their own units if they so desired. Due to manpower shortages Auchinleck enforced their stay in the Middle East.

Amidst the disbandment commotion, the CIGS ordered Laycock

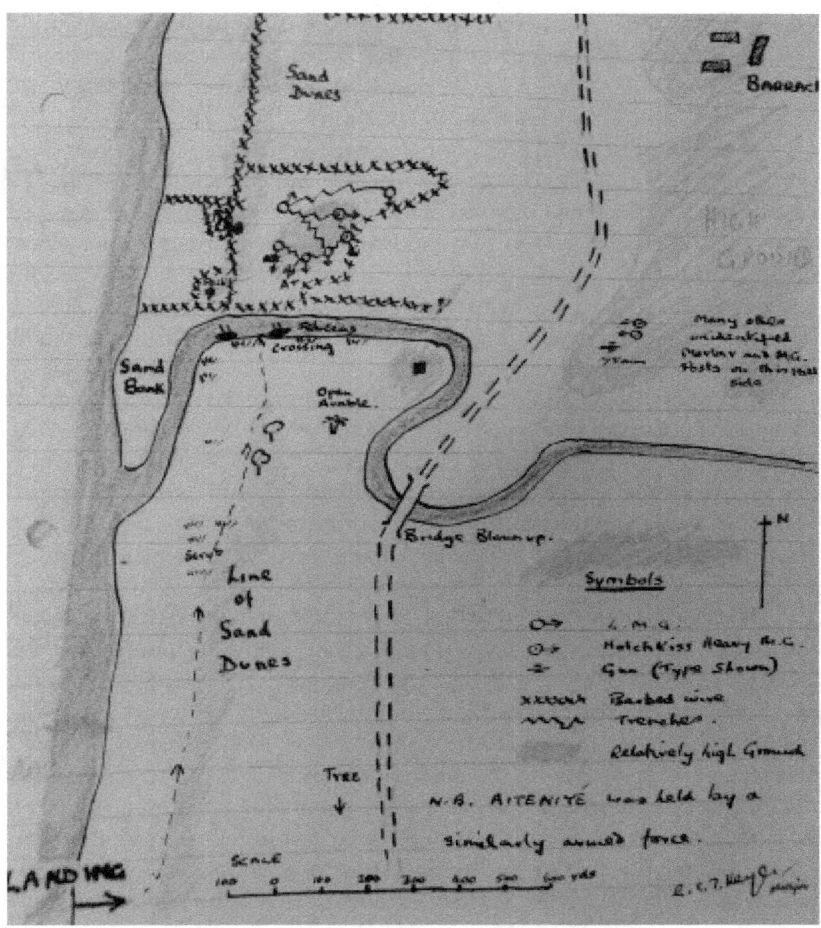

Map 3 – Italian defences on the Litani River (National Archives)

to return to England in late June. While in England Laycock lobbied for a reversal of the decision. He quickly found a supporter in the Prime Minister. Invited to lunch at Chequers by Churchill on July 19, the topic of Commandos was raised. Upon learning that the ME Commandos were to be disbanded, a very miffed Prime Minister shared that Laycock's next instructions would probably come from Churchill himself.

Days later on July 23, 1941, Churchill sent one of his famous rockets to General Ismay. "I wish the Commandos in the Middle East to be reconstituted as soon as possible," he ordered. Churchill also directed that "General" Laycock should be appointed Director Combined Operations (DCO). He further stipulated that the DCO, his forces and the three

GLEN ships be placed directly under Admiral Cunningham who should be charged with all combined operations involving sea transport. Churchill groused that "The Middle East Command have indeed maltreated and thrown away this invaluable force."[347]

Churchill's direction did not sit well with War Office staff officers. On the same day as his note to Ismay, an internal official review recorded, "To reconstitute the Commandos would involve a further drain on the Army of some 1,000 all ranks. In view of the existing serious shortage of manpower in the Middle East, it would be far better to break up the Commandos altogether and use them to reinforce existing units, as C-in-C Middle East proposes, than to reconstitute the Commandos, unless such units are vitally needed for particular operations."[348]

The concern was real. Allied forces in the Middle East were 25,000 men short of War Establishment. "Another factor which affects the immediate formation of Commandos," one senior GHQ MEF staff officer griped, "is our very serious shortage of personnel for British Units. We cannot afford luxuries."[349] The chief of staff (COS) Committee seemingly agreed. They argued, "We cannot send more Special Service troops from this country without breaking up forces held for operations."[350]

Despite the agreement of the way forward by both Auchinleck and the COS Committee the issue was far from decided. The Committee was fully aware of the difficulty they faced. "Judging by the terms of the Prime Minister's minute there would seem to be little chance of breaking up the Commandos," they cautioned the C-in-C MEF, "But perhaps you would care to represent once more the inherent disadvantages of the Commando organisation with which you are fully acquainted."[351] Subsequently, on July 30, 1941, General Auchinleck appeared before the COS Committee. "The Commandos had proved to be a most uneconomical organization," he briefed, "They were composed of excellent material but were only really suitable to execute 'coups' of a special nature. They were not as effective in combined operations as specially trained Infantry Battalions and the Officer material locked up in them would be much better employed in normal formations."[352] The minutes of the meeting recorded that "Commander-in-Chief, Mediterranean, and all responsible authorities in the Middle East with whom he had discussed this question were in general agreement with the views he had expressed."[353]

At a follow-on meeting with the COS Committee, Auchinleck argued that any combined operation which may be carried out in the Middle East "could best be done by regular units who have received training in boat work." He recommended that the Commandos should not be reconstituted. The Committee agreed and decided "in present circumstances, they [ME

Commandos] should not be reconstituted in the Middle East."[354]

Churchill refused. At a meeting at Chequers on August 2nd, at which General Auchinleck was present, the Prime Minister insisted that "the Commandos in the Middle East were to be reconstituted as soon as possible."[355] Faced with little choice, Auchinleck said "he would do his best to reconstitute the Commandos on his return to Egypt."[356] However, he requested that they be put under his direct command. The Prime Minister agreed.

Not wanting to be short-changed, Churchill sent Ismay a follow-on minute on August 16th that reaffirmed that he wanted the ME Commandos reinstated. Resistance, however, seemed to remain. MEF staff contacted the War Cabinet secretariat seeking additional guidance. "General Auchinleck is by no means clear what decision was reached with regard to the vexed question of reconstitution of the Commandos in the Middle East," the query stated, "We are quite in the dark. The Prime Minister's latest minute, which was referred to during the discussion at Chequers, appeared to visualise complete reconstitution, but we know that Middle East will find this extremely difficult, if not impossible."[357]

Despite the foot dragging, on August 31, 1941, GHQ MEF issued revised conditions of service that would allow greater leeway in the employment of commandos. These were:

- Size and composition of SS unit not decided – could be one or more.
- Commando(s) formed may be used in an SS role of any sort – not necessarily in connection with combined operations
- Commando(s) may be employed at any time, and for any period, on ordinary infantry duties.
- No guarantee can be given that any personnel volunteering for SS duties will be organised by existing or previously existing sub-units e.g., by regiments.[358]

Despite the renewed interest in Commandos, the true feeling of the conventional military chain-of-command had not changed dramatically. The rear-admiral who filled the appointment of MEF Director of Opposed Landing (DOL), bluntly informed Laycock that the "main objection to Commandos is that, being trained for one specific role, they are inactive unless fulfilling that role, in other words it means locking up valuable man power." He did throw Laycock a bone. "If, however, their strength is not too great," he proposed, "this probably can be accepted." He went on to inform Laycock that "the following recommendations will be laid before

C-in-C. (a) DOL in consultation with Intelligence Services to examine various possibilities for raids and to lay proposals before the C-in-C. (b) detailed plans and execution of the same to be the responsibility of the respective commanders."[359]

The support, however, seemed feigned. Frustrated with the bureaucratic wrangling, Laycock wrote in frustration to Auchinleck. He frankly revealed:

> At the risk of being considered outspoken, I must honestly say that the impression which I have gathered from the A branch of GHQ (from whom we must have genuine cooperation if the force is to be a going concern is that they view the formation of an S.S. unit as an unmitigated nuisance; nevertheless, they consider it politic to make a show of interest if only because they have been ordered to do so. I doubt if many of those who attended the meeting five days ago were genuinely thinking in terms of constituting the most suitable force to inflict the maximum damage on the enemy. They seemed more anxious to dispose satisfactorily on paper of the remnants of the commandos and at the same time to comply adequately with a "political whim."[360]

The note seemed to stick with the C-in-C. He informed his staff, "I am not happy about it."[361] Although initially ordering the disbandment of Layforce, Auchinleck post-his meeting with the Prime Minister at Chequers on August 2nd, now, whether genuinely or not, embraced special forces. In fact, he was soon to authorize an organization that would go on to become a military legend. Moreover, as part of his upcoming offensive, special forces were going to mount a number of missions, which if successful, could have a tremendous impact on the outcome of Operation Crusader.

CHAPTER 6
UNLEASHING THE DOGS OF WAR

FOR THE NEW COMMANDER-IN-CHIEF Middle East Forces, the challenges just kept mounting. Churchill demanded he reconstitute the commandos despite his acute shortage of manpower. As the Chief of the Imperial General Staff reminded Auchinleck in a message upon his return to Cairo, "I know you were quite clear what the Prime Minister wants."[362] In addition, the Prime Minister continually harried him to take to the offensive and drive Rommel and his Afrika Korps out of Cyrenaica, as well as lift the siege of Tobruk. As luck would have it, he was about to receive an opportunity that could kill two birds with one stone. Completely oblivious to the machinations of higher policy, events were transpiring that would lead to the creation of one of the most legendary military units of all times.

For many of the keen, young officers who joined the Commandos to have a crack at the "Hun," their expectations failed to materialize. Too many planned raids were scuttled for one reason or another, and the few missions they conducted fell short of the impact they hoped for. Lieutenant Jock Lewes was one such individual. Being frustrated with the record of raids conducted from the sea, he decided to try something different. By chance, his commander, Brigadier Laycock, authorized Lewes to experiment with some parachutes that were intended for India, but had arrived in the Middle East by mistake. Luckily, they were also able to borrow an obsolete Vickers Valentia biplane that was normally used to deliver mail.

The parachute experiment piqued the interest of another commando officer, Lieutenant David Stirling, who had transferred from the Scots Guards to No. 8 Commando. He quickly convinced Lewes to allow him to participate. None of the Commando personnel had ever jumped before. In fact, none of the non-commissioned officers (NCOs) had ever even been in an airplane. However, they did receive some assistance from a RAF jump instructor who simply told them to "dive out as though going through into water."[363] With that guidance they set off. Lacking an aircraft fitted for dropping parachutists, Lewes simply secured the static lines, which were actually designed to be attached to a steel cable that ran through an aircraft fuselage, to the aircraft seat legs. They were now seemingly ready to jump.

When Lewes checked the parachute logbooks he noticed that there was no date for the last periodic examination, which would indicate that the parachutes were actually fit for use. Nonetheless, he assessed them as functional. The following day, Lewes along with Stirling made a test flight. They tossed out a dummy made from sandbags and tent poles. The parachute opened without problem but the tent poles were smashed on landing. The final preparations included a ten-foot jump from the top of the aircraft and then some parachute control techniques. The following afternoon the intrepid group of neophyte jumpers flew in the Valentia aircraft to an inland airstrip. Guardsman Mick D'Arcy described:

We reached the landing field towards dusk, landed, fitted on our parachutes, and decided to jump in the failing light. We were to jump in pairs, Lieutenant [Lt] Lewes and his servant [batman], Guardsman Roy Davies, first, the RAF Officer was to dispatch. The instructions were to dive out as though going into water. We hooked ourselves up, circled the field, and on a signal from the RAF Officer, Lieutenant Lewes and Davies dived out. Next time round, I dived out, and was surprised to see Lt. Stirling pass me in the air. Lt. Lewes made a perfect landing, next came Davies a little shaken. Lt. Stirling injured his spine and also lost his sight for about an hour, next, myself, a little shaken and a few scratches, and lastly Sgt. Stone who seemed O.K. Guardsman Evans was unable to jump as the pilot decided to land owing to the approaching darkness. We slept on the landing field. Next morning, we jumped again, this time a stick of four, preceded by a bundle to represent a container. The previous night we had worn K.D. shirts and shorts, but from experience we decided to put on pullovers. We wore no hats. We pushed the bundle out first and Guardsmen Evans, myself, Davies and Lt. Lewes followed as quickly as possible. The first three landed quite close to each other and doubled forward to the container but Lt. Lewes in trying to avoid some oil barrels, rather badly injured his spine, Gdsn. [Guardsman] Evans also hurt his ankle. Sgt Stone who jumped after us landed O.K.[364]

Lieutenant Stirling's parachute had snagged on the aircraft's tail section as it ripped away from the static line. This mishap caused the top of his parachute to tear away. As a result, Stirling descended at a dangerous speed, almost twice the acceptable velocity, hitting the solid desert floor extremely hard. He was blind for over an hour and could not feel his legs. Stirling's own assessment was typically nonchalant. "I was unlucky," he explained, "and landed on rocky ground and severely injured my back. This resulted in two months in hospital which gave me an ideal opportunity to evaluate the factors which would justify the creating of a special service unit to carry on the Commando role."[365]

Stirling was paralyzed from the waist down. It took two weeks at the Scottish military hospital in Alexandria for him to regain the use of his legs. After a period of two months he was somewhat mobile and able to move with the aid of crutches. Up until this point Stirling's military career was anything but stellar. Most considered him to be a rather lazy, even indolent, officer. In fact, his fellow officers had given him the nickname "the Big Sloth." His tolerance for the tedium of soldiering was very low, particularly when he felt the conventional army was still fighting the last war and lacked the insight and vision to see warfare on a more far-reaching continuum. As a result, he demonstrated the least modicum of acceptable self-discipline possible.

However, while stuck in bed in the hospital he hit on the idea of raiding behind enemy lines using small teams of raiders. He believed that the Commandos were for the most part under-employed and too large and cumbersome for agile, swift raids. He thought that surprise was the key to success, not numbers. As such, he believed that a small number of men using surprise could achieve more than a larger group. He argued that 60 men, divided into five groups of 12 men each, could infiltrate behind enemy lines and destroy vital targets such as headquarters, aircraft, communications centres, railroads and supply depots. To Stirling the desert represented a veritable target rich environment. He gathered up every map of North Africa he could find and made note of all the airfields, roads, railways, ports and enemy positions he could locate. The large open tracks of desert, he quickly surmised, represented a wide-open flank. "This was the one sea," Stirling asserted, "the Hun was not watching."[366]

There remained one major hurdle – official sanction. Stirling shared his thinking with Lewes, who did not believe Stirling's plan would gain much traction with GHQ MEF. This response was no surprise as Stirling had already realized that he needed the support from the highest levels for the acceptance of any new idea. This requirement was no easy feat. He knew he had to bypass the bureaucratic headquarters staff, which he described as "layer on layer of fossilized shit" which he thought "ludicrously swollen, unnecessarily big and wholly obstructive to anything that looked like a new

Members of "L" Detachment preparing for a practice jump. (IWM, E_006404)
idea."[367]

Once he was semi-mobile, Stirling decided to take his war-winning idea to the Commander-in-Chief of the British Forces in the Middle East himself at his headquarters. His first hurdle to overcome was the fact that he did not have an official pass, without which he could not even get into the HQ. Exacerbating the problem was a sentry who could not be swayed by Stirling's persuasive and charismatic charm. He refused to allow anyone without the requisite authority to pass.

Not to be denied, Stirling waited a few metres away and nonchalantly leaned up against a tree. He surveyed the compound and detected a possible vulnerability. There was a small gap between the barbed wire fence and the guard post. He seized his chance at the first opportunity. When a staff car with officers pulled up, the sentries became temporarily occupied as they checked passes. Leaving his crutches propped up against the tree, he quickly slipped through the gap. Hobbling as hurriedly as he could, he reached the top of the steps when he heard the sentry, who by now noticed the abandoned crutches, as well as the unusually tall limping officer about to enter the HQ without a pass.

Stirling was able to make it into the building before anyone caught up with him. However, without an appointment, or an understanding of the HQ layout, he was in a bit of a pickle. To add to his problem there was an increasing amount of noise and activity building behind him which spelled potential trouble. The sentry was obviously in hot pursuit.

To shake his pursuer, Stirling swiftly made a series of turns down a number of hallways. Coming across a door marked Adjutant-General he decided to take a gamble and make this his starting point. He had chosen poorly. As he entered the office without knocking, he startled a staff major busily occupied at his desk. When the major realized the uninvited intruder was a mere lieutenant his surprise turned to disdain. The situation only got worse.

Stirling quickly broke into his pitch, explaining to the major that if he was given a small command of hand-picked men he could infiltrate behind enemy lines by parachute and destroy the German air force on the ground, as well as cause chaos and havoc. Not surprisingly, Stirling's innovative idea failed to impress the now thoroughly annoyed major who railed at Stirling's insolence. What fueled the major's anger even more was a rather unfortunate coincidence for Stirling. The major had been a guest instructor lecturing the 2nd Battalion Scots Guards at Pirbright Camp in 1939. During his lecture Stirling had fallen asleep. As he was wont to do, Stirling had partied until the early hours of the morning and he used the lecture to catch up on his sleep. Predictably, the major now ejected Stirling from his office.

To make matters worse, as Stirling was leaving the office, he heard the phone ring and the agitated major's voice repeat, "Broke past the guard post?" Sensing that matters were about to get worse, Stirling hastened down the hallway as fast as he could with his bum leg. He turned a corner and immediately spotted the sentry approaching from the far end. He quickly back-tracked and stopping briefly at another door knocked and walked in. He now found himself confronting Brigadier Neil Ritchie, the Deputy Chief of the General Staff (DCGS) Middle East Forces.

Ritchie looked up in surprise. Stirling quickly apologized for the intrusion but declared he had "vital business" to discuss. Ritchie offered Stirling a seat. Stirling then introduced himself and passed his hand-written memorandum to the DCGS. Ritchie laboured to read the scrawled note but when he had finished, he shared, "I think this may be the sort of plan we are looking for. I will discuss it with the commander-in-chief and let you know our decision in the next day or so."[368]

Three days later Stirling was summoned for an audience with General Auchinleck himself. The Commander-in-Chief had a reputation for making decisions rather quickly. Journalist Alan Moorhead described Auchinleck as a commander with "a mind of quite exceptional freshness and originality who would seize on every new idea and explore it at once."[369] Stirling now had the opportunity to pitch his idea.

Stirling himself explained, "I pointed out that the enemy was exceedingly vulnerable to attack along the line of his coastal communications and on his various transport parks, aerodromes and other targets strung out along the coast, and that the role of No. 8 Commando, which had attempted raids on these targets, was a most valuable one."[370] Stirling emphasized that the scale on which the commando raids had been planned in terms of personnel deployed and the scale of equipment and facilities used, "prejudiced surprise beyond all possible compensating advantage." Conversely, he argued "the advantages of establishing a unit based on the principle of the fullest exploitation of surprise and of making the minimum demands on man-power and equipment." Stirling claimed that his methodology would allow "a sub-unit of five men to cover a target previously requiring four troops of a Commando, i.e., about 200 men." Furthermore, he made the case that "200 properly selected, trained and equipped men, organized into sub-units of five should be able to attack at least 30 different objectives at the same time on the same night as compared to only one objective using the Commando technique."[371] Stirling outlined the unit's tasks as: "firstly, raids in depth behind the enemy lines, attacking HQ nerve centres, landing grounds, supply lines and so on; and secondly, the mounting of sustained strategic offensive activity from secret bases within hostile territory and, if the opportunity existed, recruiting, training, arming and co-ordinating local guerrilla elements."[372]

To avoid marginalization or bureaucratic inertia from a ponderous staff system, Stirling insisted that the commander of this unit would have to be solely responsible for its training and operational planning. As such, he concluded that the unit's commander must come directly under the command of the theatre Commander-in-Chief. Stirling capped his proposal with a detailed plan of how the unit could be employed in the upcoming November 1941 offensive, which apparently was not a very well-kept secret.

This turn of events set in motion the creation of one of history's most legendary units. Auchinleck authorized the creation of the unit and directed Stirling to begin planning at once. Because Stirling was only a subaltern, Auchinleck promoted him to captain and gave him the authority to recruit six officers and 60 men from the remnants of Layforce and if this did not provide the number required from specific other formations that were deployed in the desert.

Although Stirling's audacious actions and results are stirring, the fact of the matter is that the outcome is not that surprising. Stirling was well-connected and the British paid attention to the finer points of family lineage. Stirling came from one of the oldest and most imposing aristocratic

SUBJECT:- Volunteers for special S.S. Unit.

GHQ MEF
CREE/1668/AG1.
8 AUG 31.

OC, 'C' Bn LAYFORCE.

Copy to: Capt. A.D. Stirling

Will you please allow Capt. A.D. Stirling
to visit 'C' Bn LAYFORCE with a view to finding
out if there are any volunteers for a special
S.S. unit, which he is forming.

Capt. Stirling will explain the purpose of
this new unit.

Any officers or other ranks who volunteer
and who can be spared by you, will be replaced,
provided 'C' Bn is not disbanded.

Capt. Stirling will submit a nominal roll
to this HQ of the volunteers he wishes for this
new unit.

(Sgd) G. M. Thirmont.

Maj:

for Maj-Gen
DAG

SAS Recruiting Memorandum (NA)

Scottish clans. A 15,000-acre Perthshire estate had been the family seat for five centuries. His father was Brigadier Archibald Stirling of Keir and Cawdor, also a Member of Parliament. His mother was the daughter of Lord Lovat (Chief of the Clan Fraser), whose exploits at Dieppe with 4 Commando were well known. In addition, Lovat's father raised the Lovat Scouts in the Boer War. Stirling's brother Peter was in the Foreign Office, based at the British Embassy in Cairo as the Second Secretary. And if that was not enough, both Auchinleck and Ritchie were Scottish. In fact, Auchinleck was a family friend and Ritchie had been a visitor at the family estate to hunt grouse, and both had served with his grandfather in World War I.

The new unit was provisionally called 62 Commando.[373] However, the name was quickly changed. Brigadier Dudley Clarke, the individual instrumental in the forming of the Commandos, was now a staff officer in GHQ MEF responsible for deception operations. Clarke was attempting to convince the Germans that the British had a fully-equipped parachute and glider brigade in the Middle East.[374] The idea spawned from a captured Italian officer's diary after the Battle of Sidi Barrani in December 1940. The Italian officer had revealed fear that the British would land paratroopers behind enemy lines. Dudley realized the value of playing on real fears and worked towards building the illusion. He had dropped dummies into the desert and had mock-ups of gliders built and deployed across the desert to help convince enemy reconnaissance flights that the capability actually existed. Dudley called the phantom formation the 1st Special Air Service Brigade.

When he learned of the new parachute unit to be formed, he approached Stirling explaining that the new unit allowed for an opportunity to up his game with real live parachutists. Stirling acknowledged, "to humour him, we agreed to name our unit 'L' Detachment, SAS Brigade."[375] The implication being that there existed "A" to "J" Detachments. The unit, which was also colloquially known as "Stirling's Parashots," although the LRDG called them "Stirling's Parashite's" and according to Major Bill Fraser "sceptical [sic] middle ranking officers at Headquarters sarcastically named them the 'Short Range Desert Group' thinking that they preferred the close proximity of Cairo and its extensive range of bars."[376] Despite the animosity, Captain Malcolm James, a member of "L" Detachment, offered, "The work of the SAS called for initiative and an original approach, self-reliance, control, a strong sense of discipline and immensely quick thought and action."[377] For that reason, the unit consisted of a very high proportion of NCOs and was divided into five troops, each of two sections (each section consisting of four men and a NCO or officer).[378] The remainder of the personnel made up the headquarters and camp staff. Most of his personnel were recruited from the disbanded Layforce, as well as some from Stirling's own regiment, the Scots Guards.[379]

Despite support from the highest levels, Stirling, like most SOF commanders, was still encumbered by hostility from the mainstream military hierarchy. One "L" Detachment veteran recalled, "Men and equipment were given grudgingly; even his [Stirling's] eventual success bred jealousy rather than gratitude but in the end, he could not be denied."[380] Stirling himself revealed, "I found, during this and subsequent stages that the A.G. [Adjutant General] Branch was unfailing obstructive and uncooperative. Most Branches of Middle East HQ were helpful at the top level but astonishingly tiresome at the middle or lower levels. The A.G. Branch was unfortunately obstructive right up to the top and it was only by appealing to the DCGS that I could ever have made my way."[381]

Despite the bureaucratic obstacles, the unit was basically completely stood up in early August 1941 at Kabrit, giving it approximately three months to train for the upcoming offensive. Stirling took a completely different tack with regard to recruits. In the Commandos once a volunteer was selected to join a unit, that unit "had to nurse them up to the required standard."[382] However, Stirling did not have the luxury of time. Therefore, for the SAS, Stirling set a minimum standard which all ranks had to attain. Failing to do so meant returning them to their original units. At his opening address at the inception of "L" Detachment on September 4, 1941, he asserted, "We can't afford to piss about disciplining anyone who is not 100 per cent devoted to having a crack at the Hun."[383] This pronouncement set the tone and standard for the unit. Those who failed to show the requisite self-discipline and motivation would be ejected from the unit.

Although Stirling admitted that he found parachuting "most disagreeable," he believed it was an effective means to getting behind enemy lines, where "you could blow things up and find your way home by other means."[384] An early unit history explained:

Training consisted of the first parachute training and jumping in the M.E. also navigation, demolitions, languages, specialist weapons, foreign weapons, special boating, M.T., [motor transport] wireless etc. Full scale operational exercises and extensive schemes were carried out on foot in the desert, some of these exercises consisted of forced marches over difficult country with full operational load for distances in excess of 100 miles. The only water available being that carried by the men themselves.[385]

Fitzroy Maclean, an early member recounted, "For days and nights on end we trudged interminably over the alternating soft sand and jagged rocks of the desert, weighed down by heavy loads of explosive, eating and drinking only what we could carry with us. In the intervals we did weapon training, physical training and training in demolitions and navigation."[386]

The short, but gruelling, training period was not wasted. Stirling realized that the "L" Detachment's trial by fire was rapidly approaching. General Auchinleck was under great pressure from Churchill to undertake an offensive to relieve Tobruk. Importantly, Hitler's invasion of Russia made North Africa a low priority for Germany. As such, the opportunity was ripe to strike. And, Stirling's idea was about to be put to the test.

"L" Detachment's first mission was to attack five of the enemy's advanced airfields in the Gazala-Timimi area to destroy the German fighter and bomber facilities on the night prior to Operation Crusader, which was scheduled for dawn on November 18, 1941.[387] The plan called for five parties of men to be dropped into the desert on the night of November 16th, approximately 19 km south of the objectives in the Bir Temrad area between 2030 and 2130 hours. Under cover of darkness the raiding parties were to navigate their way to the rocky escarpments that ran south of the coast road, where they could hide up and observe their targets during the following day. That night they would carefully infiltrate the airfields and place their explosives. Each party was to deploy with 60 incendiary explosive bombs equipped with varied time pencil fuses (e.g., two hours, one hour, thirty minutes, ten minute and twelve second time fuses). Once their sabotage was completed, they were to march to a pre-arranged rendezvous point about 72 km in the desert interior where Captain Jake Easonsmith, commanding the R1 Patrol of the LRDG, would be waiting with vehicles to transport them to safety at the Siwa Oasis.[388]

The plan seemed easy enough. However, aside from the complexities of a parachute drop in the desert, navigating to the objective and then infiltrating a guarded airbase, there was the matter of how to best destroy the aircraft in question. The target airplanes had slippery, metal surfaces. Moreover, the raiders needed time to escape. The solution in theory was equally simple. All one required was a time bomb that, once the saboteurs had departed, would explode, igniting the fuel in the aircraft that would burn it to the ground. This requirement called for an explosive that had two fuses and a timer. Although such devices existed, they weighed over two kilograms and took ten minutes to prime. The weight and time requirement did not suit the needs of the SAS raiders. As a result, Jock Lewes, who had a basic understanding of chemistry and an unrelenting focus on the mission, experimented for several weeks with prototype

David Stirling Memorial in Dunblane, Scotland. (Author's Photo)

explosives. The end product was the "Lewes Bomb," which became part of the official British explosive inventory. It consisted of half a kilo of plastic explosive, rolled with 113 grams of incendiary thermite and some motor oil. It was triggered by a pencil detonator, which when activated allowed a slow trickle of acid that would eat through a copper wire that held the striker. Once the acid ate through the wire the striker would be released, detonating the explosives. A variety of pencil detonators were produced that allowed for different delay times. The thickness of the copper wire and the time requirement for the acid to eat through the respective copper wire provided a range of detonators designed for specific time requirements. Lewes' experimentation demonstrated the innovation and drive of the new SAS operators. It also provided them with a lightweight, versatile explosive that was sticky enough to adhere to aircraft wings and was hard to detect.[389]

The upcoming opportunity was not lost on Stirling. "Very few soldiers in the British Army," Stirling declared, "will ever have such a chance as we've got. With luck we'll polish off Rommel's entire fighter force."[390] And so, Stirling, seen by most of his peers and superiors as a torpid officer of no great promise, once given the opportunity to prosecute war as he believed it should be carried out, proved to be energetic and relentless in his focus on taking the fight to the enemy. Major-General Lloyd Owen exclaimed, "What a man! Failure meant nothing more to him than to generate fierce determination to be successful next time. He was convinced that he had only been thwarted by bad luck and certainly not by any lack of preparation or training. This intense enthusiasm, of course, spread down through him to every single man under his command and they all held him in great awe and admiration."[391] Even General Bernard Montgomery chimed in on Stirling. "The boy Stirling," he confided, "is quite mad, quite, quite mad. However, in a war there is often a place for mad people."[392] Churchill would later exclaim, "He was the mildest mannered man that ever scuttled ship or cut a throat."[393]

CHAPTER 7
A LEAP OF FAITH

CAPTAIN STIRLING'S IDEA appeared to be coming to life. He had been given command of a small group of warriors and now had a mission to prove his raiding concept. Operation Squatter, the code name for the raid, required 55 members of "L" Detachment, divided into five teams, to drop into the desert in the Bir Temrad area and attack the aerodromes at Tmimi and Gazala. To assist with these assaults, the RAF was to bomb the airstrips for the entire night of November 16/17th and at dusk on November 17th and after moonrise on the night of November 17/18, 1941.

In support of Operation Squatter, Eighth Army HQ also directed the commanding officer of the LRDG, Lieutenant-Colonel Prendergast, to organize a patrol capable of collecting Stirling's raiders at a rendezvous (RV) point agreed between the patrol commander and Stirling and transport them to a location where "L" Detachment vehicles could pick them up. In the event that all or part of Stirling's men failed to appear at the RV by 0700 hrs on November 21st, Eighth Army HQ directed that "the LRDG patrol will leave 12 gal[lons] of water in tins and 2 x 4 gal tins of dates at the RV and will then have no further responsibility for the transport of Capt.[ain] Stirling's men."[394]

Despite the careful planning and training, events seemed to conspire against Stirling. On the morning of November 16th, weather reports began to paint an unwelcome picture. The wind began to rise and it appeared that rain was likely for the next two days. By 1700 hours, the wind had reached gale force, blowing at 56 kilometres per hour. A parachute operation on a moonless night was perilous enough, but in gale force winds was beyond the pale. A brigadier serving in the MEF GHQ who Stirling had been working with, advised him to scrub the mission. However, knowing Stirling's motivation and inclination the brigadier added, "That is only my advice. We'll leave the decision to you."[395]

The brigadier at GHQ was not the only voice urging caution. The RAF also recommended calling off the drop because of the bad weather. Predictably, Stirling refused. He believed there were "enemies in high GHQ-ME staff circles" who would have greatly relished it had they canceled the mission at the last minute.[396] In essence, Stirling believed that cancelling the mission would be disastrous for morale. Many of his men were from Layforce who had experienced three missions cancelled at the last moment. As a result, he gathered his officers together and confided, "Personally, I would like to go ahead regardless of the risk. It would shake the men's confidence in the unit if we chucked in our hand at this late hour."[397] All agreed with their CO. The mission was on. Major Bill Fraser later revealed, "Those doughters [sic] at M.E.C. [ME Command] gave them every opportunity to pull out but after a conference between the L Detachment officers and the R.A.F. they decided that in due of all the previous cancellations they had met during their time in Layforce the op.[eration] must go on, which was to be met with absolute approval by all the other ranks."[398]

The decision was courageous, albeit arguably ill-conceived if not doomed. One account later described the conditions as "one of the most devilish nights North Africa has known. Rain was splashing down in icy sheets in total darkness. Even on the ground the wind was a thirty-mile gale, murderous to parachutists. It was the worst possible night."[399]

Nonetheless, at 1915 hours, at the Ma'aten Bagoush airfield, the five elderly Bristol Bombay transport aircraft from 216 Squadron that would act as the dropping aircraft started their two 1,010 hp Bristol Pegasus XXII radial engines as the SAS parachutists boarded. Surprisingly, conditions initially were good. The aircraft, travelling at 240 kilometres per hour, climbed steadily to reach their ceiling of 5,500 metres. The raiders inside the fuselage were freezing in the pitch darkness. They wrapped themselves in blankets and tried to sleep, to little avail.

As the five aircraft winged westwards over the Mediterranean, conditions rapidly deteriorated. By the time the aircraft approached the Libyan coast, after two and a half hours of flight, the winds had achieved gale force strength and a vicious thunderstorm was so loud and violent that the SAS raiders could hear the thunder over the engines, and the lightning lit the inside of the fuselage through the small windows. As they turned south to cross the coastline towards their drop zone, the flight crew now found themselves in dense, turbulent clouds that tossed and pitched the aircraft to the point that all five became separated and lost. Lieutenant-Colonel Prendergast, the CO of the LRDG, recalled, "the night of November 17th was one of the foulest of the Libyan war. Looking north from Siwa we could see the flashes of lightning along the coast though the torrential rain did not reach so far south."[400]

In fact, the pilots had great difficulty just making out the shoreline. One indicator as they crossed the coast back over land was that the aircraft were picked up by German searchlights that blinded the aircraft crews. Then flak buffeted the aircraft. One of the SAS raiders recounted, "The flak was terrible; we were all leaning back against the side [of the fuselage] and the flak was coming up through the centre. How the hell no one got wounded I don't know."[401]

The exploding flak added to the disorientation of the pilots as the shells burst in blinding light. Shells ripped through the floor and fuselage of the aircraft narrowly missing the occupants. Additionally, the storm whipped up sand and the hard, pelting rain obscured the flares that had been dropped by the RAF to assist with locating the drop zones. The poor visibility forced the pilots to descend out of the clouds to try and pick up their bearings. The cloud base was as low as 61 metres, 152 metres short of the minimum safe dropping height of 213 metres. Warrant Officer Charles (Charlie) West, one of the Bombay pilots recounted:

As the aircraft droned on, so the wisps of cloud drifting lazily across the sky thickened and deepened. Soon nothing existed in the world but cloud, rain and flashes of lightning. The smooth passage of the aircraft became a mad, bucketing switchback through the sky, and the pilots needed all their strength and skill to hold the course and airspeed. All the carefully checked navigational calculations were useless. It was impossible even to guess the force and the direction of the wind which was driving the aircraft off course and even less possible to sight the sea over which they were flying.[402]

The lack of visual or navigational aids meant that the navigators were forced to use dead reckoning for the drops. Charlie West, trying to be as accurate as possible, dropped his aircraft from 1,500 metres to 61 metres in an effort to get his bearings.[403] Despite the weather challenges the aircraft proceeded to drop their loads once they thought they were over their respective correct drop zones. Predictably, the drops, in force nine winds and complete darkness, were an utter disaster. "As far as I know," Stirling conceded, "no party was dropped within 10 miles of the selected DZs [drop zones]."[404] Lance Sergeant Robert Bennett recounted:

They got into their planes and left Kabri in the early evening flying to Bagoush airfield in order to refuel, and taking off again at about

2200 hours. Their course took them out to sea, an they turned inland when they reached the gulf of Bomba. Apart from a certain amount of flak sent up at them as they crossed the coast, they received no attention from the enemy; but the weather, which had been good when they started, deteriorated steadily throughout the flight and by now had become really foul. It was on account of this that the Air Force pilots lost their way and the men were given the orders to jump while the planes were over the wrong area. In the stormy blackness of that night, broken only by an occasional flash of lightning, the men jumped out of the planes into a wind that was blowing at half-gale strength. They drifted down fast, striking the ground heavily when they landed, and being dragged hard along the stony surface before they had any opportunity to find their feet. Little wonder then that they were widely scattered and separated, and had great difficulty in finding one another.[405]

The five groups were dropped some kilometres from their intended DZs. The conditions proved to be so bad that one of the Bombay transports never dropped their stick of parachutists. On return to base, the aircraft experienced engine trouble and the pilot conducted an emergency landing on the desert floor. Once the engine was repaired, the aircraft captain radioed for a direction finder signal to guide him home. Unknown to him, the Germans intercepted his message and promptly provided him with the requested assistance. Very quickly, once the Bombay aircraft was on the directed course, the pilot realized he was being escorted by German fighters that forced him to land with all his paratroopers still aboard, at the main fighter airstrip in Gazala. They all became prisoners of war.

The remainder of Stirling's raiders went on to jump into the desert. Fate was not as generous to them. The extremely hard landings due to high winds amongst rocks and shrubbery cacti caused injuries throughout the sticks. One SAS member recalled hitting the desert floor "with quite a bump and I was then dragged along by the wind at quite a speed. When I came to rest, I staggered rather groggily to my feet, feeling sure I'd broken something but to my astonishment I seemed to have nothing worse than my breath momentarily knocked out of me."[406] Johnny Cooper remembered:

I felt a terrific tug as my parachute opened and then I was swinging in comparative quietness ... I could see two other parachutes which both seemed to be drifting away at a vast speed. As it was impossible to see the ground I kept my legs braced, but when I hit the desert I received a tremendous jolt through my body. Before I could gather myself properly I found myself being dragged across the desert at more than thirty miles per

Operation Squatter – drop into a storm. (Artwork by Brenda Wight)

hour by the wind.[407]

Stirling, the first to jump, described his experience to Virginia Cowles, his biographer, who captured:

David was the first to jump and once he felt the jerk of his parachute opening, he was amazed at the smoothness of the descent. He could feel no pressure against his body and he wondered if there really was a high wind blowing or whether by some miracle it had stopped. After a minute he began to prepare for the landing. It was so black there was no prospect of seeing the ground. He would not know the earth was near until he hit it. But if the pilot had dropped them from an altitude of five hundred feet, as he had said he would it should come at once. He braced his body expectantly, but he continued to drift through space. Now his whole being was keyed up. Each second he expected to feel the impact of the ground, but it never came. It was almost as though the laws of gravity had stopped working and he was floating away from the earth through infinity.

Then a smashing blow obliterated his senses. He must have been unconscious for two or three minutes. He awoke to find himself being dragged very fast over rough stony ground. He knocked the release harness and rolled over on his back, free. For a moment he lay in a daze. He felt blood trickling down his face but he moved his arms and legs and was relieved to find that no bones were broken. When he stood up, he had to brace himself against a raging wind. The air was thick with dust and sand which almost choked him. He could see nothing through the black, noisy night. He shouted but the gale carried his voice away. He flashed his torch. Still, he saw nothing. He began to walk waving the torch. After a few minutes a light blinked in the distance; then off to the right was another and yet another. The group was starting to converge.[408]

Sergeant Duncan Robert (Bob) Tait recalled:

The pilot had to make several circles over the area, gliding in from the sea, coming down through the clouds right over Gazala, which was well lit up by flares dropped by the bombing force, covering our arrival. During this glide, we came in for an uncomfortable amount of A.A. We finally were dropped about 2330 hours, and owing to the high wind – I estimated this about 30 miles per hour – we all made very bad landings. I myself being the only one uninjured. Captain Stirling himself sustained injuries about the arms and legs, Sergeant Cheyne, we never saw again. We had considerable difficulty in assembling, the wind having scattered us over a wide area but finally at about 0100 hours [17 November].[409]

In the end, it took Stirling nearly an hour to assemble his stick. One was missing and the rest were in bad shape. All had cuts and abrasions. In addition, one had a broken arm, another a sprained wrist and two with badly sprained ankles. They found only two of ten parachute supply canisters, leaving them with six blankets, 12 water bottles and one day's worth of food for all. Although they had a supply of Lewes bombs, they had no fuses.

Stirling's group spent over two hours searching along the trajectory of the wind, shouting and using their flashlights, looking for the missing trooper and supply canisters. However, Stirling finally gave up. With no weapons other than the pistols they had on their person during the drop, he decided that he and Sergeant Tait would head off for the coast road to conduct some reconnaissance to at least gain some value from the mission. He dispatched the remainder of his group under Sergeant Yates to head off to the rendezvous, which he estimated was approximately 50 kilometres away. After dividing the meagre rations both groups set out. After wandering for days, Yates' group was picked up by an enemy patrol. Stirling and Tait eventually made it to the rendezvous.

Lance Sergeant Bennett, dropping with another group had a similar experience, although he was fortunate in only grazing himself when he landed. As he struggled to his feet "a fresh buffet of wind caught his chute, billowing it out and dragging him along once more." Captain Malcolm James, the medical officer for the SAS, recounted Bennett's experience as Bennett described it to him:

At last he managed to release the safety-box round his waist and rolled out of his harness. Then he got to his feet wondering what to do next. There was not a soul to be seen, nor the slightest sign of a land feature; in the pitch blackness and the blustering wind, he told me, he might have been the only person in the desert that night. It was a full half-hour before he found any one else, for under these circumstances whistle-blowing and shouting were of little value in personal location. But at length nine of the men had joined one another, although of this number two had been crippled by injuries in falling and were unable to walk. The remaining seven went out in different directions searching for the ammunition and supplies which had been dropped with them in parachute containers. They found only three of the sixteen containers which had been dropped, and from these they sorted out the explosives and ammunition they would need. When they had done this, they made the two men comfortable, leaving them most of the food and water; and then after saying good-bye, they marched off on a north-easterly bearing which by rights should have taken them to the airfield. In the remaining hours of darkness, they covered fifteen miles, and with a grey dawn lighting up the desolate scene of the open desert they began to search for a hiding-place. The weather continued to be stormy throughout the day and at five-thirty that afternoon, just as it was getting dark, there was a sudden cloudburst. They had three blankets between the seven men and they lay there shivering, doubtless feeling very miserable in their isolation. The rain kept on during the night, beating down with the wind, driving into their faces as they trudged northwards once more, until daylight the next morning showed the water fairly cascading down the rough stony slopes of the small wadis. They were wet through; but what was far worse was the depressing fact that their sticky bombs had been rendered quite useless. For this meant that they were no longer effectual as far as the raid was concerned. Accordingly, they decided to march back to the prearranged rendezvous area where a patrol of the LRDG had been detailed to stand by and pick them up. For the next two days and nights they walked south, with occasional halts for resting and sleeping. At the end of that time which had been given to them in their instructions. It should be borne in mind that these men did not know they had been dropped in the wrong place. Further one should realise that it required a considerable amount of courage and determination to decide to stay in one place like this. For their food supplies were dwindling and if the weather turned dry their water would soon become another problem. They kept a good look-out the next day and saw nothing but soon after darkness had fallen, they caught sight of a light low down on the horizon. After about half an hour it went out and thinking it to be a star they did not investigate. By now they were feeling very tired. On the following morning they noticed smoke where previously they had seen the light. Their spirits rose and they trudged wearily across the intervening miles. It was the patrol of the LRDG.[410]

Lieutenant Lewes appeared to be one of the luckier of the group leaders. Although "lucky" is relative. His drop was not without its tribulations. Lewes explained:

I hit the desert with quite a bump and was then dragged along by wind at quite a speed. When I came to rest, I staggered rather groggily to my feet, feeling sure I would find a few broken bones but to my astonishment I seemed to have had nothing worse than the wind momentarily knocked out of me. There was a sudden rush of relief but then of course I looked around and realised I was all alone and, well, God knows where.[411]

Despite his hard landing he was amazingly able to gather up his entire team, although one member had broken his back. He was given some water and a pistol and left alone, having been briefed prior to the mission on the action to be taken if anyone was injured on the drop and was unable to carry on. Lewes' team then began their march to their objective. However, the following day, navigational issues and torrential rains made further progress impossible. Jeff Du Vivier recollected:

All that night we marched or rather waded through the water which was sometimes up to our knees. We rested periodically when we could find a piece of high ground which stood out of the water, sometimes we travelled for over an hour and failing to find a dry spot just lay down in the water. Sleep came almost instantaneously but not for long, or a fit of shivering would force us to get moving. I could not explain how

LRDG Chevrolet 30cwt gun truck. (Artwork by Brenda Wight)

cold it actually was, to believe it one would have to experience it. I was not shivering but shaking. All the bones in my body were numbed. I couldn't speak, every time I opened my mouth my teeth just cracked against one another. And so, it was with all of us.[412]

With his team in a state of sheer exhaustion and suffering from exposure, Lewes decided to abort the mission and make for the rendezvous with the LRDG. The decision was timely. As Du Vivier again recalled, "we just wanted to fall out and die. We were demoralized. When you're frozen stiff, soaked to the skin, hungry ... you're not looking forward to a bright future, you just want it all to end."[413]

Notwithstanding the desperate conditions, Lewes' group marched for 40 minutes and rested for 20. Despite the terrible circumstances the raiders fell asleep as soon as they stopped. The following morning the storm had abated and the sun feebly poked through the clouds. As insipid as the sun's rays were, they did provide renewed hope and energy. Exhausted and near starvation, the group linked-up with the LRDG on November 19th. Several hours later Lieutenant Paddy Mayne and his surviving members also arrived at the RV. They also aborted the mission. Then, early the following morning, on November 20th, Captain Stirling and Sergeant Tait also finally wandered into the RV.

The LRDG patrol report captured the events:

At 0520 hours, on 19 November, LRDG Patrol "R" 1 placed two hurricane lamps on a very high point approximately a kilometre from their camp. At 0900 hours one was seen to be lifted and swung from side to side, the pre-arranged signal, this was answered by us and contact was made with the first party, Lt. Lewis [Lewes] and 9 O.R.'s." The following day at 0100 hours, the patrol saw a similar signal and Captain Stirling and a sergeant arrived. At dawn, the patrol moved to a new position that offered better cover. However, a small party remained at the RV to await stragglers. They built a smoke fire which attracted Lt. Mayne and eight other men. After an eight hour stay at the RV point, the LRDG patrol withdrew. Although "R"1 was to pass off Stirling and his party to another LRDG patrol for the return journey, they were unable to find them so HQ ordered "R"1 to return Stirling to Brigade HQ at Jerabub. This was completed at 1230 hours, on 25 November 1941.[414]

Stirling's assessment of the operation was critically objective. Shortly after the drop he told Fitzroy Maclean of the LRDG that the mission "had been a disaster."[415] In fact, Stirling himself later defined the terrible conditions:

Unfortunately, the night on which it [first mission] took place was almost unbelievably unsuitable for a parachute operation. There was no moon and the wind was so strong that on arriving in our Bombay aircraft over the Gazala coastline, the flares dropped by the Wellington bombers were quite insufficient for our navigators to pick up any fixed point on the coast because the desert sand and dust was obscuring the whole coastline. Therefore, in effect, the navigators had to take pot luck in their dead reckoning and, as far as I know, no party was dropped within 10 miles of the selected DZs. One of the five Bombays never dropped its stick of parachutists at all. ... The fate of the four other parties was a mixed one. Two men were killed on landing, owing to the severity of conditions, and of the rest only eighteen men and four officers (Paddy Mayne, Bill Fraser, Jock Lewes and myself) got to the L.R.D.G. rendezvous. Thus, the operation was a complete failure.[416]

Despite the setback, Lloyd Owen revealed that "He [Stirling] was not in any way down hearted." Lloyd Owen explained, "He was even then turning over in his mind all the mistakes that had been made and the lessons that he could learn from this abortive attempt. He was so certain

LRDG patrol. (IWM, 03532943)

that he could succeed and nothing was going to stop him – if he was given another chance."[417] This was not a given. Not surprisingly, after the mission, "their stock had gone down at GHQ."[418] Unavoidably, Stirling realized that parachuting was not necessarily the best means of reaching desert objectives and he discussed alternate means of transporting his raiders with the LRDG. The evening when Stirling was reunited with Lieutenant Lewes in the RV, he confided, "I think that's the end of parachuting for us."[419]

Despite the initial failure, Stirling's concept was not dead. Brigadier Ritchie noted Stirling's "rotten luck" with regards to the weather and accepted the idea of the SAS being attached to the Eighth Army. He also approved the concept of the SAS teaming with the LRDG to conduct raids rather than using the RAF to drop his troops into the desert. And so, regardless of their initial failure, the SAS lived to fight another day.

CHAPTER 8
TO KILL A FOX

STIRLING'S FORAY INTO THE DESERT to destroy German aircraft at their airfields deep behind enemy lines in support of Operation Crusader had resulted in utter failure. His mission, however, was not the only audacious venture the British attempted. General Auchinleck also approved another special operation that he hoped could provide a tremendous advantage to the Allied offensive. The intrepid scheme was to capture or kill the Desert Fox himself.

Auchinleck charged Lieutenant-Colonel Robert Laycock to oversee the mission. Laycock was not new to special operations. Promoted to the rank of lieutenant-colonel on July 7, 1940, he was appointed to raise and command No. 8 Commando. From the beginning Laycock emphasized a shift from the conventional mindset in his Commando. He drew his personnel mainly from the Brigade of Guards and rather than focus on "drill," his emphasis was centred on developing a "special technique," which he defined as:

- Physical fitness;
- Mental alertness;
- The offensive spirit;
- Complete disregard for danger;
- The instinct of the hunter;
- The lightning, destructive and ruthless methods of the gangster;
- Absolute self-reliance;
- A knowledge of various tricks, ruses and devices; and
- Above all, the ability to move and act at night fearlessly and noiselessly and to regard the blackest darkness as an aide rather than as a hindrance to the attainment of a difficult and hazardous objective.[420]

Appointed to command Layforce in February 1941, Laycock and his troops deployed to Crete in May to assist with the defence of the island. Following that debacle, the War Office disbanded Layforce in June with the ultimate intention of dissolving the Commandos in the Middle East.[421] However, Churchill intervened and insisted the ME Commandos be reconstituted and that Laycock become Director Combined Operations (DCO). This appointment never materialized, although Laycock was promoted to colonel and made Officer Commanding Middle East Commando Operations.[422] This reversal now set the stage for Laycock to oversee an audacious plan, which if successful, could turn the tables in North Africa.[423]

Although Laycock was nominally the approving authority for the operational plan, the actual idea, plan and raid on Rommel's supposed headquarters was the responsibility of Lieutenant-Colonel Geoffrey Keyes. The 24-year-old Keyes was the son of Admiral of the Fleet Roger J. B. Keyes, who was Director of Operations from 1940-1941.[424] Failing to gain entry to the RN due to his poor eyesight, Keyes, joined the Royal Scots Grey, his uncle's regiment, upon graduation from the Royal Military College at Sandhurst. An expert skier, he deployed to Norway as part of the British expeditionary force in April 1940; however, the rapid German advance scuttled the mission and Keyes returned to England. Subsequently, he joined the newly formed Commandos, which fell under his father's command. He was posted to the 11th Scottish Commando and upon completion of the exacting training regimen he deployed to the Middle East in January of 1941.

The Commandos seemed to be the perfect environment for Keyes. His idea of a "'happy ship' based on discipline and efficiency, were embodied by the Commandos; he liked discipline to be spontaneous and self-imposed, deriving from enthusiasm and confidence in their leaders." According to Keyes, Commandos had to be "tough as a mule and as cunning as a poacher." They had to be "killers all."[425]

On July 7, 1941, the 11th Scottish Commando departed Cyprus on *HMS Glengyle* as part of Operation Exporter, the British invasion of Vichy French Syria and Lebanon. In support of Australian 7th Division, its commander, Major-General John Lavarack, tasked the Scottish Commando with a seaborne landing at the mouth of the Litani River with the objective of seizing the bridges at Kafr Badda and Quasmiye and holding them until relieved by Australian forces. Unfortunately, rough seas delayed the landing allowing the Vichy French forces to blow the bridges.[426] Nonetheless, the Scottish Commando landed in daylight on July 9th and became engaged in substantial fighting. The resulting heavy casualties gutted the Commando. They also lost their CO, Lieutenant-Colonel Richard Pedder, which set the stage for the 24-year-old Geoffrey Keyes to be promoted and appointed CO of what was left of 11 Scottish Commando.

Keyes wasted no time seeking another mission for his new command.[427] He believed that if a raid was successful in killing or capturing General Rommel and destroying his headquarters, which was the brain and nerve centre behind the Axis war machine in North Africa, the entire Afrika Corps would be disorganized and disrupted, even if only for the critical juncture at the beginning of Operation Crusader. Furthermore, the raid, which he described as "dirty work at the crossroads," could also disconcert the Italian headquarters at the Cyrene crossroads, as well as the Italian intelligence centre at Apollonia.[428] From an intelligence standpoint, "Appollonia, Cyrene, Beda Littoria, Mameli, are known to be Nerve Centres of enemy communications and contain certain vulnerable points; these include H.Q.'s, Landing Grounds, Road and telegraph communications."[429] As such, Eighth Army HQ tasked Keyes and his Scottish Commando for a special independent mission. Unknown to them at the time, *Panzergruppe Afrika* HQ was originally established at Beda Littoria, but Rommel moved it to Ain el Gazala with an Advanced Headquarters even further forward at Gambut (between Tobruk and Bardia).

Bereft of the latest location of Rommel and his operational headquarters, planning went forward. The Eighth Army operational order clearly stated, "The Scottish Commando will attempt to land from submarines to create as much havoc and interference to communication in these areas as possible. They will attack the objectives enumerated in para 16 on the night of November 17/18th to coincide with the 8th Army's attack."[430] For the sea landings near Apollonia, Eighth Army directed that two parties, each of three officers and 30 other ranks (ORs), one of the parties to include Lieutenant-Colonel Keyes, be assigned to the task.[431]

Lieutenant-Colonel Keyes next set to the detailed planning. He organized his force into four parties:

- No. 1 Party – Commander – Lieutenant-Colonel Keyes, two officers and 22 ORs;
- No. 2 Party – Commander – Lieutenant David Sutherland and 12 ORs;
- No. 3 Party – Commander – Lieutenant Chevalier and 11 ORs; and
- HQ & Rear Link – Commander – Lieutenant-Colonel Laycock, two ORs and one Medical Orderly.
- In addition, there were two Senussi Guides attached, one for each of Parties No. 1 and 2.[432]

The plan entailed two submarines, His Majesty's (HM) Submarines *Torbay* and *Talisman*, which would be pulled from their normal patrol operations to land the raiders and their stores in rubber boats at Chesm-el-Kelb on the night of November 14/15th, in the order of *Torbay* then *Talisman*.[433] To assist with the landings, a British intelligence officer familiar with the area, Captain Jock Haselden, was to be at Chesm-el-Kelb by November 14th. He was born and raised in Egypt. His father was British and his mother was a Coptic Egyptian. Educated at King's School, Canterbury, he could transform from English gentlemen to Arab tribesman at will. Ideally suited for the mission, positioned on the beach Haselden was to indicate by signal if the beach was clear. As a redundant back-up, an SBS Folbot detachment would conduct a reconnaissance (recce) of the beach, whether or not Captain Haselden's signals were seen. In addition, the Folbot section was to provide local protection until the arrival of the first rubber-boats.[434]

Once landed and regrouped, each party had its pre-determined objectives. These were:

- No. 1 Party – a. German HQ Beda Littoria in three-storey silo; b. C-in-C's house in fir trees to west of HQ; c. Telephone lines and M.T. [motor transport] on road East and West of Beda Littoria;
- No. 2 Party – a. Italian HQ in caves NE [North East] of Cirene [sic] in escarpment; b. Graziani's villa on crest above it; c. Telegraph pole at cross roads; d. Aircraft on Cirene [sic] landing ground;
- No. 3 Party – Primary – Italian Intelligence Centre, Appollonia; b. W/T Station at Appollonia. Secondary (if above are unlocated because of lack of intelligence reports on targets) a. power station on West edge of Appollonia; b. HQ of unknown unit near landing ground; c. Aeroplanes on South edge of landing ground.[435]

Despite the specific list of targets, the Eighth Army direction stipulated that "All commanders will tackle any chance objectives or installations encountered at their own discretion to inflict maximum damage and interference to the enemy." Importantly, no objectives were to be assaulted before "Zero hour on 17/18 November."[436]

With regard to the lay-back party, Lieutenant-Colonel Laycock with Bombardier George Dunn, Private Davidson and Lance Corporal Alkin (medical orderly) were to remain at the beach landing site, which was chosen by Captain Haselden as a rear link with the submarines. Their role was to keep the beach under constant surveillance and to determine if enemy patrols located any traces of the landing and positioned troops that could hinder the re-embarkation. In this event, they would warn returning raiding parties of the danger, eradicate the threat, or if enemy forces were too great, move to an alternate beach. To allow for both contingencies, returning raiding parties were to all embark in *Torbay*, while *Talisman* deployed to the alternate beach for that contingency.[437]

Re-embarkation was scheduled for the nights November 18/19, 19/20 and 20/21. The submarines would not normally remain in vicinity of the beaches in the event of a failed rendezvous; however, if rough weather prevented re-embarkation, the *Torbay* was tasked with remaining in the vicinity until weather allowed for the remaining troops to be withdrawn. This decision also allowed stragglers who were a day or so late to attempt to regain the beach on chance that the original evacuation was delayed.[438] Failing a pick-up the orders were clear: "If for any reason anyone is left behind, he will make for the hills and endeavour to contact an Arab village. He will lie up until it is possible to contact our advancing troops. The Arabs in this area are pro-British and should at least conceal and feed any isolated individual."[439]

With the plan set, the next step was to ensure adequate preparation. The first red flag to appear was the HQ staff assessment of the actual force designated to conduct the raid. The Operations staff bluntly cautioned:

> *This Branch has recently been investigating the reports of certain operations which have been carried out by Layforce. We have arrived at the conclusion that Layforce was quite inadequately trained for some of the operations in which they took part. The DCGS is fully in agreement with this conclusion, and is now corresponding with Brigadier Macleod as to what steps we should take to put their future training on a sound basis. It is understood that a small detachment of the late 'C' Bn Layforce is being prepared to go out to the Western Desert, and I feel that a note of warning should be struck to the Western Army that this detachment cannot be considered to be a highly trained unit. This does not, of course, apply to 'L' Det SAS Bde, under Capt[ain] Stirling, who have been carrying out intensive training in night operations for some weeks.*[440]

Concerns aside, preparations moved forward. In October 1941, Captain Haselden, working with the LRDG, was landed by *Torbay* along with an Arab NCO at Chesm-el-Kelb (also referred to at times as Zaviet-el-Hamema), approximately 27 kilometres west of Apollonia. The aim of the recce was to make contact with friendly Arabs and to survey possible landing sites, particularly the beach at Chesm-el-Kelb, which was approximately 29 kilometres from Beda Littoria. Haselden was very familiar with North

Beach reconnaissance. (Artwork by Ted Zuber)

Africa. Prior to the war he had been a cotton merchant in Egypt. At the commencement of hostilities, he was employed with the Libyan Arab Force and worked for G(R) (intelligence), the branch of the MEF HQ responsible for raiding forces. Subsequently, he became the Western Desert Liaison Officer at Eighth Army HQ. Specifically, his role was to control the Arab population of the occupied territory until Civil Affairs could be established, as well as obtain intelligence from friendly Arabs.[441]

Once Haselden completed his recce, he went into Slonta, a village 19 kilometres from Beda Littoria, in Arab disguise and called on Hussein Taher, the Mudir (local governor) of the town, who assisted Haselden. After missing a number of RVs Haselden was eventually picked up by a LRDG patrol. Importantly, he reported the beach at Chesm-el-Kelb would be suitable to land the raiding party.

A second recce mission consisting of Captain Tommy Macpherson, Keyes' Adjutant from 11 Commando, as well as three officers from the Special Folbot Section attached to the First Submarine Flotilla, landed from *Talisman* on the night of October 24/25 at the preferred beach location at Ras-el-Hilal.[442] Upon completion of the recce, they failed to make contact with the submarine. They attempted an overland escape but were captured. Subsequently, the beach was ruled out as a possible landing site because it was considered compromised.

With the recce confirmed and the mission approved, Auchinleck's

HQ issued the final orders on November 9, 1941. The following day the actual raiding parties and their support elements deployed. The LRDG dispatched T2 Patrol under Captain A.D. Hunter to take Haselden, three other intelligence officers and two Arabs and drop them at a prearranged spot.[443] Hunter split his patrol into two sections of five vehicles, as he believed the complete patrol of ten vehicles would be too many for a covert infiltration. Once Hunter dropped his charges, he was to remain in hiding until the evening of November 17th when he was to begin observation of the road from Mekili to Benghazi until November 29th, at which time he was to return to the drop off point to pick up Captain Haselden and bring him back to Siwa. If Haselden was not at the RV by 0600 hours GMT on December 1st, the patrol was to return without them.

Keyes' party also deployed on November 10th. Six officers and 50 other ranks were loaded on *Torbay* and *Talisman* in Alexandria. Keyes led the team on *Torbay* and Laycock was the senior officer on *Talisman*.

Many criticized the fact that two senior officers for such a mission seemed very "top heavy." The explanation for Laycock's participation was the fact that as the officer responsible for the ME Commandos he required some personal experience on an actual commando operation.[444] He argued it was difficult to command without some field experience. Also preying on the minds of some was the fact that Keyes was only 24 years old with only four and a half years of military service behind him. Quite simply, many believed he was over-promoted.[445] Nonetheless, Laycock's participation seemed odd, particularly since he observed, "The chances of being evacuated after the operation were very slender, and that the attack on General Rommel's HQ in particular appeared to be desperate in the extreme. This attack even if initially successful, meant almost certain death for those who took part in it."[446] Despite his misgivings, he still decided to take part in the raid, albeit he agreed to stay at the landing site on the beach.

On November 13th, Captain Haselden once again called on Hussein Taher, Mudir of Slonta. The LRDG had transported him, along with two other British officers, as well as Mohammed Khaufer and Hussein Abu Jedallah of the Libyan Arab Force, from Siwa across the desert to Slonta. On arrival, he requested a horse and a trustworthy guide to take him down the coast to the landing area.

That same day, after a four-day passage, *Torbay* and *Talisman* arrived off the designated beach. The following day despite the poor weather, the raiders decided to attempt a landing at Chesm-el-Kelb. After a periscope reconnaissance of the beach, the skipper decided to dispatch a recce team to confirm all was well prior to allowing the commandos to land. Lieutenant-

Commander Anthony Miers, commanding the *Torbay,* having a reputation for "bold, determined and decisive action," recalled, "In view of the eagerness of the military [commandos] to be landed, and the improbability of the weather improving in the next few days, determined to effect the disembarkation in the prevailing conditions."[447] This decision proved to be problematic.

Initially, matters looked promising. Lieutenant Tommy Langton, one of the *Torbay's* two folbot officers remembered:

> *There was one moment none of us will ever forget. It was as we were closing the beach in Torbay. We were on the forward casing of the submarine, blowing up the dinghies and generally preparing. We could just see the dark coast line ahead. We had been told that Haselden would be there to meet us, but I think no one really believed that he would. He had left Cairo quite three weeks before, and during the interval there had been several changes of plan...When the darkness was suddenly stabbed by his torch making the looked-for signal there was a gasp of amazement and relief from everyone – in other circumstances it would undoubtedly have been a spontaneous cheer.*[448][449]

As a result of the signal, Lieutenant Ingles launched his folbot, a 16-foot two-man canvas-covered kayak.[450] Together with Corporal Severn they paddled ashore to confirm all was well. When they returned to the submarine the rough seas smashed his folbot against the submarine's hull. Fortuitously, both kayakers got back on board. With confirmation that all was well, the dinghies were brought up through the forward hatch and placed on the casing between the forward hydroplanes and the conning tower at 1830 hours. They were then inflated by foot pump as the weapons, equipment and munitions were lashed to them.[451]

Up until this point despite the conditions, all seemed to be going well. For safety, a life line was rigged both fore and aft along the casing and all ranks wore two Mae West life jackets. These safety precautions were fortunate because once the *Torbay* trimmed down to launch the dinghies, a heavy sea swell engulfed the submarine and swept four rubber boats and one commando overboard. Gunner Jim Gornal described, "As we were lying there and the submarine started blowing her tanks or what have you, there was a ruddy great wave came over the casing and some of the dinghies were swept off."[452]

Struggling against a hostile sea and Force Seven winds, the launching of boats from the submarine commenced at 2135 hours. Initially the crew

Folboat launched from HM Submarine Torbay. (Artwork by Brenda Wight)

anticipated that the entire operation to surface, prepare the boats and launch them would take only an hour. In fact, it took almost six. Adding to the delay, attempts to launch the rubber dinghies off the deck of the *Torbay* by trimming down the submarine to float them off, failed repeatedly. Finally, at 0035 hours the final dinghy was launched and Keyes' party made it ashore. Lieutenant-Commander Miers was impressed with their tenacity in light of the horrendous conditions. He wrote:

> *The operation had been completed...in spite of the weather conditions by the determination, grit and courage of all concerned on the casing, some of whom received a very severe buffeting while handling the boats alongside in the swell, and nearly all were completely exhausted at the finish. No less splendid was the spirit of the soldiers under strange and even frightening conditions. They were quite undaunted by the setbacks experienced and remained quietly determined to "get on with the job."[453]*

Meanwhile, once Lieutenant-Commander Michael Willmott, the skipper of *Talisman,* received a signal to notify him that *Torbay* had completed its unloading, he dispatched Lieutenant John Pryor, one of the SBS officers, to land on the beach and flash the letter "C" to the *Talisman* to let them know it was okay to begin the landing process. Pryor recalled:

> *I set off to do so. The Torbay party by this time had met Haselden and the venerable Arab he had with him. As there were no Italians about, they had lit a fire in a ruined house on the beach, round which the men were tryng to dry themselves. Seeing the fire, I paddled for it, and*

it drew me too far to the East. Before I could stop, we were capsized in surf on rocks. We hung on to the canoe, as we didn't want to have the wreckage about, and managed to struggle on to the rocks, but kept being sucked off by the undertow and knocked over by the waves. I began to think we might drown. [Corporal John] Brittlebank said, "I don't think this canoe is much more use, sir." I said "no – dam the thing," so we let it go....We got ashore in a little rectangular bay, and found Haselden and his Arabs sitting around the fire with the men from the Torbay.[454]

Once Keyes and his party were ashore, *Talisman* attempted to launch its commando party at 0137 hours. Initially it seemed that the seas and wind had quieted and the unloading process would go much more smoothly. However, suddenly the seas became extremely angry once again and the swells played havoc with the submarine. Lieutenant-Commander Willmott decided to ground his ship to assist with the unloading. Unfortunately, as the submarine touched the sea floor and they were about to launch the first dinghy, a heavy sea swept over the casing resulting in most of the dinghies and 11 men being swept into the sea. "There was a heavy thud as the ship grounded and started to roll over on her side," Corporal Charles Lock recalled, "the next instant a solid sea came thundering over us, submerging everyone in a welter of water black and furious."[455]

The crew of the Talisman now tried to assist the commandos and they threw the remaining boats into the water, hoping the commandos could climb inside and paddle to shore. One dinghy "got away in this manner." However, the remainder of the boats capsized and / or had difficulties with the current. As a result, many swam back to the submarine. The Talisman spent until 0400 hours recovering men and boats.[456] The skipper of the *Talisman* later reported:

Touched bottom, ground swell increased without warning and first wave went over the casing...This sudden transformation of an orderly scene on the casing to one of confusion was most demoralising... Lieutenant Sutherland was told by me to throw in the remaining boats clear of the submarine and get his men to jump in after them. The men very pluckily carried out this order but only one boat got away the right way up with the men on board. The remainder got into difficulties through being carried out to sea by the current and gentle breeze off shore which had just got up.[457]

By this point, both time and weather negated any further attempts of launching dingies. *Talisman* now used its remaining time surfaced to retrieve the boats and men that were still in the water and move out to sea to recharge their batteries. As a result, only Laycock and seven others were able to paddle to the beach. [458]

Extremely wet and cold, the landed commandos waited until it was clear that no one else was coming ashore. The dinghies were then hidden in a cave near the beach. Significantly, all the folbots were destroyed so they could not bring the grass line ashore with which they had planned to haul the dinghies back to the submarines. As a result, they had to hide the dinghies on shore.[459] Once this was done, they moved approximately a kilometre and a half inland to a wadi that had been selected as an assembly area. They laid up here while Lieutenant Pryor, the SBS officer, and his fellow kayaker remained on the beach.

To this point, the mission was filled with turmoil. Captain Robin Campbell revealed.

> *Whatever he may have felt like inside himself, Geoffrey certainly appeared confident and cheerful as we set off at about 8 p.m. He took the lead with the guide and Corporal Abshalom Drori [a Palestinian] the interpreter, leaving Laycock with a beach party of Pryor, Brittlebank and two men with Bren guns to guard the stores in the Wadi and keep in touch with the Torbay. The Talisman was to lie off an alternative beach. [This arrangement, however, had been cancelled and she returned to Alexandria with seventeen Commandos on board].*
>
> *The raiding party reached the top of the first escarpment (which is about half a mile inland) about 9.15 after a fairly stiff climb, and all that night we marched inland over extremely difficult going, mostly rock-strewn sheep tracks. Our guide left us about midnight, fearing to go any further in our company.*
>
> *Geoffrey then had the difficult task of finding the way by the aid of an indifferent Italian map, his compass and an occasional sight of the stars. In spite of this responsibility, he kept the heavily laden party going with my help and that of Lieutenant Roy Cooke [both he and Campbell were attached only for the operation]. Here was another disappointment for Geoffrey-none of his own officers had been able to land. At the end of the night Geoffrey was carrying more than his own equipment.[460]*

After a short spell of rest, while darkness still prevailed the commandos had to make preparations to hide in a waiting area during daylight until it was time to deploy on the raid.

Captain Campbell described, "Just before first light, Geoffrey gave the order to assemble the stores and personal kit, and follow him inland to a wadi he had previously selected from the map as a good place to lie up during the following day. The men were dispersed in various old ruined houses and caves all round the bed of the little dry stream, where they huddled together and slept – as cold as charity."[461]

The operation was off to a rocky start. Even before the mission had even fully begun, the raiding party was down considerably in personnel. Keyes had only 36 men in total. In addition, they were short rations and ammunition and their two Senussi guides and interpreters were believed drowned. As a result, according to Lieutenant-Colonel Laycock's report, he adjusted the objectives. He explained:

> *First, I had been definitely instructed by Eight Army that any operations would be of the greatest value to our own main forces if carried out on the night D-1/D1[17/18 November], and secondly the weather now looked far from promising...I therefore modified the plan as follows: I limited the primary objectives to the two considered most important and placed Lt.-Col Keyes in command of No. 1 detachment. As originally planned, he was to attack the German HQ*

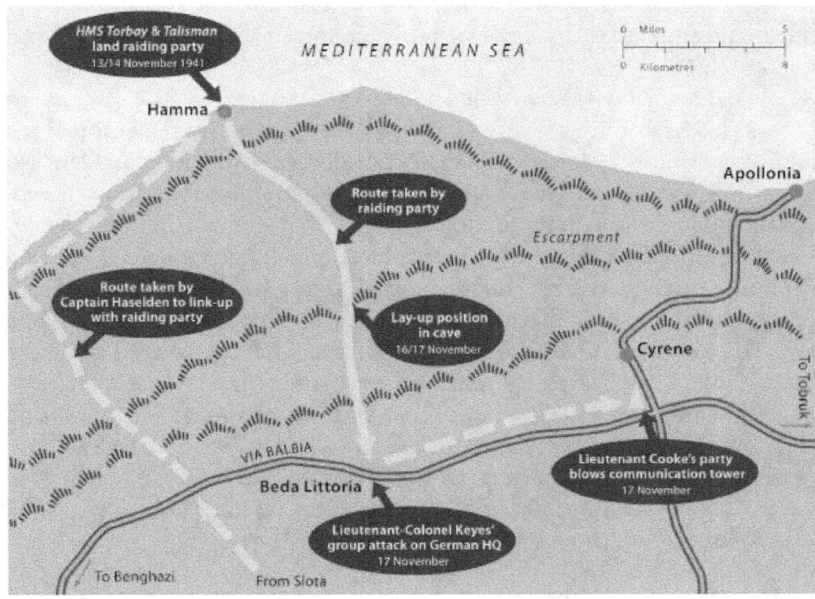

Map 4 -Routes taken by the Commandos during OP Flipper.

*and General Rommel's house. He had with him Capt. Campbell and
17 ORs.*

*Lt. Cook commanded No. 2 Detachment with orders to sabotage
the communications at the cross roads south of Cirene [sic]. I allotted
him 3 ORs from Torbay and 3 of the ORs who had landed from
Talisman.*[462]

Although many sources actually credit Keyes with making the decision, the
end result was the raiding party was now divided into two groups instead
of the original four. Party No. 1, commanded by Keyes now consisted of
Captain Campbell and 17 ORs. Their target was what was believed to be
Rommel's villa and the German HQ at Beda Littoria. Party No. 2 was led
by Lieutenant Roy Cooke and six ORs. Their objective was the Italian
HQ at Cyrene. However, Keyes hedged his bet. They would travel as one
group to the target area and, if Keyes could spare Cooke and his party, he
would cut them loose. If not, they would remain with Keyes to assault the
primary objective. Captain Campbell detailed, "In the afternoon Geoffrey
summoned his men, and after explaining the new plan in outline, supervised
the opening, repacking and distribution of the ammunition, explosives and
rations. Although his original plan had been very thoroughly upset and
his force lacked guides, two, or it may have been three, officers and some
twenty men, Geoffrey gave no sign of being disturbed by this and none of
the men seemed to realise how seriously hampered the operation was from
the outset."[463]

Haselden, who was scheduled to depart to rejoin the LRDG, agreed to
provide his Arab guide to Keyes. However, the Arab quickly abandoned the
raiding party after guiding them for a few kilometres inland. Haselden also
undertook to conduct demolitions on other communication infrastructure
on the road from Lamluda to El Faidia. Importantly, before leaving,
Haselden informed Keyes that the building previously identified as housing
Rommel's quarters and HQ had changed. Originally, Haselden briefed that
Rommel and his staff officers lived in a house at Sidi Rafa (the Arab name
for Beda Littoria). He now informed Keyes of what he believed to be the
current structure housing Rommel. Keyes adapted his plan accordingly.[464]

The raiding party moved out at 1900 hours to a more secure waiting
area. Having moved to the new location in the dead of night over
treacherous terrain, the raiding party hunkered down to try and grab some
sleep. Early on the morning of November 16th, Captain Campbell awoke
in drizzling rain to the sound of a commotion. He described:

Keeping out of sight I crawled over to where Geoffrey was sitting wrapped in his Arab blanket to await developments. Presently Drori, the Palestinian interpreter, came running up to Geoffrey and reported that they were surrounded by armed Arabs. Raising our heads cautiously above the scrub we saw a few rascally-looking Arabs, one or two brandishing short Italian rifles. However, Geoffrey decided that they did not appear either particularly formidable or implacably hostile, so he gave the order for the chief of the band to be brought to him for a talk. Shortly afterwards a villainous-looking Arab with a red head cloth wound round his head was brought up by the Palestinian interpreter and a sentry.[465]

Keyes now gambled that he could convince the Arab chief of his bona fides. Keyes showed the chief a letter from Seyed Idris, the exiled chief of all the Senussi. Although the Chief could not read, Keyes was able to convince him that the letter instructed Idris' subjects, the people of Cyrenaica, "to render every aid to our friends." Fearing the Arab would abscond and warn the Italians, his salesmanship was clearly important. Once Keyes had finished talking the Chief "was soon grinning happily and offering to do anything he could to help."[466] Keyes then requested cigarettes. Amazingly, after giving the Chief some money, he went to the Italian canteen and bought them. Several hours later a boy arrived in camp with the cigarettes. After prolonged haggling, Awad Mohammed Gibril of the Masamir tribe, agreed to guide the raiders to the *Prefettura* in Beda Littoria for a sum of a thousand Italian lire.

The raiders holed up for the day and then once darkness descended moved closer to their objective on the night of November 16th. That night, the third behind enemy lines since they landed, a local Arab guided them to a cave hidden in a dense wood of juniper and lentisk, called Karem Gadeh at Carmel Hassan – approximately 16 kilometres from Beda Littoria, where they spent the night. This location was designated as the rendezvous point for after the attack. The interior of the cave was roomy and dry, albeit it had a ghastly smell of goats. Nonetheless, it was a perfect location to stay hidden for the remainder of the night. The only downside was that the guide cautioned Keyes and his raiding party to depart before dawn because local goatherders often brought their flocks to the cave during inclement weather. As such, prior to sunrise Keyes moved his men to a small wood nearby.

Once deployed to the new hide, Keyes left Captain Campbell in charge. Along with his guide, Sergeant Terry and Lieutenant Cooke, the designated leaders of the other attacking parties, Keyes now set off on a recce. As they made their way to the objective, a violent thunderstorm began dumping torrential rain on the small recce party. Adding to the difficulty, the guide refused to take them in Arab disguise into Beda Littoria because of all the enemy spies and agents. Instead, he took them to a wood nearby, where unfortunately, they could see very little. As a result, they returned to the hide in the woods near the cave.

On return Keyes decided that the risk of moving back inside cave and being discovered by locals, in order to stay warm and get some rest prior to the raid, trumped hiding in the wood and suffering from exposure. Captain Campbell described:

> *Every now and then the clouds seemed to open and a deluge of rain fell. The country we had to march over turned to mud before our eyes. Little torrents of muddy water sprang up all over he countryside we could see from the mouth of the cave, and a rivulet ran into the cave, which sloped down from the opening. The roof began to drip. Spirits were sinking – at least I know mine were – at the prospect of a long, cold, we and muddy march before we even arrived at the starting point of this hazardous operation.*[467]

With weather continuing to create issues and due to the fact that the recce was of little use, Keyes asked the Arab guide to send his boy to Beda Littoria "to spy out the lie of the land." The boy returned hours later with a windfall of information. His report allowed Keyes to draw an excellent sketch map, which proved to be extremely accurate. It included such details as the outbuildings and parking lot, as well as a guard tent on the HQ grounds. Their fortunes seemed to have improved.

CHAPTER 9
WHEN IT RAINS IT POURS

AS THE RAIDERS RESTED IN THE CAVE in preparation for the assault, torrential rains continued off and on. The impact of the rain was immense. It was the worst rainstorm the area had experienced in almost 40 years. The rain when it came was a savage, driving sheet of misery turning every wadi and creek into a raging river. The pitch darkness was pierced by jagged bolts of lightning. To add to the harsh conditions, the accompanying wind, despite the physical exertion of the raiders, chilled them to the bone.

Despite the poor conditions, the raiding party departed at 1800 hours, November 17th, with blackened faces. Keyes left himself five hours to travel the eight kilometres to the objective due to the inclement weather. They quickly disappeared into the dusk and pouring rain. Sergeant Fred Birch recalled, "Six miles as the crow flies, but following the winding path over the escarpment, knee-deep in rushing water it was nearer nine miles." He described, "The night was moonless and pitch-black, making it necessary to hold on to the bayonet scabbard of the man in front to keep in contact, the whole party being in single file."[468] Campbell reminisced:

The going became so bad that we were compelled to go in single file to avoid knocking one another over as we slipped and stumbled through the mud, and it became so dark it was only just possible to see the man in front. We had to hold on to one another's bayonet scabbards in order to keep in touch. Every now and again a man would fall, and the whole column would have to halt while he picked himself up. From time to time the middle of the column would lose touch with the man in front of him and we would have to stop and sort ourselves out again.

We reached the bottom of the escarpment at about 10.30p.m. without serious mishap. After a short rest we began our climb of about 500 feet of muddy turf with outcropping rocks. About half way up the noise of a man slipping and striking his tommy gun against a rock roused a watch-dog, and a stream of light issued from the door of a hut as it was flung open about a hundred yards away on our flank. As we crouched motionless, hardly breathing, we heard a man shouting at the dog. Finally, the door closed, and we resumed our way upward. At the summit we found a car track which the guides said led straight to the back of the German headquarters. We halted for a rest and Geoffrey re-formed the men, some twenty-four all told.[469]

At this juncture, the Arab guides became uneasy and wanted to leave. They confirmed to Keyes that the current track they were on led directly to the German HQ. Keyes pulled out his revolver and told the interpreter to explain to the guides that they were to proceed until told otherwise. However, the translation was not required as Keyes' body language reinforced by the pistol were self-explanatory. The guides carried on.

The raiding party now followed the darkened, muddy track until they reached a bush beside the fork in the track. They were now about 400 metres from Beda Littoria. They paused here for a last cigarette. Subsequently, with weapons at the ready, they cautiously proceeded until they came to the point where the track led down a slope towards the back of the village. Halfway down the slope, Lieutenant Cooke detached his party and led them to the main road to strike their objective.

At this point Keyes confirmed the location of the six-story objective, which the Italians called the *Prefettura*. At this point the Arab guides refused to go any further. Keyes directed them to wait there until the raiding party returned, at which time they would receive their money. However, once the shooting started, the guides disappeared into the night, although they later swore they waited in vain for the commandos to return.[470]

Keyes then led the party closer to the objective. At one point a searchlight or flashlight from the HQ parking lot, approximately 300 metres away, suddenly illuminated them. Keyes quickly whispered, "stand still!" Luckily the torrential rain obscured them from any inquisitive eyes. Once the light went out, Campbell formed up the raiding party in the shadow of an outbuilding while Keyes and Sergeant Terry conducted a brief reconnaissance.

During Keyes' absence, the mission was almost torpedoed. One of the commandos tripped over a tin can, which stirred a dog that began to bark uncontrollably. Someone in a nearby hut began to yell. Within minutes an Italian in a Fascist uniform and an Arab officer of the Italian Libyan Arab Force emerged from another hut and approached the raiders.

Upon questioning, Drori translated what they said in German to Captain Campbell who replied in German, in as an arrogant and authoritative voice as possible that they were German troops on patrol and that they should keep the dog quiet and go away. The ruse worked and the enemy officers returned to their hut.[471]

After the brief recce of the objective, Keyes felt he could tackle the target without the assistance of Cooke and consequently dispatched him to take out the communication mast in Cyrene. Along with Drori and three commandos, Keyes moved out. During his brief recce, Keyes discovered that the torrential rain had pushed the German sentries inside the main building, and as a result the large bell tent being used as a guardroom was empty. Therefore he reassigned the three commandos who had been responsible for its neutralization to accompany him as he began to position the raiding party for the attack.

As they approached the building, despite the fact that the cypress trees that lined roadway made the garden very dark, Keyes still spied a single guard standing at the entrance to the driveway. Leaving the four others with him in the shadows, Keyes stealthily moved forward alone and killed the guard at the gate. Having dispatched the sentry, he directed the three commandos to watch the back door of the house and fire on anyone who came out. He then went to get the remainder of his raiding party.

Although they carried a large quantity of explosives, enough to blow up the HQ and the electric-light relay plant nearby, Keyes was concerned that the persistent heavy rain may have compromised the explosives. Time would tell.

He sent one group to act as a blocking force to stop any attempts by the enemy garrison to reinforce the HQ. Then, just before midnight, Keyes, Captain Campbell, Sergeant Terry, Drori, Bombardier A. Brodie and Keyes' batman, Lance Corporal Denis Coulthread, all moved to within striking distance of the HQ. There was still a light visible in a window at the top of the house, therefore they patiently waited until it was extinguished.

Now with the building appearing dark, using his excellent German, Captain Campbell hammered on the front door and demanded entry. When the door was finally opened, Keyes jammed his revolver into the ribs of the startled soldier behind it. Fortunately, or unfortunately, depending on perspective, the German guard, Rifleman Jamatter, was well-trained and courageous. He began shouting warnings at the top of his lungs and, overpowering Keyes, he grabbed the revolver and began to wrestle with the Commando leader. Surprise was now totally lost. Campbell shot the struggling German over Keyes's shoulder, ending the struggle. Keyes now flung the door open and his six-man assault party stormed inside. Chaos

Keyes prepares to enter the HQ he believed belonged to Rommel. (Artwork by Brenda Wight)

now ensued as the main floor of the house reverberated with the sound of submachine gun and pistol fire, shouts of alarm, the slamming of doors and the panicked sound of men running on stone steps.

Off the left of the main hall, a door started opening and Keyes kicked it wide open. Inside, five Germans froze in startled shock.[472] Keyes emptied his pistol into the room as Campbell appeared at his elbow with a grenade. Keyes quickly hauled the door shut while Campbell prepared the grenade by pulling the pin and letting the fuse burn down a bit. Then Keyes opened the door once again and Campbell tossed in the grenade followed by a burst of the Thompson submachine gun. Simultaneously, a single shot fired by one of the Germans cracked from the interior of the room. Keyes was flung back and hit the floor heavily. The bullet had struck him just above the heart. He was dead within seconds.[473]

Campbell later described the assault and ensuing chaos:

Geoffrey then led us through a hedge into the garden, and we found ourselves at the back of the house. He posted Corporal [Joseph] Kearney and Private [Malcom Edward] Hughes at the back door, which he had already tried and found locked. All the ground floor windows were high up and barred with heavy wooden shutters, so it was impossible to get in that way. There was no alternative but to use the front door. We followed him round the building on to a gravel sweep in front of the house. The front door was set back inside a porch, at the top of a flight of stone steps. Geoffrey ran up the steps. He was carrying a Colt, and I knocked on the door for him, demanding loudly in German to be let in. The door opened on a second pair of glass doors, and we were confronted by a German (officer I think) in a steel helmet and overcoat. Geoffrey at once closed with him, covering him with his Colt. The man seized the muzzle of Geoffrey's revolver and tried to wrest it from him. Before I or Terry could get round behind him, he retreated, still holding on to Geoffrey, to a position with his back to the wall and his either side protected by the first and second pairs of doors at the entrance. He started to shout. Geoffrey could not draw a knife and neither I nor Terry could get around Geoffrey as the doors were in the way, so I shot the man with my .38 revolver, which I thought would make less noise than Geoffrey's Colt. Geoffrey then gave the order to use tommy guns and grenades, since we had to presume that my revolver shots had been heard. (Geoffrey said that his arm had gone numb; perhaps the shots had chipped his elbow, or it may have been the wrestling match with the German had damaged it.)

We found ourselves, when we had time to look round, in a large hall with a stone floor; it had a stone stairway leading to the upper stories on the right.

There were several doors leading out of it, one on the right of the entrance, and two down the left-hand wall, while on the far side glass doors led to the back premises. The hall was very dimly lit by a single electric-light bulb hanging in the centre; but Terry saw the farthest door on the left open a little way – a gleam of light shone out for a second before it hurriedly shut again.

We heard a man in heavy boots clattering down the stairs, though we could not see him nor he us, as he was hidden by a right hand turn in the stairway. He was shouting, "what goes on there?"

As he came to the turn and his feet came in sight, Sergeant Terry fired a burst with his tommy-gun. The man turned and fled upstairs.

Geoffrey had been flinging open the doors on either side of the hall. We looked inside and found the rooms were empty. He pointed to a light shining through the crack under the next door and inside were about ten Germans with steel helmets, some sitting and some standing. He fired two or three rounds with his Colt .45 automatic. I said, "Wait, I'll throw a grenade in."

He slammed the door shut and held it while I got the pin out *of the grenade. [Sergeant Terry, who had closed up behind them, afterwards said he could hear the sound of heavy breathing inside the room.]*

I said "Right" and Geoffrey opened the door. I threw in the grenade, which I saw roll to the middle of the room, and Sergeant Terry gave a burst with his Tommy-gun. Before Geoffrey (who said "well done" as he saw the grenade go in) could shut the door the Germans fired. A bullet struck him just over the heart and he fell unconscious at the feet of myself and Terry.[474]

As the melee erupted, Lance Corporal Coulthread fired a couple of bursts at the man's silhouette on the staircase. He then turned back towards the main door and left Bombardier Brodie to guard the stairs. While the action was ensuing, another German, following the path leading towards the house using a flashlight with red filter, moved toward the apparent commotion. The man was in pyjamas but armed. Coulthread saw the light and moved to the back door and waited so that he could get the drop on the individual once he entered the house. However, Drori, who was guarding the back door, also saw the light and went outside and hid in the garden. When the man was a few metres away, Drori stepped out and shot him. The German silently fell, apparently dead. Coulthread then turned back into the hall.

While Coulthread was busy with his own part of the battle he heard the shout "grenade," followed by Keyes' revolver clattering to the floor as he was hit. Campbell shut the door and he and Terry flung themselves to one side; immediately afterwards the grenade went off with a shattering explosion. "This was followed by complete silence, and we could see that the light in the room had gone out," recalled Campbell. He explained, "I decided Geoffrey had to be moved, in case there was further fighting in the building [and because they intended to blow it up], so between us Sergeant Terry and I carried him outside and laid him on the grass verge to the left of the front door. He must have died as we were carrying him outside, for when I felt his heart it had ceased to beat."[475]

Having carried Keyes outside, Campbell then went back into the house. At that point, Campbell and Terry heard shots outside so they deployed by the door with hand grenades at the ready. Drori stayed with the body of Keyes, as well as the German he shot who was still breathing. At one point, he thought he heard Sergeant Terry call him so he left to look for the others.

When Drori met up with Terry he found out that Campbell too had now been wounded. Campbell had gone around to the back of the house to ascertain the status of the cut-off force. Unfortunately, he forgot that the sentries had orders to shoot anyone coming from that direction unless they gave the password. As a result, he was shot by one of the sentries, which resulted in a ghastly wound and a broken leg.[476]

This latest accident now left the raiding party without an officer. As a result, Campbell ordered Sergeant Terry to retreat after placing the remainder of the explosive charges. The two explosives they left in the house were enough, according to the Germans later, to have killed everyone in the building. Kearney and Coulthread both carried three sticks of gelignite in canvas ammunition bandoliers. They were bound together at each end, primed and fused ready for use. On the end of the fuse was a large brimstone head (similar to a match) which in theory only needed a matchbox rubbing across it to start the fuse burning. Hughes also had a self-igniting incendiary, the type that starts to burn when the head is smashed. Kearney threw the gelignite through the window into what appeared to be an office and Hughes tossed his incendiary after it, but there was no sign of a fire behind them when they looked back. The fuses apparently did not function.

Next, Brodie and Coulthread tried to get into the powerhouse to destroy it, but it was solidly built of concrete with a large flush-fitting steel door. Therefore they looked to explosives, but Brodie informed Sergeant Terry that the fuses were too soaked. Terry then directed Brodie to use grenades as an ignitor. Subsequently, Brodie pushed all the charges down the pipe and then dropped a grenade after them. They travelled approximately 20 metres, the charges exploded and all the lights went out.

Sergeant Terry now blew his whistle, the signal for the withdrawal. The men quickly gathered around Terry. One group came from the town hall where they had thrown hand grenades through the window. Sergeant Charles Bruce was busy in the HQ parking lot, leaving time bombs in all the vehicles. Although the soldiers offered to carry Captain Campbell back to the rendezvous, he realized that it was unrealistic to carry him 18 kilometres with a descent of approximately 610 metres to the coast in the current terrible conditions. Campbell was gravely wounded. His leg was shattered below the knee, and was later amputated. With no realistic hope of an evacuation, Campbell ordered the men to leave him behind. They gave him morphine and left him propped up behind the house. The Germans found him there when they searched the grounds. With his fluent German, he understood their discussion on whether to execute him or take him prisoner. As difficult as it was, he pretended he did not understand what they were talking about.

For the other raiders the return trip was quite despondent. The consoling thread was the hollow boom of the time bombs detonating in the car park. Nonetheless, the lashing rain had not let up and it was dark as coal, and to add to the misery a thick mist descended on them. Not surprisingly, they quickly lost their bearing and became lost. Having gone less than a kilometre, Sergeant Terry suddenly disappeared. He fell off the edge of a cliff, but luckily was able to hang on to a bush. However, he did lose his Thompson submachine gun but managed to save himself. After his men hauled him back up, they decided to stop until daybreak. As soon as it became light enough to see, the raiding party quickly scrambled down the escarpment, took a compass bearing and made for the beach.

Meanwhile back at the assembly area, Private Robert Fowler, who was left with the raiding party boats and stores, sensing something had gone wrong, decided to head back to the beach RV. Shortly thereafter he met an Arab who deceivingly led him to the enemy. Sergeant Bruce's party, who had not heard Sergeant Terry's withdrawal whistle, made their own way back to the cave at Carmel Hassan, but by the time they arrived, no one and nothing remained. The locals had made off with all of their boots and supplies.

Concurrently, Lieutenant Roy Cooke and his party of five, who had accompanied Keyes to the HQ building because of the lack of manpower, were eventually released by Keyes and they set off up the road to attack the communications pylon. Due to the delay of first accompanying Keyes, as well as the terrible weather, they were unable to rendezvous with the LRDG transport from Slonta who were to transport them to the actual objective. As a result, they had to march the 24 kilometres to the target. En route, two of the commandos dropped out because of their feet, which by now had become quite injured (one individual had actually lost his shoes). Although the group tried to hijack a vehicle, the plan fell flat. Despite all the trepidations as dawn emerged on November 18th, they reached their objective. However, the rain had done additional damage. "Unfortunately," explained Lieutenant Cooke, "all matches, etc. for setting off the charges were soaked, even inside the oilskin pouches – it had rained for some sixteen hours very solidly." With the growing light of dawn, time was now of the essence. Cooke tried a grenade under the charge but it was a dud. Fortunately, one of the commandos had a self-igniting incendiary detonator. Sergeant Birch explained, "I attached two new lengths of Bickford fuse and a detonator to the cordtex, struck the incendiary on a stone, laid it on the fuse and retired." They had only withdrawn five metres when "the incendiary burst out and the whole place was lit up over an area of about hundred yards diameter."[477] They ran for approximately 150 metres and threw themselves on the ground in the wet, low scrub. After approximately a minute the charges went off and they heard cables hitting the road. "We set it off," Cooke simply recounted, "and up she [communications pylon] went in fine style."[478] However, once the smoke cleared it became evident the cable mast had been damaged and was skewed at a severe angle, but it had not toppled.

Meanwhile, as the raiding party elements scrambled to return to the evacuation site, there was no sign of the Arab guides. According to Hussein Taher, who assisted the raiders (and who in 1945 became the Mudir of Sidi Rafa):

> *Both the Arabs [guides] remained at Zidan until dawn but as none of the party appeared, Awad decided to see what had happened. When he reached the Suk el Zabat market, he perceived German and Italian soldiers with armed police spread out like locusts going northwards. He asked one of the Arabs what was the matter and was told that the British had attacked Rommel's House, but unfortunately Rommel was not there.*
>
> *Awad looked for the party, but as he could not find any of them, he retraced his steps to the cave where he found the sentry who asked for the rest of his companions. Awad told him he could not find them and offered to guide him to the shore, where he left him so as not to be seen with him.*[479]

This account was discounted by the raiders who believed their Arab guides abandoned them as soon as they parted company.

Meanwhile, Sergeant Terry's group slogged-on all day. Although they were on a different path than the one they used to move from the beach to the objective, they were certain they were on the correct trajectory. During the afternoon they ran into a group of six to eight armed Arabs. Although Drori's explanation resulted in the Arabs allowing them to pass, the party was not sure that he was able to lull their suspicions entirely. They sensed that the Arab patrol followed them at a distance and reported their presence to the Italian Carabinieri.[480]

Finally, at approximately 1700 hours, the exhausted party led by the nineteen-year-old Sergeant Terry spotted their landing beach, where they found Lieutenant-Colonel Laycock waiting for them. Terry quickly briefed Laycock on the happenings of the raid.

More misfortune now befell the group. Although with evening the wind and the sea had calmed and it seemed conditions were acceptable for a withdrawal to the submarines, a major problem emerged. The dinghies had disappeared. Apparently, for some unexplained reason friendly Arabs had moved them from the cave where they were hidden. However, with the myriad of caves along the escarpment they could not be found.

Calamity continued to plague the group. While in the wadi an unfriendly Arab came across the group. He hastily turned around and using cover as best he could, he quickly disappeared. Their Senussi guides had warned them that some of the tribes living close to the coast were unfriendly and would report them to the Italians. Although until now they had been careful to move only at night and hide during daylight hours, the completion of the mission and their expected departure resulted in a lapse of security. Although shooting the man may have been an option, Sergeant Terry wisely decided not to start a war with the local Arabs.

Once Laycock was told of what happened, he ordered all the men down to the caves on the beach. He calculated that they may be able to evade their pursuers if they in fact the enemy came to search the wadi. As night began to fall, Laycock went to the beach and scanned the sea with his binoculars. Shortly after dark, he spotted the *Torbay* fully surfaced approximately 400 metres from shore. Through signals he requested a folbot, , be sent to shore with life jackets and a grass-line.[481] He explained the dinghies had gone missing.[482]

The *Torbay* did not return the signals. It had been previously agreed for security reasons that only the beach party would send signals. With the missing dinghies, Lieutenant-Commander Miers suspected the proximity of enemy elements. As a result, he sent Lieutenant Ingles and Corporal Severn in a dinghy loaded with life jackets, food and water.

Once again, there were great difficulties launching the dinghy from the submarine and the boat broke loose before either Ingles or Severn could get in. Fortuitously, the sea swell swept the dinghy to shore within 20 metres of where Lieutenant-Colonel Laycock stood.

Confusion now set in. Not receiving an acknowledgement of his signals, Laycock returned to the cave and told the men evacuation was off for that night. Concurrently, the friendly Arabs who had moved the boats arrived and were prepared to show them where they were. Then, the sentry told Laycock the submarine was signalling. Laycock rushed back to the beach but neither side could understand each other's messages. Finally, at 2315 hours, the *Torbay* used a shaded lamp to send its signals. Laycock understood Miers to say that the sea was unsuitable for sending a folbot. *Torbay's* commander, unaware that the raiding party had found their dinghies and life jackets, suggested he bring the submarine close to a spit of land at the head of the bay at dawn and that the men could swim out to the submarine.

Laycock, however, believed the men were too tired to swim out to the submarine and feared many would drown.[483] He also realized that trying to paddle the dinghies out to the submarine in the Force 4 winds and heavy sea swell would lead to the same effect. As a result, he decided to risk staying on shore for one more day and attempt the withdrawal the following night. Although in disagreement with Laycock's decision, Miers had no choice but to submerge and leave the area as dawn was quickly approaching.

As dawn slowly emerged Laycock ordered a "stand-to" and an all-around defensive posture was taken. He then walked the perimeter with Lieutenant Pryor and deployed additional sentries to ensure they had good observation on all the possible approaches. He also laid out defensive arcs of fire for the remainder of the men. He had two detachments of men guarding the flanks of their position at the caves; three men were left to observe the wadi and the main body remained at the caves.

What Laycock had not known was that the Italians had captured two of the commandos near Beda Littoria on November 18th, who, contrary to Keyes' orders, had marked their map with the landing beach. As a result, the enemy now knew where to find any other remaining commandos.[484] Not surprisingly then, around mid-day Laycock and Pryor had just sat down to eat when chaos erupted. Pryor recounted, "BANG went a shot from our western sentry, and we ran in a fusillade of pops to action stations in a ruined house on a knoll back of our cave."[485] The remainder of the main body similarly ran from their caves to their defensive positions. In the distance, the raiders could see a number of "Arabs in red turbans crawling towards us."[486] Pryor then recalled, "Everybody fired and they fired back, there were a few bigger bangs that I imagined were from a mortar, and I remember thinking 'our old wall doesn't look a bit bullet proof.'"[487]

There did not at first appear to be many native troops so Laycock and Pryor conjectured that they could defeat this Arab force, which were just Carabinieri Arabs, and still get away that night. After all, the wind had let up and the sea had become calmer. Laycock then ordered Sergeant Bruce to take two commandos and outflank the Arab enemy force. Pryor, armed only with a .38 revolver and a grenade, accompanied by another soldier quickly moved off to outflank the enemy from the seaward side. Matters quickly disintegrated. The Thompson machinegun carried by the commando with Pryor quickly jammed and he was unable to clear it. "I looked around," Pryor recalled, "and saw that my man had managed to get his Tommy gun jammed solid. I poked it about a bit and banged it, but it couldn't budge." Now incensed, Pryor fumed, "Well try and clear it for God's sake – I'm going on."[488]

Pryor then ran on by himself but quickly ran out of cover. He also noticed that there were Italian soldiers with the group, which numbered approximately 40. He decided to withdraw and report to Laycock, but on his attempt to pull back was quickly hit in the foot and leg. Nonetheless he made it back to Laycock and reported the situation.[489] Based on the report, Laycock decided to break into small teams and each group try to make their escape. Lieutenant-Colonel Laycock later recounted in his report:

[On 19 November 1941] *All was quiet until about mid-day, when a few shots were heard from the direction of the wadi and from the Westernmost sentry-group. At first the only enemy to be observed were "Carabinieri" Arabs known to be stationed at Hania, about eight miles to the west. This did not worry us unduly since we were confident that we should be able to drive them off until darkness allowed us to retire to the beach for evacuation, which now seemed feasible as wind and sea were rapidly abating.*

I sent two small parties from the main body to outflank the enemy but it soon became evident that they were not on a wide enough front or in sufficient numbers, as detachments of Germans now appeared moving south towards us down the Western side of the wadi, whilst further Carabinieri forces came from the West. Later, what appeared to be a considerable party of Italians showed themselves on the skyline about a mile to our North but took no part in the battle. Fairly accurate fire was brought to bear on us, but we were behind good cover and suffered no casualties, though it was feared that the party in the wadi had been over-run.

The detachment sent to outflank the enemy to the East was held up after advancing a few hundred yards, but succeeded in rejoining our position. The detachment to the West advanced about a quarter of a mile before the tommy-gunner's gun jammed and became useless. He and the private with him were pinned to the ground, but Lieutenant Pryor gallantly continued to advance single-handed and, using cover and firing his revolver, he attempted to deceive the enemy into thinking that an outflanking operation was still in progress. He was eventually shot through the thigh, but managed to limp back to the main position.

Although the enemy were not equipped with automatic weapons, they were maintaining a steady advance, and bringing a considerable volume of rifle fire to bear on and around our position.

It was now evident that it would be impossible to hold the beach until dark against such superior forces, and that our only remaining line of retreat would soon be cut off.

At about 1400 hours I therefore reluctantly decided to abandon the position and to adopt the alternative plan of hiding in the Jebel until we could rejoin our advancing main forces [the 8th Army].

Nothing could be seen of our Western detachment whose original position was now occupied by the enemy and, as a runner sent to reconnoitre returned with negative information, I presumed that they had been kill or driven off Westwards.

I ordered the main body to split into parties of not more than three men each, to make a dash across the open, and to retire through our Eastern detachment to whom they were to pass on my orders.

They were then to gain the cover of the Jebel and to adopt whichever of the three alternatives seemed most propitious:

- Under cover of darkness to return later to the alternative beach, off which Talisman would be lying until just before first light on the night of 20/21 November.
- To make their way to the area of Slonta in which vicinity the Arabs were known to be friendly and where there was a chance of being picked up by Long range Desert Group.
- To hide in the wadis north of Cyrene escarpment until news of our forces was received.

Leaving a Medical Orderly with Lieutenant Pryor, whom I feared might otherwise bleed to death, I ordered them to surrender, and made good my escape.

On reaching the position originally held by our Eastern detachment, I found Sergeant Terry waiting for me and we set off together. The first half mile of the withdrawal was unpleasant owing to the open nature of the country, but the enemy's marksmanship seems to have been particularly poor, and although we had some close shaves, I do not think we suffered a single casualty, since Sergeant Terry and myself would almost certainly have observed any which had occurred.

Sergeant Terry and myself attempted to gain the alternative beach on the first and second nights, but were frustrated by the enemy whom we contacted near the original beach and considerably to the Northward. We therefore abandoned the project and retired Eastwards.

We found little difficulty in avoiding search parties since the cover in the Jebel is excellent and, having a good pair of field glasses I could usually spot Germans or Italians at considerable distances. Our greatest fear was being stalked by the Carabinieri Arabs who moved much more cleverly by tracking us, and who got close to us on several *occasions during the first few days.*

Later, however, having made friends with the Senussi tribes, we adopted the enjoyable policy of moving each night into the very wadis which the enemy were known to have searched during the day.

Our greatest problem was the lack of food and, though never desperate, we were forced to subsist for periods which never exceeded two and a half consecutive days on berries only, and we became appreciably weak from want of nourishment. At other times we fed well on goat and Arab bread, but develop a marked craving for sugar. Water never presented a serious problem, as it rained practically continuously.

Our failure to obtain reliable information of the advance of the British forces we found aggravating in the extreme.[490]

Corporal Dori, the interpreter described:

At noon an Italian Carabinieri (Police) patrol composed of Italians and natives encountered us. On the first shot of our sentry, they fell to the ground and hid themselves behind some stones on top of a facing hill. Lieutenant Colonel Laycock asked for volunteers to go round them and see their strength. Two men and myself went for it separately. The two men made a big circle and I made a small one. I reached a hiding place behind the Italians and kept watching them, I don't remember for how long but when some time had elapsed, I heard Colonel Laycock calling me to return...The Italians who up to that moment had hardly fired a shot, trying as much as possible to conceal their hiding place, opened up with a barrage of fire when they saw our men making off. I did not attempt to catch up with the running men, but lay hidden in the bush. It took the Italians some hours before they advanced although a white flag was hoisted where our position was by a wounded officer and a medical orderly, who had been ordered to stay behind with him. Taking the wounded officer and the orderly the Italians retreated to their position. At night I crept down from my hiding place towards the beach, hoping for the return of the submarine.[491]

Lance Corporal Bill Pryde evoked:

While fighting was going on Private [Frank] Varney came dashing into the cave I was in (that made five in our cave), bringing Colonel Laycock's orders to scatter. The mouth of our cave was facing the enemy and we were in a difficult position. Ammunition was going fast, and we knew we would have to give up, or try to run. We started running from the cave one at a time, and Corporal Radcliffe was the only casualty; but it was only a flesh wound.

We managed to reach the hills, and lay in the undergrowth with Radcliffe, who was losing a good deal of blood. While we lay there the enemy passed within thirty yards, but did not see us. We waited until dark. All the food we had was one tin of bully beef.[492]

They were captured two days later and taken to prisoner of war camps in Italy.

Lance Corporal Hughes, who had been in one of the caves, heard shooting but had not seen any enemy. Upon getting the order to split up into small groups and escape, he ran for the interior "rough country" where he met up with Bombardiers George Dunn and Brodie, Denis Coulthread, Privates James Bogle and Bob Murray, as well as Lance Corporal Joe Kearney. The group, however, was in a bit of a predicament. They had only approximately 20 rounds of ammunition between them and two days rations for one person, as well as ten emergency bars of chocolate. Luckily, friendly Arabs provided some assistance and food. Dunn recalled:

On the morning of 26th November 1941, just eight days after the raid, we were practically at the end of our tether. We roasted by day, and freezing cold at night; we were also rather hungry, our rations having finished three days before. We had plenty of water – the rainy season had started. The only signs we had seen of the enemy were a couple of armoured vehicles in the distance....We moved on until we spotted Mekili in the distance – it looked somewhat like a large fort - and took cover.

We found out later that the Long Range Desert Group had paid the place a visit that very day. They dropped a few shells into it. There was a strong Italian garrison. The shelling put them on the alert, and they picked us up with field glasses while we were still a long way off.

After lying low for about half an hour, we spotted movement on the top of a hill which lay to the left of the fort. All of a sudden from out of the fort itself came three whippet tanks, four motor cyclists, and a lorry mounting a Breda gun and filled with men. ... However, as there was a possibility that they were only a patrol, we lay perfectly still, but they came straight for us. At least the truck and Breda did, the motor cyclists worked round to our rear, and the light tanks onto our flanks.

They got within a couple hundred yards of us, so we did the only thing left to do. We put down our guns and stood up and waited for them.[493]

Luck seemed to elude the escaping commandos. Sergeants Bruce and Nichol reached the Tobruk perimeter before they were captured. As for the remainder of men who scattered, with the exception of Bombardier Brittlebank who made it back to friendly lines, nothing was heard from them until they came home from various prisoner of war camps after the war.

One team, however, dodged capture. Laycock teamed up with Sergeant Terry and managed to evade the enemy cordon, heading south into the Jebel Akhdar. The hostile country provided ample cover, with rocks, bushes, wadis and caves. They could lie up during the day and move at night. They developed a system of determining what areas had been searched during the day and then moving there at night, somewhat confident that the areas would not be revisited. They had little in the way of provisions, subsisting off berries and rain water. The discovery of a cave one evening gave them the opportunity to light a fire and warm up.

One night, breaking from their practice, no one stood guard and both slept. Suddenly, they both awoke, hearing a noise at the entrance. They lay still but the individual entered the cave. Fortunately for them, he was a member of a local Senussi tribe, which was hostile to the Italians but favourably inclined to the British. The Senussi brought them unleavened bread, and on one occasion a goat that they made last for days. With the eventual advance of Operation Crusader, after 41 days on the run, Laycock and Terry spotted what appeared to be British troops. They were immediately evacuated to Eighth Army HQ.

Captain Haselden and his group also achieved success and escaped. They blew their targets en route and safely reached the LRDG RV. Unfortunately, the LRDG patrol T2, while waiting for Haselden, was discovered by German patrols and attacked. The patrol lost its commander and two men before it could make its escape.

The *Torbay* did return the following night.[494] No signal was seen so Lieutenant Tommy Langton and Corporal Cyril Feebery paddled in to shore to reconnoitre the beach. They capsized in the surf but ended up on shore with their boat. They searched the beach for about 400 metres but saw no one. They then paddled along the beach and shone their torch as a signal, but still did not find anyone. A giant breaker caught the duo once again and brutally tossed them ashore. As a result, they lost one of their paddles and their boat broke up. Then they saw the glow of a cigarette. They realized immediately that it was the enemy as no commando would be foolish enough to openly smoke behind enemy lines. Therefore they decided to return to the *Torbay*, which was a feat in itself with one paddle and a sinking, broken boat.[495] Miers later reported, "They were making water fast and the boat was only just embarked in time to prevent her sinking."[496]

Drori, the Palestinian interpreter, who had returned to the bush for concealment, missed the rescue party. An Italian patrol captured him the following morning.[497] The *Torbay* also returned the next morning. Langton witnessed groups of Italian soldiers on the beach through the periscope. The mission was now clearly over. The *Torbay* reported:

> *Regret to report failure to re-embark. Day 1. In touch with 22 on shore in unfavourable weather conditions. Party unwilling to swim. Day 2. No signals seen and reconnaissance boat failed to contact. Day 3 and 4. All beaches strongly held, considerable air patrols. Operation definitely created diversion, invasion seemed feared. Bombarded landing ground 1600 21*[st]*, destroying aircraft on ground near Ras Amer.*[498]

In a letter to Keyes' family after the war, Ernst Schilling, the commander of the German Headquarters that Lieutenant-Colonel Keyes attacked, revealed:

> *[The targeted] HQ was the Second HQ for German Panzergruppe Africa – residence of the superior staff for supply. It was not used by Rommel generally. He resided at Casa Bianca at Ain Gazala, about 50 kilometres from Tobruk. He occasionally visited Beda Littoria, where a house was reserved for him and other high officers. This house was named "Rommel-Haus. ... Whether it was the death of the commander [Keyes] or the arrival of our assistant group, the fact is that the English did not attempt to advance in the upper rooms where really important plans and secret papers could have been found. There too were the leading officers. ... Though it was only the H.Q. II being touched, and no really success having been attained, I must confess that the sudden attack of a Headquarters 200 kilometres behind the front had made nervous almost all leading officers; and in the following time numerous rumours influenced the activity of all supplement troops. In this view the raid was in fact a success.*[499]

At the time the Germans did not immediately link the raid to a British attempt to kill Rommel. The War Diary of the *Panzergruppe Afrika* O.Q. Department recorded, "There is no doubt that the British attack on this Headquarters was for the purpose of capturing important documents."[500] Extracts from the German intelligence report to the Chief of the General Staff of Rommel's HQ on November 18, 1941 described:

> *On the 18 Nov. 41 at about 0030 hrs about 6 to 8 men sprang upon the sentry, Rifleman Jamatter, who was posted in the centre of the steps at the entrance to the Prefettura...Alarmed by the noise Lieutenant Kaufholz, Sergeant Artificer Leutzen, Staff Sergeant Major Bartl and Rifleman Kovacic, all of whom slept in the workroom (office) W u G [administration & supply] leaped out of their beds. Sergeant Leutzen opened the door of room W u G and shone his torch down into the entrance hall. At the same moment a man stepped in from the main entrance, approached Leutzen and wounded him with a pistol shot. Leutzen jumped to one side and tried to take cover. Lieutenant Kaufholz, who by now had stepped up next to Leutzen, returned the fire, but fell to the ground having been hit himself several times. Two of the intruders chose this moment to enter the room and throw two hand grenades. The resulting explosion knocked out all the occupants of the room.*[501]

As the chaos engulfed the bottom floor, officers and NCOs seated upstairs, upon hearing the commotion sounded the alarm by telephone. They then secured all documents and armed themselves to defend the staircase. When the commandos blew the generating house, the lights in the building went out. German reinforcements arrived quickly and conducted a careful search of the area. The severely wounded Captain Campbell was discovered and given medical attention. Although they attempted to interrogate Campbell his serious wounds made questioning impossible.

A German intelligence report assessed:

> *Judging by the evidence, it can be assumed that the raid had been carefully planned. It has not been possible to establish whence the Englishmen came nor how many of them there were. Once can conclude form the notes in the small brown pocket diary that the force consisted of twelve men in all, including the Captain. ...Judging by their clothing, one comes to the conclusion that the Englishmen had been dropped from the air and belonged to an Airborne Unit. Both*

had not shaved for several days, and one could conclude that they had been dropped some time ago and had chosen this day of particularly heavy rain as favourable for their undertaking.[502]

Rommel's aide-de-camp, Heinz Schmidt, confided, "[the raid] was a fearless exploit by the British ... the pity of it from their point of view was that they had been so badly misled."[503] Lieutenant-General Fritz Bayerlein, Chief of Staff of the Afrika Korps, later described the raid in his contribution to the *Rommel Papers*. He wrote:

During the night 17-18 November, British Commandos, in a raid of great audacity, tried to wipe out what they supposed to be Army Headquarters in Beda Littoria – 200 miles behind our front – as a prelude to their offensive. The place they attacked was actually occupied at the time by the Quartermaster staff, who lost two officers and two other ranks. It is interesting to note that Rommel had in fact formerly had his H.Q. in this house. He himself had had the first floor and his A.D.C.s [aide-de-camp] the ground floor. The British must have received knowledge of this through their intelligence service. The British Commandos answered the sentry in German. Although they did not know the password, the sentry did not fire, thinking they were Germans who had lost their way. The British were wearing no insignia which might have identified them as enemy. Suddenly one of them drew his pistol and shot the sentry. They pressed quickly into the house, fired a volley into the room on the left of the entrance door killing two Germans, and tried to get up the first floor. Here, however, they were met by German bullets. One British officer was killed and a German fatally wounded. The remainder of the British Commando withdrew.[504]

General Presti of the Libyan Colonial Police concluded in his report of the raid, "the enemy is attempting to draw troops from the front and spread panic among the people by acts of sabotage and terrorism, brought about by means of coast landings, parachutists and long range raids by motor vehicles along the Southern roads."[505] Yet another German account was given by Oberst (Colonel) Schleusener, who was a prisoner of war and gave his account in 1946. At the time of the raid, he was Oberquartiermeister (QM) of Rommel's army. He confirmed the house Keyes raided was the administrative HQ of the army and he stated General Rommel had never been there. The Operational HQ was near Gambut. Some days before the raid the local military police had reported some abandoned collapsible boats on the beach West of Beda Littoria and after this a sentry was posted on the HQ which had up to that point been unguarded. Schleusener stated, "the raid failed totally. The Commander, Lieut. Colonel Keyes, was killed immediately after entering the house. His deputy, a captain, was wounded in the leg and remained down. The whole success was the death of a lieutenant and of a premier-lieutenant of my staff. The men vanished and were captured during the following days." The Italian HQs, which were close by, were not raided. The raiders third objective was a cable mast with four concrete pillars. One pillar only was damaged. Schleusener said that there may have been some mistake in identity, since he and the Senior Medical Officer were of much the same build as Rommel and wore similar uniforms.[506]

In the final tally, the raid failed in its primary mission, although like all raids deep behind enemy lines, the psychological toll on the enemy and their subsequent actions to protect rear areas cannot be underestimated. One German diarist noted, "the unexpected sudden death of good comrades has produced a depression which cannot be avoided." Italian reports on the raid also reflected the panic and alarm of being attacked in a perceived safe area 400 kilometres behind the front lines. In addition, the attack so unnerved the Germans that the Army Chief of Staff, Generaloberst Franz Halder directed that the Quartermaster section of the HQ be moved to a new location.[507]

Nonetheless, they missed the Desert Fox. Rommel had flown back to Germany two weeks early for a rest and to celebrate his fiftieth birthday.[508] Even if the location had been correct, they would have missed their man. The end result was, of the 29 British commandos all ranks, two were killed (Lieutenant-Colonel Keyes and Corporal Peter Barrand, who was swept off the *Talisman* and drowned) and two wounded (Captain Campbell and Lieutenant Pryor).[509] The remainder of the commandos (less Lieutenant-Colonel Laycock, Sergeant Terry and Bombardier John Brittlebank who made it back to Allied lines) were captured and spent the war in prisoner of war camps. In a final nod to Rommel's professionalism, he had Lieutenant-Colonel Keyes buried beside the four German soldiers that had been killed, with full military honors.

Notwithstanding the ultimate failure of the mission, Lieutenant-Colonel Keyes was awarded the Victoria Cross for his leadership and example and Sergeant Jack Terry earned a Distinguished Conduct Medal.[510] Lieutenant-Commander "Crap" Miers received the Distinguished Service Order. Aside from the awards the raid did not impress GHQ Middle East Command. The Brigadier General Staff was dismissive of its results. He scribbled, "I doubt whether this operation achieved anything very great" on Laycock's formal report.[511]

Lieutenant-Colonel Laycock later, on January 3, 1942, asked Lady Hermione Ranfurly to take down his account of the raid. He now recorded the aim of the attack "...was to cause maximum damage and interruption to German installations and communications and, incidentally, to raid a house at Sidi Rafa where Rommel was known to stay frequently with the German 'Q' General."[512] The mission statement was changed. By this time, he knew the intelligence on Rommel had been wrong. This error of intelligence has been played down in the aftermath of the raid. Some accounts, much like Laycock's later narration, make a point of noting that the attack was never intended to target and kill Rommel. However, the orders of the mission and contemporary accounts clearly articulate that the British believed Rommel to have had his quarters in Beda Littoria.[513] For example, Major-General Rowan-Robinson wrote, "A Commando, led by Lieut.-Col. Geoffrey Keyes – a son of the Admiral of the Fleet Sir Roger Keyes responsible for all commando operations as the Commander of Combined Operations Command - surprised the German G.H.Q.; but unluckily, the Nazi leader was away on tour. A number of staff officers were indeed shot up and much destruction caused."[514] Similarly, Major-General I.S.O. Playfair wrote, "A party of No. 11 (Scottish) Commando was put ashore from the submarines *Torbay* and *Talisman* near Apollonia with the idea of attacking the house in which it was (wrongly) thought that General Rommel was living. Overcoming many difficulties, the party reached their objective and a hand-to-hand fight ensued."[515] And finally, Elizabeth Keyes in her biography of her brother wrote, "In the official communiqué it was announced that the object of the raid was 'to capture Rommel.'"[516]

CHAPTER 10
HOW THE STORY ENDS

GENERAL AUCHINLECK'S GAMBLE on special forces missions to give his Operation Crusader offensive a decided advantage, failed to materialize. Neither the SAS gambit to raid German airfields, nor the Commando scheme to capture or kill Rommel led to any substantive immediate support to the attack. Notwithstanding their failure, the initial launch of the Crusader offensive appeared to prove quite promising. And, as always, Prime Minister Churchill applied pressure through his exuberance and enthusiasm on his commanders and soldiers. His message prior to the deployment of forces stated:

> *For the first time British and Empire troops will meet the Germans with an ample equipment in modern weapons of all kinds. The battle itself will affect the whole course of the war. Now is the time to strike the hardest blow yet struck for final victory, home and freedom. The Desert Army may add a page to history which will rank with Blenheim and with Waterloo. The eyes of all nations are upon you.*[517]

The actual operation began on November 18, 1941 on a 105-kilometre frontage spanning Sollum to Jarabub. The British War Cabinet announced General Auchinleck's intentions as:

- to bring about a tank battle, with the particular object of destroying the German 15th and 21st Armoured Divisions; and
- at the same time, to roll up the enemy's forces in the frontier area Sollum-Bardia-Sidi Omar from the south and south-west.

The War Cabinet further explained that "to provoke the tank battle, the plan was to advance on Tobruk with cruiser tank formations via Fort

Maddalena and El Gobi with the object of forcing the enemy to leave his laager positions and fight in the open. The Tobruk garrison was to co-operate."[518]

Despite the build-up of forces and the materiel advantage, Auchinleck still banked on surprise, and not solely depending on the special forces missions he authorized. During November 16-17, the entirety of the Eighth Army was on a long approach march. The Eighth Army stealthily deployed 100,000 men, 600 tanks and 5,000 other vehicles.[519] Using supply dumps and leaguers that were deep in the desert, the main British Force conducted a wide flanking movement around the German-Italian fortified position near Sollum on the coast route. General Auchinleck deployed seven divisions (including the Tobruk garrison) against Rommel's three German and seven Italian divisions. In terms of tanks, the British fielded five brigades of armour against two German and one Italian armoured brigades. In aircraft the British had a further advantage of 1,100 against 120 German and 200 Italian airplanes.[520]

Importantly, the British advantage in materiel was also enhanced by the element of surprise. Although at the strategic level the Germans were anticipating a British counter-offensive, it nevertheless tactically came as a surprise. This shock was a result of the failure of German aerial reconnaissance from the end of October 1941, to actually penetrate into Egypt, as well as the Allied ability to conceal all general preparations and signal traffic. The Cairo *communiqué* reported, "So skilfully had our fighting troops been insinuated into their concentration area, so good were the arrangements for deception, camouflage and dispersal, that the enemy observation and interference from the air, prior to and during the advance on November 18th were negligible."[521] Churchill extolled, "In spite of the immense preparations, complete tactical surprise was achieved."[522]

The offensive, which opened at dawn on November 18th, also gained a degree of surprise based on the fact that it coincided with extremely adverse weather. Although it hampered the bombing of enemy aerodromes to the extent planners had hoped for, the heavy rain that had fallen in Cyrenaica had turned the usually passable areas into mud. Importantly, the rainfall had been much heavier on the coast than inland and as a result, the German communications, landing grounds and leaguers were more adversely affected than the desert areas in which the British troops had concentrated.[523]

Nonetheless, the weather was a factor that also impacted the Allied forces. As noted in earlier chapters, the vicious storm scuppered the special forces missions. It also impacted the Eighth Army. The ragged flashes of lightning lit up the desert sky and the desert floor. One individual described the bolts of lightning as presenting a "cold, green, flickering radiance, while overhead the thunder boomed and roared, then crashed out with the startling suddenness of cannon-fire." He added, "Then the rain came. Squalls of bitter sleet swept across the huddled army, lancing down through every tear in fabric, gap in lacing, open windshield or gun-port; soaking inexorably through serge or drill to transform it into icy poultices to chill the flesh and blood."[524] The storm ended before dawn, with a brooding, overcast sky remaining for the entirety of the following day.

Despite the storm, British armoured forces crossed the frontier south of Sidi Omar and penetrated 80 kilometres into enemy territory by evening. Concurrently, Allied forces pressured the enemy defences in the Sollum-Sidi Omar-Bardia triangle.[525] Strict wireless silence was preserved during this stage of the operations. To this point "serious battle had not been joined, but all available evidence pointed to the fact that the enemy had not yet appreciated either the scope or weight of the offensive."[526]

Part of the British success was due to Rommel's fixation with Tobruk. As late as November 19, 1941, Rommel was still preoccupied with the capture of the port of Tobruk. As early as October 26th, Rommel felt confident he had the strength to take the objective. As a result, he formulated his plan and issued orders. Preparations were complete by November 15th, but the attack was planned for the 20th to coincide with favourable moonlight. When the British attacked, Rommel surmised the offensive was an attempt to forestall him from his goal. As a result, he directed *General der Panzertruppe* Ludwig Crüwell to destroy the British thrust before it could interfere with his plan.

Not surprisingly then, for most of the first two days all seemed to go the British way. Armoured forces reached the escarpment at Sidi Rezegh, only 51 kilometres from the besieged garrison of Tobruk. The first clashes between armoured forces occurred on the afternoon of November 19th, when 18 Italian tanks were destroyed near Bir el Gobi and one of the leading Allied formations met some 60 German tanks of the 21st Panzer Division, 20 miles north-west of Sidi Omar. In the latter action 26 enemy tanks were destroyed and 20 British tanks were lost. Meanwhile the Allied formation in the centre had pushed on unopposed in the direction of Sidi Rezegh, south-east of Tobruk.[527]

On November 20th the armoured battle was joined in earnest. The Allied formation on the right took up the pursuit of the enemy forces with which it had been engaged in the Bir el Meliba area on the previous afternoon and drove them off in a north-easterly direction, inflicting a loss of 34 tanks and nine tank transporters. Meanwhile the centre formation had encountered 200 tanks of the 15th Panzer Division, which appeared to try and cut their way out to the west. In the action which developed to the south-east of Sidi Rezegh the Germans lost 70 tanks, 33 armoured cars and several hundred prisoners before withdrawing.[528]

In addition, 19 Axis aircraft that were previously damaged by British fighters, were captured at the Sidi Rezegh airfield along with their crews. German and Italian tank losses on November 19th and 20th amounted in all to 130 tanks, 33 armoured cars and nine tank transporters. At the time the British believed that this represented approximately half of the German armoured strength in Cyrenaica.[529]

On the evening of November 20th, Auchinleck dispatched tanks from his reserve to replace those that had been lost during the opening engagements. While the various battles were in progress, increasing pressure was being exerted on the Axis forces in the Halfaya-Sidi Omar region. Some of the Auchinleck's forces engaged the enemy in the north while another part attempted to outflank the enemy defences to the west, directed on Sidi Aziz, 19 kilometres to the south-west of Bardia.[530]

Undoubtedly, the offensive caught the Germans off guard. Major-General Von Mellenthin later recorded that the British attacked with 748 tanks (213 Matildas and Valentines, 220 Crusaders, 150 cruisers of an earlier model and 165 Stuarts). He stated that the Germans met the attack with 249 German (70 Panzer IIs armed with a 2cm gun and a heavy machine gun, 35 Panzer IVs and 139 Panzer IIIs along with five captured

British crusader tank passes a burning German tank. (IMW, E_006751)

Matildas), as well as 146 Italian (47mm low velocity gun and inadequate armour) tanks.[531] The *Rommel Papers* put the German tank strength at the time at 260 German tanks and 154 Italian tanks. German tanks consisted of 15 Panzer I, 40 Panzer II, 150 Panzer III (50 percent still with the 37mm gun) and 55 Panzer IVs.[532]

The British overestimated the German capability. They understood that the German armoured divisions were on a colonial establishment and contained only one armoured regiment each (in addition to infantry regiments, supporting artillery and other combat support). Furthermore, British intelligence believed that the 132nd Armoured Division "Ariete" was about the equivalent of a British armoured brigade. In all, the British estimated that the Axis forces consisted of approximately 387 tanks, apart from obsolescent and very light tanks.[533]

Adding to the Allied advantage was the fact that throughout November 19th and 20th, the RAF were extremely active and steadily gained air superiority which by the 21st appeared to have become almost complete. Importantly, the cooperation between the Air Force and the armoured formations was excellent. For example, a distress call for ammunition made at 1230 hours on November 20th resulted in aircraft picking up the ammunition from Mersa Matruh and delivering it to the respective formation at the scene of battle four hours later.[534]

Significantly, on November 20th alone, nine fighter sweeps, totalling 177 sorties, were flown over the battle area. Nine German Junkers (Ju) 87

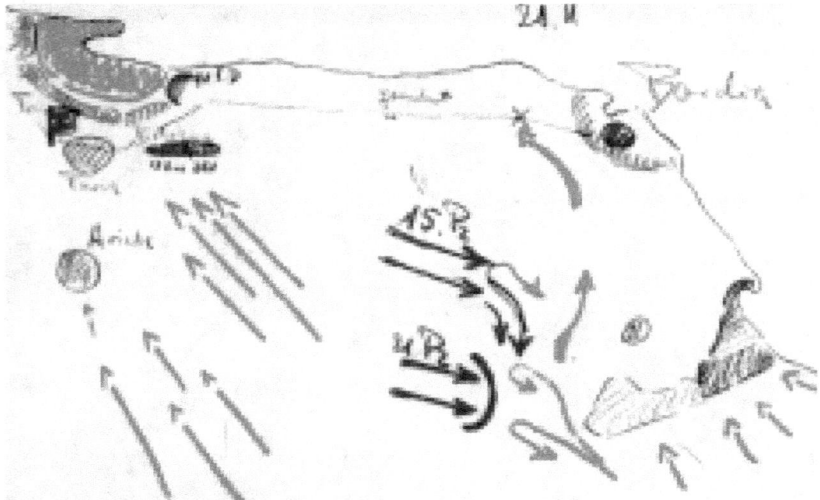

Map 5 – Rommel's sketch map of the British November 20, 1941 attack (Rommel Papers)

Stukas, escorted by 15 Messerschmitt (Me) Bf 109s, were attacked and forced to jettison their bombs. Seven Ju 87s, four Me 110s and one Me 109 were shot down during the day for the loss of seven British fighters and three pilots. On the 25th, 20 Curtiss P-40 Tomahawk fighter aircraft intercepted a mixed force of about 60 German and Italian bombers, which were escorted by fighters. The Allied effort destroyed ten of the enemy aircraft and damaged numerous others with the loss of only two friendly planes. Since the start of the offensive the Allied air forces shot down 52 aircraft and destroyed a further 40 with the lost of 24 of their own.[535]

In addition to the support of the armoured formations and the struggle for air supremacy, the Allied air forces also staged a bombing campaign to disrupt the Axis lines of communications. On the night of November 19th/20th, 43 tons of bombs were dropped on Derna and ten tons on Bardia. On the following night 32 Vickers Wellington medium bombers attacked the aerodrome and landing grounds at El Gazala. Additionally, from November 22-25, Allied bombers attacked Benghazi, as well as the aerodromes of Berca and Binina. Allied aircraft were marshalled from Egypt and Malta and the focus of the attacks were fuel and munitions dumps, railways, infrastructure and military headquarters.[536]

Assisting the Allied air effort was the heavy rain and floods that made German aerodromes unserviceable and communications difficult. This state of affairs hampered the operation of the Axis air forces, which under the Allied onslaught were forced to focus their efforts on protecting their air bases and supporting their ground forces. As a result, very few operations were taken against the British fleet off shore, Allied formations or lines of communication.[537]

Although total surprise was achieved and the ground and air battle appeared to be going well, it was only a matter of time before the Desert Fox gauged the British intent and reacted accordingly. He received assistance from the British Broadcasting Corporation (BBC). Rommel was at his advanced headquarters in Gambut and at the time paid little heed to the British offensive, which he believed to be diversionary. His focus was on his planned attack on Tobruk. Incredibly, on the evening of November 20th, the BBC announced that the "Eighth Army, with some 75,000 excellently armed and equipped men, had invaded Libya with the object of destroying the remainder of the Axis forces in Africa and that the operation was proceeding successfully."[538] Once Rommel realized his mistake he pivoted immediately, dropping his move against Tobruk and counter-attacking the British penetration.

The speed and violence of the counter-thrust now caught the British off guard. Rommel, true to form with his daring outlook, quickly struck at

Sidi Rezegh. Major-General Lloyd Owen described:

All went very well at the start of the fighting. Armoured forces swept over the frontier and drove towards Tobruk. On the 19ᵗʰ November they got on to the escarpment at Sidi Rezegh, captured the airfield there and were within thirty miles of Tobruk. Relief of the garrison seemed in sight. But on 20ᵗʰ November the enemy fought back and retook Sidi Rezegh from us. There then followed some very confused fighting in that area and some of the most gallant armoured actions of the whole campaign in the desert were fought. Over the next four days the battle went on indecisively but the garrison in Tobruk were beginning to tear their way out and join hands with the leading elements of the Eighth Army.[539]

Heavy fighting continued throughout the 21st. This turn of events was to be expected once the German High Command had recovered from the shock of their original surprise. By midday a strong German armoured force engaged Allied armoured formations south of Sidi Rezegh.[540] By nightfall on November 21st, the Afrika Korps had destroyed the 7th Hussars, inflicted considerable damage on the 2nd and 6th Battalions Royal Tank Regiment, destroyed a large number of the Support Group's guns and

British Hurricane fighter flying over the desert (with the Mediterranean Sea on the left). (WO, MoI, 1941)

wiped out the Support Company of the Rifle Brigade. In addition, it had halted both the break-out by the Army Tank Brigade from Tobruk and the 7th Division's attempt to advance and link-up with the besieged Tobruk garrison.[541]

The entire front now fell into chaos and a savage battle of attrition that roiled both Allied and Axis forces. On November 22nd, 15th Panzer Division captured the headquarters of 4th Armoured Brigade. The 15th Panzer War Diary captured the feat:

> [The Regimental Commander] burst through the enemy leaguer in his command vehicle and ordered No 1 Company to go round the left and No 2 Company round the right to surround the enemy. The tanks put on their headlights and the commanders jumped out with their machine-pistols. The enemy was completely surprised and incapable of action. Thus far there had been no firing. A few tanks tried to get away, but were at once set on fire by our tanks and lit up the battlefield as bright as day. While the prisoners were being rounded up an English officer succeeded in setting fire to a tank. This coup on our part got the rest of 4 British Armoured Brigade with light casualties to ourselves. The Brigade Commander, 17 officers and 150 other ranks were taken prisoner. One armoured command vehicle, 35 tanks, armoured cars, guns and self-propelled guns, other fighting vehicles and some important papers fell into our hands.[542]

Captain Stephen Hastings, serving with the 2nd Battalion Scots Guards, captured the mayhem. "The Crusader battle swung backwards and forwards," he wrote, "The German tanks came right through us. All was confusion, dust and lead."[543] He noted, "We wound up eventually, not far from the start point of Operation Crusader in what was known as the Gazala line."[544]

The struggle, however, was not all one-sided. The following day, November 23rd, New Zealand troops captured General Crüwell and his Afrika Korps headquarters. Crüwell lost almost all of his wireless vehicles and his entire cipher staff, as well as 200 personnel.

By the evening of November 23rd, the offensive appeared in peril. Lieutenant-General Alan Cunningham's Eighth Army, most importantly his armoured element was spread out over the desert. A great deal of it was destroyed, the remainder disorganized and shattered into a multitude of small fragments. Confusion was rampant throughout the battlefield. Von Mellenthin reported, "the battle of 23 November ended with the Afrika Korps in a state of great confusion."[545] General Fritz Bayerlein observed, "the wide area south of Sidi Rezegh had become a sea of dust, fire, and smoke. [When darkness fell] hundreds of burning vehicles, tanks, and guns lit up the battlefield. Not until midnight was it possible to gauge the results of the battle, to organize the formations, to assess losses and gains, and to appreciate the general situation."[546]

To add to the chaos, Rommel now delivered an unexpected blow. At 1030 hours on November 24, leading the 21st Panzer Division followed by 15th Panzer, he struck east towards the frontier in what has been dubbed "the dash to the wire."[547] Rommel simply told his commanders not to be concerned with their flanks. The audacious thrust made Rommel's Italian allies apoplectic. He dispatched a column of tanks and motorized infantry across the Egyptian frontier in the neighbourhood of Sidi Omar and turned north and attacked the British lines of communication. The German armoured force dealt a severe blow and caused substantial damage. The German counter-attack then advanced westwards to join the remainder of their armoured forces east of Sidi Rezegh. Rommel assessed:

> The greater part of the [enemy] force aimed at Tobruk has been destroyed; now we will turn east and go for the New Zealanders and Indians before they have been able to join up with the remains of their main force for a combined attack on Tobruk. At the same time we will take Habata and Maddalena and cut off their supplies. Speed is vital; we must make the most of the shock effect of the enemy's defeat and push forward immediately and as fast as we can with our entire force to Sidi Omar.[548]

Rommel, who possessed a greater number of medium tanks at this point, was now in a position to potentially cut off a sizeable piece of the Allied army. If he could achieve this feat, he could threaten the Suez delta itself as there were few British forces in between to stop him. Essentially, Rommel decided to take the offensive and exploit the British confusion and disorganization. He scraped together a weak holding force to maintain the siege of Tobruk and marshalled all of his mobile forces for the pursuit. It burst into the British rear and caused panic and confusion.[549]

Clearly, the British offensive was blunted with a great part of the army destroyed. Lieutenant-General Cunningham had contemplated halting the offensive and withdrawing to the frontier to reorganize on the 23rd. The previous two days had proven to be an unmitigated disaster in his estimation. His immediate concern was not to risk the army being completely destroyed. Cunningham argued that all British forces should be withdrawn immediately from Libya to take up a defensive position to protect Egypt from Rommel's advance.

Providentially, General Auchinleck arrived by air from Cairo and overruled Cunningham's plan. Cunningham argued that the offensive must be halted and a defensive posture taken. Auchinleck rejected the idea. Auchinleck gambled that Rommel's forces were just as disorganized as the Eighth Army. Where the British had a robust resupply system, Rommel did not. Auchinleck staked his career on Rommel running out of resources, specifically fuel, tanks and ammunition. In his estimate of the situation, Auchinleck wrote to the Eighth Army Commander, "...it is clear to me that after the fighting of the last few days, it is most improbable that the enemy will be able to stage a major advance for some time to come." Therefore, he ordered, "continue to attack the enemy relentlessly using all your resources

Rommel briefing staff. (Bundesarchiv, 1011-786-0315-34A)

even to the last tank. Your main immediate object will be as always to destroy the enemy tank forces."[550] Major-General Lloyd Owen recounted:

> *Meanwhile the great offensive by the Eighth Army was beginning to lose some of its impetus after our armour had swept over the frontier, got to the escarpment of Sidi Rezegh and fought their way to within ten miles of the besieged garrison in Tobruk. Relief seemed at last in sight, but Rommel realised the danger in time and fought back to retake Sidi Rezegh from us, before launching a typical all-out thrust across the Egyptian frontier with the object of forcing the Eighth Army to reduce its line of communication by withdrawing. This was a boldly desperate stroke, which came a little too late, and which the Eight Army was just able to contain. But it was a close thing.*[551]

Lloyd Owen would later reveal, "These [24 November on] were very anxious days."[552]

Quite simply, Auchinleck wagered that Rommel did not have the resources to sustain his attack; risking the survival of the Eighth Army he ordered it to continue the advance. But first, Auchinleck sacked Cunningham because "[he] has now begun to think defensively, mainly because of our large tank losses."[553] Auchinleck replaced him with Lieutenant-General Sir Neil Ritchie. It was now a case of brinksmanship - which force could survive the longest on vulnerable extended lines-of-communication.[554]

Auchinleck's reasoning was sound. As he identified, he had a robust supply chain whereas Rommel did not. And, since the Afrika Korps failed to discover the British supply dumps south of Gabr Saleh, Rommel's gamble to push to the frontier was doomed. Von Mellenthin later remarked, "Very fortunate for the British, General Auchinleck had arrived at Eighth Army headquarters; he disagreed with Cunningham, and ordered the continuation of the offensive. This was certainly one of the great decisions of the war; Auchinleck's fighting spirit and shrewd strategic insight had saved the Crusader battle and much else besides."[555]

With the outcome of the battle teetering on the brink of disaster, Auchinleck quickly turned to his special forces for assistance, specifically the LRDG. At the outset of Operation Crusader, Eighth Army headquarters deployed six LRDG patrols with the main object of watching the enemy's reactions to the Eighth Army's advance. The direction was to "report in detail what the enemy does behind his front line."[556] Wireless timings were allotted to each patrol, which governed patrol movement to some extent because each detachment required time to set up aerials to call in. If a timing was missed, they could call in anytime with the exception of calling during another patrol's allotted time unless it was an emergency.

However, by November 24th, the situation was desperate. General Auchinleck wrote to the Eighth Army Commander, "Use the Long Range Desert Group patrols offensively to the limit of their endurance against every possible objective on the enemy lines of communication from Mechili to Benghazi, Jedbaya and beyond to the west. ... The advantages to be gained by a determined effort against the enemy lines of communication are worth immense risks which will be taken."[557]

The change in tasking was recorded in the LRDG War Diary on November 24, 1941. "Heavy fighting is taking place between Tobruk and Sollum," the War Diary revealed, "Orders have been received from Adv[anced] HQ 8 Army to cease our watching and reporting role and to attack and harass enemy transport and any other suitable targets within our reach. Patrols will therefore proceed immediately to the following areas and operate either singly or together against enemy transport, particularly eastbound fuel tankers"[558]

Lloyd Owen recounted, "It was on 24th November, when the fate of the main battle was in the balance, that the Army Commander decided to change the role of the LRDG patrols and ordered us to operate offensively in the hope that we, too, could threaten the enemy on his lines of communication and force him to dissipate his strength for their protection. It was an attempt to play Rommel at his own game."[559] Captain Shaw recalled events similarly. "On November 24th we received a signal, on 'Emergency Ops' priority, which afterwards became a household word – 'Advance and attack'." He added, "that was all it said, but a second message was more explicit, 'Act with utmost vigour offensively against any enemy targets or communications within your reach.'"[560]

The LRDG now created more chaos across the desert. By the morning of November 25th, all still remained in disarray with German and British units spread across the battlefield. The tide was about to turn. That morning Churchill dispatched a message to Auchinleck alerting him that the 1st Armoured Division had landed at Suez. Always willing to share his thoughts, Churchill quickly added, "Ram it in if useful at earliest without regard for future. Close grip upon the enemy by all units will choke the life out of him."[561]

In the interim the battle raged on throughout November 25-26, with neither side fully aware of the entire situation. "The dust clouds raised by charging tanks and moving columns," Von Mellenthin described, "added to the obscurity, and, as Auchinleck says, 'at times the fog of war literally descended on the battlefield.'"[562] Crusader descended into a series of thrusts and counter-thrusts.

The immediate battle, however, came to a decisive moment on November 26th. Rommel's staff were finally able to convince him of the serious situation the Axis forces were in. The German and Italian forces were strung out at the end of a long supply chain and undeniably the British now had superiority of forces, particularly fighters and bombers. His attempts at outflanking the entire Eighth Army had failed. It was now elements of his Afrika Korps that faced potential annihilation due to the continued Allied advance towards Tobruk. Specifically, General Hermann Boettcher's small force left to stop the advancing British forces from relieving Tobruk now faced being crushed. As a result, Rommel halted his counter-offensive and deployed his forces to the west to alleviate the threat near Tobruk and prevent the Afrika Korps from being shredded.

Auchinleck had won. His gamble had turned a possible defeat into a victory. The result was not hard to understand. By the end of November, the British had developed a decisive advantage. They could feed fresh troops and equipment into the fray. The Germans could not.

The Allies, however were not yet out of the woods. On November 27th, 15th Panzer Division captured 800 prisoners, a huge supply dump, six field guns and the entire headquarters of the 5th New Zealand Brigade, including its commander. Despite the most recent success, Rommel still realized his "dash to the wire" was an overreach. He continued his withdrawal back towards Tobruk.

By November 29th, by Von Mellenthin's account, "The situation was now extremely complicated and confused, and both sides were almost at the end of their tether. The conditions were very severe; the troops were fighting in bitterly cold weather, and in waterless country where the normal supply system had virtually broken down."[563] By November 30th, although the Germans judged they had won the Crusader battle, Von Mellenthin acknowledged, "The price paid was too heavy; the *Panzergruppe* had been worn down, and it soon became clear that only one course remained – a general retreat from Cyrenaica."[564]

Von Mellenthin concluded, "The supply position was causing grave anxiety, and we were at a hopeless disadvantage in the air."[565] Crippling indeed was the German's supply situation. Von Mellenthin explained, "In July 1941, 17 per cent of the materiel sent to Africa was lost, and in August 35 per cent. In September shipping losses on the African route had risen to 38 percent of the traffic, comprising 49,000 tons sunk and 14,000 damaged. Of 50,000 tons of material and supplies dispatched to Libya in October, only 18,500 tons reached their destination. On the night of 8/9 November a convoy of seven merchant ships protected by Italian cruisers

Two LRDG members conducting Road Watch. (IWM, E_012434)

and destroyers was wiped out by the British without loss to themselves."[566] In fact, 14 of the 22 ships carrying over 500 tons of equipment dispatched from Italian ports to North Africa during November, had been sunk, representing a loss of 60,000 tons of supplies. Significantly, fuel tankers were particularly hard-hit allowing for only 2,500 tons of aviation and motor fuel to arrive in-theatre. Adding to the dire situation was the fact that the Italian shipping that was sent to the bottom of the Mediterranean could not be easily replaced.[567] With this scale of loss, the Axis position in North Africa was in jeopardy.

Nonetheless, Rommel inflicted considerable damage on his adversaries. According to a report from Rommel to his higher headquarters, he conveyed that the continuous heavy fighting between November 18th and December 1st resulted in 814 Allied armoured fighting vehicles and armoured cars being destroyed, 127 aircraft shot down and in excess of 9,000 prisoners taken, including three generals.[568] However, the Germans had also suffered grievously. Their losses included 16 commanding officers killed or seriously wounded, a proportionate number of junior officers lost, 3,800 other ranks killed or wounded, 142 panzers destroyed, 25 armoured cars and 390 trucks demolished, as well as a large number of artillery pieces and heavy weapons lost.[569]

Despite the savage war of attrition, it appeared the battle was not quite over yet as it dragged into December. By December 4th, it was now

Rommel who feared being outflanked once again. Therefore he disengaged and withdrew his forces further west. However, he was not content to remain on the defensive. Two days later, on December 6th, the Afrika Korps launched yet another attack.

The latest assault went in without their Italian allies. "The Italians," General Bayerlein revealed, "reported that their troops were exhausted and no longer fit for action."[570] With such undependable allies, it is not surprising that Rommel regularly kept information about his intentions secret from his Italian superiors. In fact, Rommel entrusted to his diary his frustration that "Italian headquarters could keep nothing to themselves and that everything they wirelessed to Rome got round to British ears."[571]

Despite the aggressive spirit, by this point in the battle the British were far superior in ground forces and aircraft. Moreover, the Germans were dangerously short of fuel and ammunition. As a result, by the end of day December 6th, Rommel realized he had to halt his offensive and withdraw to prepared defensive positions on the Gazala defensive line. On December 7-8, German forces around Tobruk disengaged and they reached the Gazala position on December 12th.[572]

The siege of Tobruk, which had lasted eight months, was finally lifted. The Australians had held out for 242 days against the German blockade. Aside from the tremendous morale value in Britain, it was now possible to open airfields in Tobruk and surrounding areas. This access now ensured that the Allied Desert Air Force could provide fighter cover further west. Equally important, with the siege lifted, by November 25th the port was handling 18,000 tons of shipping a month, half of which was gasoline and aircraft fuel. By the end of December, the port was handling 600 tons a day and the rate was continually increasing.[573]

The British now pushed their advantage. By December 11th, a New Zealand formation was in contact with the German main position. Auchinleck ordered Indian troops, supported by "I" tanks, to bypass the Gazala defensive position to the south and advance in a north-west direction across the Axis line of withdrawal. Concurrently, he deployed mixed mobile columns of tanks, armoured cars, artillery and motorized infantry in a wide sweep around the enemy's southern flank towards Derna, Mekili and Tmimi. Auchinleck now planned to annihilate the Afrika Korps.

The plan was not without heavy cost. Throughout December 12-13th, while the Kiwis steadily made progress penetrating the Gazala position, a series of heavy counter-attacks were launched on the Indian formations attempting to cut off the German line of withdrawal. By the evening of December 15th, the situation was terribly confused. The bulk of Rommel's

Rommel outside of Tobruk. (Bundesarchiv, 146-1991-031-25A)

forces were now committed to the Gazala battle. The following day, Rommel, to avoid being cut off by a British thrust from Mechili to the coast, ordered a withdrawal from Cyrenaica. His intent was to buy time for the Afrika Korps to regroup. By withdrawing further west he also forced the British to fight on extended supply lines. "I fully realized that this would mean the eventual loss of Cyrenaica and that political difficulties might result," Rommel confided to his personal papers, "But the choice I was faced with was either to stay where I was and thus sacrifice the Panzer Group to destruction – thereby losing both Cyrenaica and Tripolitania – or to begin the retreat."[574]

As a result, on the night of December 16/17th, the remnants of the two German armoured divisions succeeded in slipping away from the battlefield and made their way to the vicinity of Derna.[575] The remainder of the German forces stayed in their position until the morning of the 17th when they, too, began to withdraw. The British pursued the withdrawing Axis forces for over 50 km.

Continued pressure by the Eighth Army forced the Germans to withdraw to Benghazi on December 24th. Three days later, the British 22nd Armoured Brigade advanced once again but was checked by German forces, as well as fuel shortages. These factors basically stopped the Allied pursuit and exploitation. Additionally, on December 28th, the Germans launched yet another vicious counter-attack that forced the British to withdraw and refit.

The Crusader battle was basically over. On January 1, 1942, Rommel fell back to El Agheila.[576] The British forces also depleted from the prolonged fighting lacked the resources to react to the latest development. It was not until January 13th that the Eighth Army was able to re-establish contact with the enemy. However, by this time the Germans were well-established in a defensive position and the Allied forces did not have the necessary strength to force a breakthrough. And so ended Operation Crusader.

After almost two months of fighting, Operation Crusader was arguably a British victory as it relieved Tobruk and drove the Axis forces out of Cyrenaica with heavy casualties. However, in the process the British lost considerable manpower and equipment and basically exhausted themselves. As always, actual statistics are difficult to nail down. Historian John Strawson puts the Operation Crusader cost at approximately 38,000 casualties for the Axis and British / Imperial forces losses at about 18,000.[577] Historian Barrie Pitt, in his detailed history of the North African campaign calculated the casualties as of December 27, 1941, for the British / Imperial forces at fifteen percent or 17,700 and the Axis casualties at twenty percent or 24,500.[578] Finally, Churchill tabulated the losses in his history of the war at: German – 13,000, Italian – 20,000 and a combined 300 tanks lost; UK and Imperial troops to mid-January – 2,908 killed, 7,339 wounded, 7,457 missing and 278 tanks lost.[579]

Although the special forces' missions, less the LRDG tasks, at the opening of Operation Crusader failed, they did redeem themselves over the course of the battle. As noted, on November 24th, The LRDG sprang to the offensive and wreaked havoc on the German lines-of-communication (LoC). Information obtained from captured German documents demonstrated that the "reports made by victims of the LRDG exploits during the second phase had given the enemy an exaggerated notion of the strength of its patrols; and had caused them great anxiety about the safety of their LoCs."[580]

Furthermore, Stirling and his neophyte SAS eventually proved his concept. In the aftermath of the disastrous parachute operation, in December, Stirling utilized the LRDG patrols to deliver his raiding teams close to German airfields and then they marched to their objectives and set their explosives. The SAS attacked airfields at Tamet, Agheila and Agedabia with varying results. However, they succeeded in destroying a fuel dump and a total of 61 aircraft.[581]

Although the war was far from over in the North African desert, special forces proved their worth in the cauldron of the Crusader battles. They carried on the fight well behind enemy lines for the remainder of the North African campaign and well into other theatres of operations.[582]

CHAPTER 11
CHARLATANS OR
SPECIAL WARRIORS?

ANY PERSPECTIVE ON SPECIAL FORCES in World War II risks spiralling into an emotional debate between their supporters and the wider military institution at large. One consistency with special forces and military elites in general, is that historically they have faced rancour, if not outright hostility, from the conventional military institution. "Almost all of the elite [SF] units we have studied," Professor Eliot Cohen revealed, "faced considerable bureaucratic hostility - enmity translated into effective harassment."[583] Similarly, historian Damien Lewis concluded regular army officers viewed "special duty raiders as truly a villainous bunch – a band of ragged, renegade, warn-torn desperadoes."[584] It has only been the intervention of well-placed champions, either political or military, that have ensured that some of these elite military organizations were able to be created and maintained.

This institutional resistance to special forces is well documented. In World War II, the aggressive, combative Prime Minister Churchill had a difficult time establishing commandos and other unconventional organizations. He explained, "In my experience of Service departments, which is a long one, there is always danger that anything contrary to Service prejudices will be obstructed and delayed by officers of the second grade in the machine."[585] Churchill groused, "The resistances of the War Office were obstinate and increased as the professional ladder was descended." He explained, "the idea that large bands of favoured 'irregulars,' with their unconventional attire and easy-and-free bearing, should throw an implied slur on the efficiency and courage of the Regular battalions was odious to men who had given all their lives to the organised and discipline of permanent units."[586] Frustrated with the seemingly endless resistance from within the military, Churchill suggested to Anthony Eden, his Secretary of State for War, that an example should be made of "one or two" of the reluctant officers.[587]

Churchill was not wrong. One official report acknowledged that "Home Forces have consistently used their predominating influence at the War Office to thwart the efforts of those well disposed to us [special service brigade]."[588] In trying to raise the Special Air Service, Lieutenant David Stirling admonished that "I found during this and subsequent stages, that the A.G. [Adjutant General] Branch was unfailingly obstructive and uncooperative."[589] Dick Holmes of the SBS similarly acknowledged:

The rest of the British army hated us. They disliked us intensely. I mean, no doubt about it, we were arrogant bastards. We walked around with scarves on, carried guns, and most of us had shoulder holsters and on thing or another that we'd picked up along the way, guns concealed in our pockets somewhere – little Berettas and stuff.[590]

Field Marshal Sir William Slim was representative of the traditional military mindset at the time. "Private armies," he proclaimed, "are expensive, wasteful, and unnecessary."[591] His disdain for their ideas and what they represented was clearly evident in the profile he painted. He stated that these "racketeers" were in essence of two kinds, "those whose acquaintance with war was confined to large non-fighting staffs where they had had time and opportunity to develop their theories, and tough, cheerful fellows who might be first-class landed on a beach at night with orders to scupper a sentry-post, but whose experience was about the range of a tommy-gun... Few of them had anything really new to say, and the few that had, usually forgot that a new idea should have something to recommend it besides just breaking up normal organization."[592] Slim added, "The trouble was that each [Special Force organization] was controlled from some distant headquarters of its own, and such was the secrecy and mutual suspicion of their operations that they sometimes acted in close proximity to our troops without the knowledge of any commander in the field, with a complete lack of coordination among themselves, and in dangerous ignorance of local tactical developments."[593]

Field Marshal Bernard Law Montgomery held analogous beliefs. He explained that special forces drew away promising material from the conventional forces and that the investment was not worth the return. He posed the rhetorical question, "You want only my best men; my most experienced and dependable men ...What, Colonel Stirling, makes you assume that you can handle these men to greater advantage than myself."[594] Similarly, Major-General Orde Wingate asserted, "As far as SEAC [South East Asia Command] is concerned, all evidence goes to show that well trained infantry units would be just as suitable as special troops."[595]

In fact, a War Office study dated July 10, 1945, concluded that "most conventional organizations and their senior leadership disagreed with the SOF [Special Operations Forces] concept."[596] Moreover, the Director of Operations argued that "continued maintenance of any form of Corps d'elite is most undesirable."[597] Similarly, a Director of Infantry report stated, "The War Office directors have agreed that the formation of a specialist corps such as the SAS have tended to reduce the normal infantry man's standing and prestige. Difficult to eradicate this tendency until such specialist forces are abolished."[598] As one special forces soldier observed, "Private armies were frowned upon by the Sam-Browned, spit-and-polish General Staff newly out from England, who regarded anything not in the textbook as 'frightfully infradig. [sic]"[599] The American approach was no different. General Douglas MacArthur successfully refused to allow Office of Strategic Services (OSS) operations in the Pacific.[600] American Army historian David Hogan observed that "except for some isolated instances, conventional US generals discarded special operations in Europe and focussed almost totally on conventional warfare once their forces had consolidated beachheads in North Africa, Italy, and France."[601] "They [senior US Army officers] were outright hostile to a clandestine presence," one senior OSS senior officer explained, "by most of the old hard-bitten regulars, we are not part of the Army, and never will. We are not regulation and therefore a pain in the neck."[602]

The question becomes, were special forces a group of ill-disciplined rogues and charlatans or were they indeed special warriors? For many it is an emotional issue. However, arguably, events tell a different story. Despite the institutional hostility, due to highly placed champions, special forces were established and went on to make a name for themselves. Although, with the exception of the LRDG, special force missions designed to support the commencement of Operation Crusader failed to deliver the punch that was intended, all three entities, the LRDG, "L" Detachment SAS and the Commandos, all went on to make substantial contributions to the war effort. The LRDG proved to be a resilient and highly effective force from start to finish. They conducted the tedious but highly important task of road watch, undertook critical reconnaissance missions and carried out sabotage and raids. They proved to be a vital enabler for conventional forces and they tied down enemy troops required for convoy and rear area security. An LRDG intelligence officer learned from interrogating prisoners that "in addition to the casualties - and these were at least five to one in our favour - nuisance value was very great."[603]

Furthermore, a news release at the time noted that "The commander of the Eighth Army has stated that the operations of the LRDG behind the enemy's lines during the offensive were of great value. The psychological effects on the German and Italian Command of these constant thrusts were evident." It explained, "The nimbleness of the LRDG patrols who would strike in one place on Monday and again a hundred miles away on Tuesday, caused the enemy to waste time, personnel and valuable fuel in fruitless hunts for their tormentors."[604]

In the aftermath of Operation Crusader, the LRDG continued to carry out its essential task of road watch on the Tripoli to Benghazi Road, reconnaissance deep behind enemy lines, as well as ferrying SAS patrols to and from raids on Axis airfields. Additionally, LRDG patrols laid mines and attacked enemy vehicles on the German lines-of-communication. In September 1942, the LRDG reverted from Eighth Army control to under the command of GHQ MEF.

After the Allied victory in North Africa, the LRDG was deployed to Lebanon in May 1943, to undertake mountain warfare training. However, following the Italian armistice on September 3, 1943, the LRDG was dispatched to Leros in the Dodecanese islands where they participated in the Battle of Leros.

In December, the LRDG re-organized into two squadrons of eight patrols, each patrol consisting of one officer and ten ORs. Patrols conducted shipping watches and raids in the Dalmatian islands, as well as reconnaissance, raids and assistance to resistance groups in Yugoslavia, Albania and Greece. Although the LRDG leadership requested a deployment of the organization to the Far East at the end of hostilities in Europe, the War Office declined and the LRDG was disbanded in August of 1945.

"L" Detachment, SAS, also survived its Operation Crusader debut. Although most believed that the SAS would be disbanded after the fiasco of Operation Squatter, General Auchinleck gave Stirling and his neophyte command a new lease on life. Although Stirling admitted that he found parachuting "most disagreeable," he did initially believe it was an effective means to get behind enemy lines, where "you could blow things up and find your way home by other means."[605] However, after his initial foray he realized that parachuting was not necessarily the best means of reaching desert objectives. Rather, he felt that the LRDG, who ferried them home, would be a most effective manner of delivering his raiders close to the enemy airfields.

Between December 1941 and March 1942, the SAS conducted 20 raids against various targets, primarily enemy airfields. Stirling wrote, "We destroyed 115 aircraft and a considerable amount of enemy road transport

LRDG Patrol. (IWM, 03532942)

– we concentrated particularly on heavy diesel and petrol-carrying vehicles."[606] These raids were conducted in conjunction with the LRDG who were able to accurately deliver the sabotage teams within striking distance of their objectives.[607] "In the months that followed," SAS member Fitzroy Mclean wrote the SAS achieved, "a series of successes which surpassed the wildest expectations of those who had originally supported this venture."[608] Paddy Mayne, Stirling's right-hand man, alone in a twelve-month period destroyed over a hundred enemy aircraft on the ground with his own hands.[609] By the end of June 1942, "L" Detachment had raided all of the more important German and Italian airstrips within 500 kilometres of the forward area at least once or twice. As a result, due to their experience with navigation and travel in the desert, the SAS developed the concept of using jeeps on their own without LRDG support armed with two sets of twin Vickers K machine guns (originally aircraft-mounted) or alternatively one twin Vickers and one Browning .50 calibre machine gun. Stirling boasted, "the astonishing agility of the jeep enable us to approach a target at night over almost any country. The technique turned out to be most successful and enable the Unit to be very much more flexible in its methods of operation."[610]

The autonomous jeep-mounted SAS continued to raid German airfields and harass the enemy lines of communication for the rest of the North African campaign. By January 1943, they conducted raids behind enemy lines as far as Sfax in Tunisia. One official report noted, "These Jeeps used to operate as far as 500-600 miles in enemy held territory, destroying aircraft, mining roads, blowing up supply trains, cutting signal & phone communications, strafing road convoys, attacking camps & leaguers, at night and isolated enemy posts, etc."[611] In short, the SAS had evolved from parachute insertion, to being ferried by the LRDG and finally to conducting jeep raids themselves. Throughout the campaign the focus was always on the mission – destroying the German war capability.

In total, David Stirling's SAS raids in North Africa were credited with destroying nearly 400 aircraft, numerous hangars, workshops, railway lines, vehicle transports and telegraph communications.[612] The SAS success in the desert is undeniable. One account of the SAS raids revealed:

The Italian commandant was frantic. The world had gone mad tonight. He couldn't believe his eyes, still fogged by sleep, for it was three o'clock in the morning. His airdrome garrison town seemed to be under heavy attack and half of it was already blazing. His bewildered brain told him it was impossible. The damned British were at least 250 miles away, no planes have been sighted ...The gasoline dumps went up with a might roar. One by one a line of airplanes began exploding into flames, apparently by themselves...the planes had been brand-new.[613]

The SAS success was also evident by Hitler's wrath. He issued a directive that clearly stated, "Captured SAS Troops must be handed over at once to the nearest Gestapo unit ...these men are very dangerous and the presence of SAS troops in any area must be immediately reported...they must be ruthlessly exterminated."[614] Lord Haw-Haw, the Nazi propagandist, described the SAS as "Churchill's cut-throats."[615] This description may not be far off as Auchinleck's chief of staff described the SAS as "small raiding parties of the thug variety."[616] An American journalist observed, "today, at 25, the erstwhile subaltern is one of the youngest majors in the British Army and his command has become fantastically daring, an exquisitely trained pack of killers, thieves and saboteurs – all in a good cause. The British Army of the Nile admiringly calls them, 'Bloody fools,' arguing that nobody else would be mad enough to operate as much as 600 miles inside the enemy lines."[617] Similarly, Mike Sadler a member of the SAS recalled:

Shortly before we set off, a brigadier turned up to speak to us or wish us luck or something. But when he set eyes upon us, he was horrified because some members of the patrol hadn't shaved for two weeks, our hair was thick with dust and we were wearing all different types of

SAS Patrol, 1943. (IWM, E_021341)
   uniform. He looked at us and said, "oh my god!"[618]

With regards to SAS impact on the Axis forces, Rommel noted in his diary that Stirling and his SAS caused "considerable havoc and seriously disquieted the Italians."[619] Further, he recounted how some of his troops managed to surprise a "British column of the Long-Range Desert Group in Tunisia and captured the commander of 1ˢᵗ S.A.S. Regiment, Lieut.-Co. [Lieutenant-Colonel] David Stirling" in January 1943. Poorly guarded, Stirling escaped and made his way to some Arabs. He offered them a reward if they would spirit him back to British lines. However, the Arabs traded him back to the Germans for 11 pounds of tea. Rommel concluded, "the British lost the very able and adaptable commander of the desert group which had caused us more damage than any other British unit of equal strength."[620]

   The prestigious assessment of the SAS ability, however, was not shared by their own headquarters. At the end of the North African campaign, GHQ in Cairo told Major Paddy Mayne, then commander of the SAS after Stirling's capture, that "there was no more useful work for the SAS." He was given the choice of disbanding or carrying on in a new role as a special raiding squadron, but at a reduced establishment.[621]

   Paddy decided on survival and the SAS continued to evolve as a result. The original "L" Detachment, which had absorbed Free French paratroopers, a Greek Squadron and the Special Boat Section to form 1st SAS Regiment in late 1942, was transformed into the Special Boat Squadron and the Special Raiding Squadron.[622] Along with the 2nd SAS Regiment, they went on to conduct long-range penetration patrols and seaborne raids during the Sicilian and Italian campaigns. On the island of Salonika, Captain Anders Lassen, with 40 SBS raiders, a solitary Willys jeep and a handful of unreliable local guerrillas, through bold, audacious action was able to project an image of a force so large that he convinced the German garrison to withdraw prior to completing their intended demolitions. Prisoners confirmed the German estimate of forces opposing them was at least 1,000 men with automatic weapons."[623]

Additionally, when the Allies invaded occupied Europe in June 1944, SAS personnel conducted deception operations and they worked with French Resistance forces to harass German lines of communication and relay intelligence. Later, SAS personnel dropped into Belgium and the Netherlands, and conducted operations in conjunction with Allied forces during the battle for Germany. In December 1944, SAS elements worked with Italian partisans and when hostilities ceased in May 1945, the SAS Brigade assisted with disarming Germans in Norway.

In a testimony to their success, General Dwight D. Eisenhower asserted, "The ruthlessness with which the enemy have attacked Special Air

SAS Jeep destroyed by German JU 87 Stuka dive bomber. (Artwork by Brenda Wight)

Service troops has been an indication of the injury which you were able to cause to the German armed forces both by your own efforts and by the information which you gave of German dispositions and movements."[624] Nonetheless, with the war in Europe over, the War Office disbanded the SAS on October 8, 1945. However, the following year the War Office decided that a deep-penetration reconnaissance unit was required. As a result, in January 1, 1947, the War Office established the 21st Battalion, SAS Regiment, (Artists Rifles) as part of the Territorial Army.

Finally, despite the failure of Operation Flipper, Commando fortunes did not die as a result. Actually, the Commando record of achievements both prior to, and after, Operation Crusader are rather impressive. Thirty-eight commandos from "X" Troop, 11 Special Air Service Battalion parachuted in the dead of night into south-eastern Italy on February 10, 1941, as part of Operation Colossus. Their objective was to blow up the Tragino Aqueduct and then make their way to the coast for extraction. Although the mission was only partially successful, blowing only one pier and causing minor physical disruption to the Italians, the attack inside of Italy so unnerved Mussolini that he diverted valuable manpower and resources in its aftermath for the protection of every vital point in the country.[625]

Commando raids in Norway provided similar success. The Lofoten Raids on March 4, 1941, yielded technical equipment such as an Enigma

SAS Patrol. (IWM)

machine and code wheels, as well as a wealth of documents and the destruction of German equipment and war materiel.[626] Similarly, the Vaagos Raid on December 26, 1941, produced the master code for the whole of the German Navy, in addition to the destruction of infrastructure and equipment important to the German war effort.[627] Significantly, the raiding policy in Norway had another tangible payback. Aside from the destruction and intelligence coups, it resulted in a diversion of enemy manpower that totalled 372,000 troops by June 1944.[628] These forces would have been extremely helpful both in France and on the Eastern Front.

Special operations conducted by commandos and other special forces continued to have great success in 1942. On the night of February 27/28, special forces conducted Operation Biting (also known as the Bruneval Raid), designed to capture sensitive secret German radar equipment. Specifically, Director Combined Operations assigned "C" Company of the 2nd Parachute Battalion the task of securing details and components of the German Würtzburg radar that was used to control German night fighter aircraft in their intercept of Allied bombers. In addition, they were to capture technicians familiar with the use of the technology.

The raid was a spectacular success. The operation highlighted the possibilities of inter-Service cooperation and delivered material that proved invaluable to the electronic warfare research being undertaken by Britain at the time. In fact, Allied researchers were able to develop counter-measures, code named "Window" (or chaff – thousands of small, thin aluminum strips that were dropped to reflect radar beams and simulate a large number of aircraft in the air), which was used to great effect during the Normandy invasion.[629]

Major, later Major-General, John Frost, the commander of Operation Biting reflected, "The Bruneval Raid came at a time when our country's fortunes were at a low ebb...Many people were disgruntled after a long catalogue of failures, and the success of our venture, although it was a mere flea-bite, did have the effect of making people feel that we could succeed after all."[630]

Yet, another example of a successful commando raid was the attack on the French port of St. Nazaire, Operation Chariot, on the night of March 27/28, 1942, that destroyed the only dry dock on the Atlantic coast large enough to service the German battleship *Tirpitz*, which the Allies feared could slip into the Atlantic as a surface raider and play havoc with the vital Allied convoys from North America. In a remarkably bold attack, an old destroyer, the *HMS Campbeltown*, laden with five tons of explosives bluffed its way past the enemy defences and rammed the dry dock. Although very successful, very few of the raiding force returned to England.[631]

Commando raids evolved over time. Only three were conducted in

"Operation Collossus" (Artwork by Brenda Wight)

1940, ten in 1941, and 21 in 1942. By 1943, they reached a high of 31 raids.[632] However, by this time, the momentum of the war had swung irretrievably into the Allied camp and large-scale conventional operations were now not only possible but also more favourable. The Allied steam roller had begun to push the Axis war machine back to its borders. At the Special Service Brigade Headquarters on January 15, 1943, during the Commanding Officers' Conference, the Brigade Commander revealed:

> *Owing to the general change in the war situation it was apparent that raiding for the sake of raiding was unlikely to be undertaken. Therefore, Commando must be prepared to carry out a role as specialized and highly trained infantry, possibly for protracted operations. In view of this it was necessary to think ahead of the likely requirement of units, and consequent changes of establishment.[633]*

Not surprisingly, as a result, commando organizations became fixed and they began to increasingly resemble regular line battalions. Moreover, Commando operations became more conventional in nature, specifically to assist with large attacks and normally being used on the flanks or as specialized amphibious assault troops, to overcome difficulties that would stymie regular troops with less training and motivation. In addition, their preferred status for personnel also evaporated as manpower became scarce, particularly as commando requirements increased due to a high amount of casualties, normally resulting from their employment in conventional operations.

By the end of the war, the commandos attained a strength of 30 units and four assault brigades. Commandos served in every theatre of war including the Arctic, Europe, the Mediterranean, North Africa, Middle East and South East Asia. At the end of hostilities, all British Army, Royal Navy and Royal Air Force, as well as some Royal Marine Commandos were disbanded. This purge left only three Royal Marine Commandos and one assault brigade remaining.

Despite their eventual demise, the commandos made their presence felt by their enemies. One German commander spoke of the commandos and the SBS, "The British come like cats and disappear like ghosts."[634] The impact of their raids was such that it drove Hitler to take extreme action. On October 18, 1942, he issued his infamous "Commando Order," which directed that "all men operating against German troops in so-called Commando raids in Europe or in Africa are to be annihilated to the last man." This desperate directive provides further testimony to the effectiveness of the commandos and the raiding policy. So incensed was the German dictator by their constant attacks that he ordered them killed "whether they be soldiers in uniform...whether fighting or seeking to escape...even if these individuals on discovery make obvious their intention of giving themselves up as prisoners." He insisted that "no pardon is on any account to be given."[635]

The contribution of special forces to the eventual Allied victory in World War II is still a topic of heated discussion. Many argue that special forces were of limited value, assisting only in the attrition of enemy forces. This suggests that the return achieved by them was not worth the investment. Yet an examination of the achievement of special forces and special operations in general tells a different story. Quite simply, special forces tied down hundreds of thousands of enemy troops for defensive tasks; supported conventional forces by seizing key bridges, airfields and defensive positions. They also captured strategic materials such as radar components and Enigma cipher equipment, as well as codebooks and classified documents. Finally, they destroyed enemy materiel (e.g. aircraft, ships, locomotives and railway cars) and infrastructure (e.g. factories, bridges, rail lines, fortifications); shut down the German atomic weapon program; and raised, trained and equipped, as well as in some instances led, secret armies and resistance networks.

Rather than the myth that special forces are costly and a drain of resources, the opposite is true. Namely, a small number of highly-trained and motivated individuals achieve results well-beyond their numbers. This assessment is based on their wartime accomplishments.[636] Importantly, special forces maintained the offensive spirit and buoyed public morale in the early years of the war when Allied forces were largely on the defensive and rebuilding their shattered armies.[637] During this period, aside from the Royal Navy and strategic bombing, Britain and its allies had little with which to strike back at the Germans. Special forces provided the needed tonic to demonstrate a fighting spirit and force the Axis forces to dedicate resources to defending their territory and military forces.

Equally important, special forces conducted special reconnaissance that assisted in tracking German defences and movements and provided information for the planning of operations. This vital information provided crucial intelligence that allowed commanders and planning staffs to make timely decisions for the most effective use of forces. For example, General Montgomery wrote to the commanding officer of the LRDG on April 2, 1943, "I would like you to know how much I appreciate the excellent work done by your patrols and by the SAS in reconnoitring the country up to the Gabes Gap. Without your careful and reliable reports the launching of the 'left hook' by the N.Z. [New Zealand] Division would have been a leap in the dark; with the information they produced the operation could be planned with some certainty and, as you know, went off without a hitch."[638]

Additionally, direct action in the form of raids, ambushes and sabotage had an important impact on the Allied war effort. The destruction of vital war material, weapons, equipment, munitions, installations, as well as enemy personnel, had a cumulative effect on the Axis forces, who did not have the same industrial or resource base as the Allies. The constant drip of losses, not to mention the requirement to dedicate resources to defend against the continual attacks, created a strain for Germany and her allies. Brigadier H.W. Wynter in his study of special forces operations in North Africa concluded:

> *There can be no doubt that the short-range operations of the SAS parties against the enemy's exposed Southern flank and long lines of communication, were of the greatest assistance to our main Army;*

and were particularly valuable immediately before and during the last battles on the El Alamein position in the Autumn of 1942. Success was due to the enterprise, energy and daring of all concerned; and the frequent raids that were made not only inflicted heavy losses on the enemy's supplies of all sorts, but also reduced the strength of his Air Force, and caused him to withdraw troops from the front to strengthen the defence of landing grounds, roads and tracks.[639]

Similarly, Lieutenant-Colonel T.S. Airey from the MEF General Staff asserted, "The diversionary value of operations of this sort [LRDG / SAS operations]...The fact that it becomes known that saboteurs are operating in the back areas during a critical period causes the enemy considerable nervousness, makes them detach patrols and increase guards." [640] Captain Shaw reflected, "The scale of the attacks, here today and fifty miles away tomorrow, made mostly at night when accurate observation was impossible, was greatly exaggerated, especially by the fearful Italians." He explained, "At times all traffic after dark was stopped. Transport drivers, many of them from semi-civilian contractors, were terrified, not knowing when their turn would come. Troops, armoured cars and aircraft had to be diverted from their proper use to convoy protection work."[641] Rommel himself conceded, "they [Special Forces] caused considerable havoc, and seriously disquieted the Italians."[642]

The full impact of behind-the-lines sabotage and raids is sometimes lost because of the small-scale nature of individual acts. However, it is important to consider the cumulative effect of the constant strikes. For example, examining the SOE actions alone from March to December 1942, reveals an impressive tale. During this period the SOE had 385 agents in the field. In May 1942, three Norwegian SOE agents landed by fishing boat and destroyed the Bardshaug electric converter station that supplied power for the Orkal pyrite mines and the railway serving the mine. In addition, during this timeframe the SOE destroyed the only magnesium factory in Italy at Mestre and burned a large dump of Axis grain and fodder near Gorizia.[643]

From October 12th to December 31, 1942, the SOE attacked and damaged German barges and merchant vessels in France. They also damaged factories and port facilities, as well as destroying locomotives and railway lines.[644] SOE success in France continued into the spring. Between March 1943 and May 1943, the SOE continued with the destruction of locomotives, trucks, trains, barges, electric motors, transformers, munitions trains, as well as the killing of German officers and soldiers (i.e. 583 in April alone), and the destruction of fuel (i.e. 300,000 litres of oil and 200,000 litres of petrol in May alone). The SOE observed that their efforts had created "a general feeling of alarm and despondency among the German troops dealing with the *Maquis* [French Resistance]."[645]

The SOE also had an impressive record in Greece. Their April 1943, monthly summary revealed that SOE actions achieved:

- a two-thirds reduction of Chrome output;
- an attack on German and Italian troops prompting reinforcement by troops outside of Greece;
- the destruction of the Gorgopotamos Viaduct;
- the derailment of trains;
- the destruction of road and railway bridges;
- the destruction of ships in harbour;
- the sabotage of 20 aircraft;
- the organization of strikes;
- power houses in Salonika and Athens rendered ineffective; and
- the placement of mines in Corinth Canal.[646]

SOE success in other theatres was also impressive. In Norway, in April 1943 alone, the SOE sank with limpet mines the 2,000 ton *Ortelsburg* and the 1,460 ton *SS Sanen* and holed and grounded the 5,500 ton *Tugela*. During the approximate same period in Poland, SOE-sponsored activity reported to have damaged 202 locomotives, 937 trucks and destroyed a

"Midnight Rendezvous" (Photo artwork by Silvia Pecota)

petrol train and inflicted 28 interruptions to rail traffic headed to the Eastern Front.[647] A letter from a German soldier on the Eastern Front to his parents revealed, "Now the Partisans have started their activities in Poland and hardly a train reaches its destination, everything is being blown up."[648] In fact, the Polish Home Army is credited with having put over 5,000 locomotives out of service.[649]

By June 1943, the SOE had 650 agents in the field. It had created secret armies that amounted to an impressive number including:

- Poland 100,000 personnel;
- France 30,000;
- Norway 20,000;
- Holland 10,000; and
- Belgium 5,000.

In addition, the SOE supported a large number of guerillas in the field, specifically 180,000 in Yugoslavia and 20,000 in Greece.[650]

Meanwhile, SOE's "F" Section continued to deliver results. From July-September 1943, SOE's activities were responsible for:

- Members of the French Resistance, with SOE support, killed 650 German officers and men, wounded 4,000, destroyed 150 locomotives, 1,200 railway wagons and 170 lorries;
- 445 attacks on Axis personnel or premises;
- 171 train derailments and acts of railway sabotage;
- 289 acts of incendiarism;
- 219 acts of sabotage in factories or against public works;
- 141 acts of subversion;
- Destruction of the Lannemezan aluminium factory in July 1943 (as of end October operating then at only fifty per cent capacity);
- Sinking of a minesweeper in Rouen;
- The burning of 3,600 tires at Michelin works in Clermont-Ferrand; and
- The destruction of 1,000,000 litres of aviation fuel and 10,000,000 litres of oil.[651]

October was rated as a "record month to date for sabotage including the blowing up of aircraft, transformers, break-down trains, lock-gates, locomotives and powder factories."[652] In addition, 5,000 tons of munitions were destroyed at Langres.

The remainder of the year for SOE activity in France was no less successful. SOE actions achieved the substantive destruction of:

- Lock gates, which immobilised 50 barges;
- Pimento's power plant;
- 35 locomotives;
- 50,000 litres of ether;
- 14 tankers;
- 800 aircraft wings;
- 19 transformers; and
- A steel works.[653]

In addition, many smaller targets were attacked, including 44 locomotives, three trains, and numerous vehicles, pylons and electric motors. The Peugeot factory in Sochaux, France that made tank turrets was also put out of commission by sabotage.

The snapshot of major accomplishments in France and a few other countries begins to paint a larger picture.[654] These persistent strikes had a cumulative effect on the German war effort, as well as morale. The "war of the flea" is both physically and psychologically exhausting. As such, SOE operations alone were making themselves felt.

Undeniably, SOE, OSS and SAS efforts provided the Allies with a major boost during the invasion of occupied Europe (D-Day) and the subsequent Normandy Campaign. For instance, after the coded announcement by the BBC on the night of June 5/6, 1944, special forces-supported Resistance cells conducted hundreds of sabotage attacks in preparation for the invasion. The French Forces of the Interior (FFI) cut the French railways at 950 points.[655] In total, there were 3,000 confirmed rail cuts in France and Belgium between June 6-27, 1944.[656]

One immediate impact of the special forces actions was to deny the Germans the ability to rapidly counter-attack. For example, the 2nd SS Panzer Division *Das Reich* was short of fuel due to the attacks on petrol dumps. As a result, it turned to the railway but found the lines between Toulouse, where it was stationed, and the frontline cut. A normal three-day trip took 16 days. Similarly, the 11th Panzer Division took three days to move from the Eastern Front to the Rhine River. It then took three more weeks to reach Caen on the Normandy coast.[657]

Special forces teams also arranged the reception of three-man Jedburgh teams that were designed to assist local resistance networks to coordinate their efforts. The Jedburghs provided a wireless link, supplied arms and ammunition and provided training on the use of weapons and basic tactics. Fourteen teams dropped into Brittany alone and helped organize 20,000 resistors. A large part of the German effort was needed simply to fight the resistance forces.[658] Significantly, 8,000 Frenchman were fighting in Massif Central alone.[659]

The Chiefs of Staff Committee acknowledged:

There can be no doubt that at a time when the Germans were exerting every effort to obtain more manpower, the dispersion of troops in protective and internal security duties had an effect on the land battle. In June 1944, the Germans were forced to employ 5,000 troops to disperse the guerillas in the Correze and approximately 11,000 with artillery, were engaged against resistance in the Vercors in July. On 20th July, the 11th Panzer Division was still operating against resistance groups in Dordogne.[660]

By June 10, 1944, the special forces commanders could claim a degree of success. An internal assessment reported, "Virtually all organisers have carried out successfully their D-day tasks, which have included the derailment of at least two trains in tunnels, the mining of road bridges over which German armour was expected, the blowing up of transformers supplying power to electric railways, and the cutting of telecommunications in widespread areas."[661] Their assessment was understated. The Chiefs of Staff Committee was far more generous in its praise. It acknowledged that the SOE, as well as other special operators who supported Resistance cells, assisted Allied operations as follows:

- It sapped the enemy's confidence in his own security and flexibility of internal movement;
- by diverting enemy troops to internal security duties and keeping troops thus employed dispersed;
- by causing delay to the movement of enemy troops concentrating against the Normandy beachhead and regrouping after the allied break-out from the beachhead;
- by disrupting enemy telecommunications in France and Belgium
- by enabling Allied formations to advance with greater speed through being able to dispense with many normal military precautions, e.g., flank protection and mopping up;
- by furnishing military intelligence; and
- by providing organised groups of men in liberated areas able to undertake static guard duties at short notice and without further training.[662]

A Supreme Headquarters Allied Expeditionary Force (SHAEF) report issued just after D-Day lauded, "The actions of the Resistance groups in the

"Landing by moonlight." (Photo artwork by Silvia Pecota)

South resulted in an average delay of forty-eight hours in the movement of German reinforcements to Normandy, and often much longer. The enemy was facing a battlefield behind his own lines."[663] The Supreme Allied Headquarters later elaborated, "The widespread and continuous sabotage caused outside the capabilities of Allied air efforts ...it [sabotage] succeeded in imposing serious delays on all the German divisions moving to Normandy from the Mediterranean, and forced the enemy to extensive and intricate detours ... both main railway lines up the Rhone Valley were closed for a good part of the time, the route on the right bank at one time for ten consecutive days."[664]

Of immense importance to the Allied war effort, special forces-supported Resistance action provided a major contribution towards the attrition of the German pool of locomotives, as well as the destruction of irreplaceable machine tools and heavy cranes. In fact, sabotage in France alone between September 1943 and September 1944 accounted for almost as many locomotives as the total disabled by air action during the same period. The increase in repairs made necessary by sabotage overwhelmed the repair facilities. It forced the deployment of railway and reserve troops, defence workers and German railwaymen to guard and rebuild the vital lines and thereby overwhelmed the German administrative system for the occupied countries.[665] As well, special forces, through their connections with the *Société National de Chemin de Fer*, encouraged slow-downs, absenteeism and strikes. In fact, the German Director of French Railways cited this as one of the significant contributory factors that led to the German failure to maintain transport facilities adequately to contain the Allied bridgehead in Normandy.[666]

Special forces achieved similar results during Operation Dragoon, code name for the landing operation of the invasion of Southern France, in August 1944. The American 3rd Infantry Division history noted, "A major factor aiding the speed and success of our movement was the activity of the French resistance groups...Whole towns were seized and held to await our coming. In addition to this sabotage activities were coordinated with our movements. If the Air Force failed to destroy a bridge, that bridge might be demolished anyway – from the ground and with hand-laid demolitions. Speeding convoys of enemy reserves ran into mysteriously laid roadblocks and ambush."[667] The 3rd Infantry considered the efforts of the special forces-supported resistance network equivalent to that of four to five divisions.

In fact, with regard to Operation Dragoon, British General Sir Henry Maitland Wilson, Supreme Allied Commander in the Mediterranean, acknowledged that the FFI "reduced the fighting efficiency of the *Wehrmacht* in southern France to forty per cent at the moment of the Dragoon landing operations."[668] In addition, the FFI were credited with capturing approximately 42,000 German prisoners of war during the operation.[669]

Special forces operations in Denmark provide another informative snapshot. Major operations included the attack on the Burmeister & Wain power station in Copenhagen, which was engaged in U-boat production in 1943 and was consequently out of commission for nine months; the destruction of 30 German aircraft and the workshop and special tools at the Aalborg West airfield in 1944; the destruction of materiel and machinery of the factory in Copenhagen that was engaged in V1 and V2 rocket manufacturing; the destruction of the "rifle syndicate" armament factory; and the complete destruction of the Always Radio factory during U-Boat production. In addition, there was also minor sabotage, particularly against Danish railway traffic. During February 1945, for instance, as the

CHARLATANS OR SPECIAL WARRIORS | 197

Germans were attempting to withdraw forces from Norway to reinforce their crumbling front-lines elsewhere, they were repeatedly attacked and stalled in Denmark. The 223rd Reserve Panzer Division and the 166th Infantry Division were successfully attacked over 100 times. In fact, in a period of one week, more than half of their 44 trains were immobilised in Denmark.[670]

The narrative to this point has provided only a snapshot of actions conducted by special forces. As noted earlier, the cumulative total of activities clearly had a disruptive impact on the German war effort. It is incomprehensible to deny that a force of 750,000 special forces-supported resistance fighters and partisans operating in Europe and the Balkans alone would not create a substantive military problem for the Germans.[671] In fact, an official report rightly assessed special forces "provided organization, communications, materials, training and leadership without which 'resistance ' would have been of no military value."[672] It is for this reason that a SHAEF report to the Combined Chiefs of Staff on July 18, 1945 acknowledged, "It can be fairly concluded, therefore, that SOE activity forced the Germans to retain considerable forces in areas of no immediate military value to us. The forces could have been usefully employed elsewhere and were contained by an economical expenditure of effort."[673] Major-General Colin Gubbins explained:

Admittedly there were all over France from the moment of German conquest individual Frenchmen and French women determined to resist, but I think to be quite fair, that it was primarily the British who slowly gave to the Nation a will to resist. It sounds a hard criticism of the French to say this, but without the parachuting into France of British leaders, instructors, Wireless Operators, Couriers, etc., and the example they set (even though many fell into Gestapo hands through lack of security, and so on) which gave the necessary rallying point or focus, little would have happened.[674]

The SHAEF report also commented on the impact of special forces. The Supreme Commander's staff assessed that special forces assisted Allied operations by:

- sapping enemy morale;
- diverting troops to internal security;
- causing delay to movement of enemy troops;
- disrupting telecommunications / lines of communications;
- furnishing military intelligence; and
- providing organization to groups of men in liberated areas to

undertake guard duties
- prevention of demolitions - counter scorched earth.[675]

The SHAEF report conclusively singled out the SOE and stated, "SOE operations made a substantial contribution to the victory of the Allied Expeditionary Force."[676] General Dwight D. "Ike" Eisenhower, himself noted in his memoir, "without their [Special Forces assisted resistance groups] great assistance the liberation of France and the defeat of the enemy in western Europe would have consumed a much longer time and meant greater losses to ourselves."[677] Eisenhower also wrote to Major-General Gubbins and Colonel David Bruce, head of OSS European Theatre, at the end of the war and commented:

In no previous war and in no other theater during this war, have resistance forces been so closely harnessed to the main military effort. While no final assessment of the operational value of resistance action has yet been completed, I consider that the disruption of enemy rail communications, the harassing of German road moves and the continual and increasing strain placed on the German war economy and internal security services through-out occupied Europe by the organized forces of resistance, played a very considerable part in our complete and final victory.[678]

Eisenhower went so far as to say, "the Resistance in France shortened the war by nine months."[679] One of General George Patton's corps commanders agreed. He wrote, "SF operations, including the employment of FFI personnel in support of this corps and that continuing support of this corps, have been particularly effective ...It is believed that a very definite role has been created for SF personnel in support of this corps and that continuing support will definitely be gained from their activities."[680]

His opinion was supported by General Eisenhower and his SHAEF headquarters. They assessed that special forces operations "made a substantial contribution to the victory of the Allied Expeditionary Force. Widespread and continuous sabotage against railways and telecommunications supplemented the air effort and completed the confusion of the enemy." They went on to state that there were four types of activity that paid impressive military dividends, specifically, attacks on railways, diversion of enemy forces through guerilla activities, prevention of demolitions and the provision of supplementary manpower for the Allied Expeditionary Force.[681] Moreover, Colonel "Wild" Bill Donovan, the Director of the OSS, observed that the value of special forces, particularly the SOE and OSS was not just "in its role in hastening military victory, but also in the development of the concept of unorthodox warfare which alone constitutes a major contribution."[682]

The spike in support for special forces after the D-Day invasion is not totally surprising in light of their accomplishments. In fact, their achievements garnered some wider support within the chain-of-command. One official report affirmed, "A force of some 2,000 strong [Special Forces] operated with such outstanding success that the Supreme Commander circulated reports to all United States theatres of war as an example of what could be achieved."[683] Furthermore, a War Office study dated July 10, 1945 conceded that most conventional organizations and their senior leadership disagreed with the special forces concept. However, the War Office acknowledged that "some form of SAS organization must exist in peace time which will be capable of forming the nucleus for a rapid expansion on the outbreak of war. It must also be ready to plan, prepare and mount SAS operations immediately."[684] It went on to assert, "The dividends paid by introducing small parties of well trained and thoroughly disciplined regular troops to operate effectively behind the enemy lines can be out of all proportion to the numbers involved.[685] It explained, "Generally speaking a party of three or four specialists is as good as a party of twelve or fifteen normal good soldiers led by one officer. The size of the party is little guide to its operational efficiency."[686]

The report also noted, "The SAS idea is as yet only in its infancy. The very fact that such operations have already paid dividends with the application of a very small allocation of troops, aircraft and naval craft should encourage us to enlarge the scope of this type of operation in the future." In fact, it went so far as to emphasize, "Our experiences in this war, prove that we shall want SAS troops from the very start of the next war."[687]

Despite the accolades provided and the conclusions drawn in the report, the recommendations held very little sway as the conventional military establishment marginalized and dismantled special forces from the order of battle at the end of hostilities. Nonetheless, in the final analysis, special forces in World War II were neither rogues, nor charlatans. Rather, they were courageous and highly-trained warriors who made a significant contribution at the strategic, operational and tactical levels. They reinforced the words of Yasotay, the Mongolian warlord, that, "When the hour of crisis comes, remember that 40 selected men can shake the world."[688]

APPENDIX 1
VICTORIA CROSS CITATION
LT COL GEOFFREY KEYES

Lieutenant-Colonel Keyes commanded a detachment of a force which landed some 250 miles behind the enemy lines to attack Headquarters, Base Installations and Communications. From the outset Lieutenant-Colonel Keyes deliberately selected for himself the command of the detachment detailed to attack what was undoubtedly the most hazardous of these objectives—the residence and Headquarters of the General Officer Commanding the German forces in North Africa. This attack, even if initially successful, meant almost certain death for those who took part in it.

He led his detachment without guides, in dangerous and precipitous country and in pitch darkness, and maintained by his stolid determination and powers of leadership the morale of the detachment. He then found himself forced to modify his original plans in the light of fresh information elicited from neighbouring Arabs, and was left with only one officer and an N.C.O. with whom to break into General Rommel's residence and deal with the guards and Headquarters Staff.

At zero hour on the night of 17th-18th November, 1941, having despatched the covering party to block the approaches to the house, he himself with the two others crawled forward past the guards, through the surrounding fence and so up to the house itself. Without hesitation, he boldly led his party up to the front door, beat on the door and demanded entrance.

Unfortunately, when the door was opened, it was found impossible to overcome the sentry silently, and it was necessary to shoot him. The noise of the shot naturally aroused the inmates of the house and Lieutenant-Colonel Keyes, appreciating that speed was now of the utmost importance, posted the N.C.O. at the foot of the stairs to prevent interference from the floor above. Lieutenant-Colonel Keyes, who instinctively took the lead, emptied his revolver with great success into the first room and was followed by the other officer who threw a grenade. Lieutenant-Colonel Keyes with great daring then entered the second room on the ground floor but was shot almost immediately on flinging open the door and fell back into the passage mortally wounded. On being carried outside by his companions he died within a few minutes.

By his fearless disregard of the great dangers which he ran and of which he was fully aware, and by his magnificent leadership and outstanding gallantry, Lieutenant-Colonel Keyes set an example of supreme self-sacrifice and devotion to duty.[689]

APPENDIX 2
GERMAN SPECIAL OPERATIONS

THE GERMANS ALSO ATTEMPTED to use their own special forces in North Africa. Initially, the Abwehr (German military intelligence) focused on information gathering to collect as much knowledge as possible about Libya and the Sahara Desert. When the war began to turn against the Italians in North Africa, Germany began planning should they need to send assistance. The first mission was in March 1941, to Murzuk in southern Libya. This mission, codenamed Operation Dora, consisted of almost entirely scientific personnel, including astronomers, geologists and cartographers. As the Italians did little to protect the Abwehr personnel, the Germans deployed a small security section equipped with a few armed Steyr trucks and a pair of SdKfz 222 armoured cars.

In support of the intelligence efforts, also commencing in March 1941, was a special detachment under Major Nikolaus Ritter, Chief of Air Intelligence in the Abwehr, who worked through the Secret Service Centre at *Fliegerkorps X*.[690]

Much of the German desert patrols were done by aircraft by Sonderkommando (special detail) Ritter and later replaced by Sonderkommando Blaich.[691] Connected to Major Ritter was the Hungarian Count László Almásy who was a desert explorer before the war. He had amassed a special knowledge of Egypt and the Arabs. Almásy continued to run agents until the summer of 1942.

In June, the Abwehr deployed elements of their Brandenburg special forces unit (Brandenburgers) to North Africa to conduct reconnaissance, specifically to determine British front lines, strength and equipment. In July, the Abwehr dropped the Gauleiter of Mannheim (which was a pseudonym for the German spy) into Palestine to attempt to foment an uprising against the British among the Arabs. However, a Palestinian farm worker reported spotting a parachutist landing near Ramleh. He observed that the parachutist buried a number of items in a series of holes. The German agent was eventually captured. The British also discovered the holes which contained Palestinian currency, a shortwave transmitter complete with codes, identification signals and specified transmission times. This information was then used to send bogus messages to the Germans.

During the month of October 1941, Brandenburger agents made two attempts to infiltrate Cairo. The objective was to make contact with Arab nationalists and assist them to mount an insurrection against the British. The first attempt to reach Cairo was conducted by a seaborne infiltration. This attempt failed and the team returned to its base in Libya. The second attempt was by parachute insertion close to Cairo. This mission also ended in failure. A final attempt in making contact with key Arab leaders was successful. A team of Brandenburger agents using vehicles crossed the Egyptian frontier and the Nile near the town of Asyut. Nonetheless, the insurrection never transpired.

In late October 1941, a half-company of Brandenburgers arrived in North Africa and towards the end of 1941, as the front lines in Africa began to solidify, were deployed in the most southern regions of the German sector where the LRDG and SAS operated. The Abwehr reinforced their Brandenburg troops on January 22, 1942, when First Lieutenant Helmut von Leipzig's Brandenburg company of 100 men and 24 captured British vehicles, which were taken after the German seizure of Tobruk, arrived in theatre. Operation Dora (retitled Sonderkommando Dora) now took on a more military focus as the Brandenburgers were tasked with determining if the Free French forces in Chad represented a threat to Rommel's Afrika Korps.[692]

The Italians, fearful of a French attack, requested that the Brandenburgers be located at El Gatrun. As a result, the Germans established an airfield with a collection of aircraft, including a captured Spitfire, which were used for reconnaissance work. From El Gatrun, Sonderkommando Dora deployed three patrols to explore the mountains and passes of southeastern Algeria, northern Niger and the Tibesti mountains of Chad. The first mission, led by Lieutenant Becker, travelled into Algeria where they discovered a German dressed as an Arab, who had deserted from the French Foreign Legion when the war began. He provided Becker with detailed information about the area. Becker's patrol continued on into Algeria where his men, disguised in British and French uniforms, slipped through the thin French picket line along the border. However, their ruse failed when they bumped into a much stronger French force.[693] A firefight broke out and four of the Brandenburgers were killed and two trucks destroyed. The survivors piled into the remaining vehicles and withdrew to the Libyan border and returned to El Gatrun.

First Lieutenant von Leipzig led the second expedition in the summer of 1942, dressed as British soldiers to avoid suspicion. This group moved into Niger to check out the Tümmö Pass. The patrol was stopped at a French roadblock, but von Leipzig bluffed his way through. They then determined that the pass was heavily guarded and believed that several divisions would be required to break through. With that, von Leipzig returned to El Gatrun.

A third mission, led by Sergeant Stegmann, ventured the furthest into enemy territory. He slipped through French outposts guarding the frontier and made it to the Tibesti Mountains. With the assistance of the local Tibbu Bedouins, who despised the French, he infiltrated the town of Bardai, which held a major French military garrison. He quickly discovered that the base, which was manned by a company-sized French garrison, was about to be reinforced by a large number of troops. Stegmann decided to withdraw back to El Gatrun, but he chose to travel north through the mountains rather than attempting to sneak through the French lines once again.

Concurrently, the Germans used their captured Spitfire to take aerial photos of the French forces in northern Chad in support of the Brandenburger missions. All three patrols added to the German understanding of the terrain and enemy activity. The patrols accurately mapped out the terrain and roads that could be used in the future to raid the British land-based supply convoys in Egypt and the Sudan. The patrols also confirmed that the French strongly held the mountain passes, and a major effort was required to capture them. Importantly, they also determined that the French posed no real threat to Rommel's forces in the north.[694]

On May 16, 1942, the Brandenburgers achieved one of their most successful operations in Cairo when they covertly met with the Grand Mufti of Jerusalem. The objective was once again to attempt to convince the Arabs to mount an insurrection against the British. However, despite the coup in arranging the meeting, the mission failed to trigger a revolt.

The Brandenburgers continued with their covert warfare. On December 26, 1942, First Lieutenant Friedrich von Koenen's commando team of 30 men departed from the Bizerta airfield in Libya in three gliders. They were released close to their target, the thirty-seven-metre-long railroad bridge near the village of Sidi bou Baker that spanned the Wadi el-Kbir in central Tunisia. Although guarded by French troops, the Germans successfully destroyed the bridge. The Brandenburgers then proceeded to march 190 km back to German lines.

Concurrently, a second team of ten Brandenburger commandos, under the command of Lieutenant Hagenauer, assaulted another bridge near Kasserini in southern Tunisia. Although they destroyed the bridge, on their return to German lines they were intercepted by a Free French armored reconnaissance platoon. All ten German commandos were captured.

Later, on January 18, 1943, a team of Brandenburgers led by Lieutenant Fuchs destroyed the bridge over the Wadi el-Melah in southern Tunisia, which supported a key Allied supply line. Unfortunately for the Germans, the Allies had by this time amassed such superiority in theatre that the loss of the bridge had little impact on their offensive.[695]

After the German defeat at El Alamein and Rommel's withdrawal to Tunisia, Sonderkommando Dora was recalled to Tripoli, where it met up with fellow Brandenburgers, von Koenen's battalion. The two units fought a fighting withdrawal and at Wadi Zemzem, they battered elements of the LRDG and Popski's Private Army before safely withdrawing to Tunisia.[696] Shortly before the capitulation of all German and Italian forces in North Africa, the surviving members of the Brandenburgers were withdrawn and returned to Germany.[697]

British archives provide some information on what British Intelligence knew. They identified that Special Unit 288 and Lehrregiment Brandenburg 287 (also referred to as the Special Desert Unit) had deployed to the Mediterranean theatre. In fact, they assessed the Special Desert Unit was "probably fitted for sabotage, for raising rebellion in Iran and Irak [sic], and possibly for preventing demolition of oil-wells." The approximate strength was estimated at 3,396 all ranks.[698] British assessments determined that "Units 287 and 288 appear to be not more than highly equipped battle Groups, not intrinsically different from other formations of the German Army...They are particularly fitted for carrying rapid destruction and disruption into an invaded country where a fifth column may be expected. This is where the German-Arab Lehr Abteilung in 287 is doubtless meant to find its role."[699]

British intelligence also identified Operation Wido (also under Abwehr I like Dora), which was under the command of Major von Griesheim. Wido's primary area was identified as west and south-west of Tripoli including French North Africa (Operation Dora's sector was more to the south and south-east). Griesheim ran a network of agents that maintained liaison with Italians and was concerned with intelligence collection on the Sahara. Griesheim's agents used camel and vehicle patrols. They also carried Swiss wrist watches to "charm simple natives." They reported mainly on Anglo-Gaullist troop concentrations, as well as weather reports, political intelligence and cartographic details based on their recces.[700]

British intelligence also noted that General der Flieger Hellmuth Felmy "has been labouring since 1941 to collect intelligence and raise insurrection in the Arab lands...in 6/41 he hopefully landed at Aleppo for the rising in Irak...He was transferred in 9/42 to Armavir, with a new motorized Special Detachment 287, including a 'German-Arab Lehrabteilung.'" However, from October 1942 to January 1943 this formation was used to fight the Soviets under 1st Panzer Army.[701]

Finally, British intelligence believed that the German efforts at covert warfare were largely unsuccessful. They attributed this failure to the organizational and operational dysfunction at all levels of the two rival German intelligence services, namely the Abwehr and the Sicherheitsdienst (SS Security Service or SD).

NOTES

CHAPTER 1

1. Major-General I.S.O. Playfair, *History of the Second World War. The Mediterranean and Middle East. Volume I "The Early Successes against Italy (to May 1940)* (London: Her Majesty's Stationery Office, 1954), 89.

2. Erik Larson, *The Splendid and the Vile. A Saga of Churchill, Family, and Defiance During the Blitz* (New York: Crown, Kindle Edition, 2020), 436.

3. Ibid., 436.

4. Robert Woollcombe, *The Campaigns of Wavell 1939-1943* (London: Cassell, 1959), 9.

5. Winston S. Churchill, *The Second World War Vol I. Their Finest Hour* (Toronto: Houghton Mifflin Company Boston Thomas Allen Limited, 1949), 419.

6. Ibid., 371.

7. Playfair, *Vol 1, The Mediterranean and Middle East*, 37.

8. The experimental brigade (5 Brigade) under Major-General Fuller was responsible for testing methods and doctrine for combined arms operations, specifically the use of armour, aircraft with infantry and artillery.

9. Playfair, *Vol 1, The Mediterranean and Middle East*, 188-189.

10. Woollcombe, *The Campaigns of Wavell*, 17; and Playfair, *Vol 1, The Mediterranean and Middle East*, 93. Wavell also had 9,000 troops in Sudan and 8,500 men in Kenya approximately 3,200 kilometres away. Under his command he actually had 86,000 troops, which also included garrisons in Aden, British Somaliland and Cyprus. Ibid.

11. Playfair, *Vol 1, The Mediterranean and Middle East*, 69.

12. Ibid., 95.

13. John Strawson, *The Battle for North Africa* (London: B.T. Batsford, 1969), 19. The Duke of Aosta surrendered his forces on May 16, 1940. Wavell reported, "conquest of Italian East Africa had been accomplished in four months, from

the end of January to beginning of June. In this period a force of approximately 220,000 men had been practically destroyed with the whole of its equipment, and an area of nearly a million square miles had been occupied." Cited in Ibid., 51.

14. Playfair, *Vol 1, he Mediterranean and Middle East,* 95-96.

15. Count Galeazzo Ciano, *The Ciano Diaries 1939-1943: The Complete and Unabridged Diaries of Count Galeazzo Ciano, Italian Minister of Foreign Affairs, 1936-1943,* henceforth *The Ciano Diaries,* edited by Hugh Gibson (Arcole Publishing, 2017, Kindle Edition), loc 4965. Although Ciano was Mussolini's son-in-law, the Duce still had Ciano shot by firing squad in 1943 for his part in the coup to oust the dictator.

16. *Il Duce,* derived from the Latin *dux,* translates to "the leader." This was a title adopted by Mussolini.

17. *Ciano Diaries,* loc 5209.

18. War Cabinet, "General Directive for Commander-In-Chief, Middle East." NA, CAB-66-11-wp-40-330-10.

19. Cited in Woollcombe, *The Campaigns of Wavell,* 18.

20. Major-General H. Rowan-Robinson, *Auchinleck to Alexander* (London: Hutchinson & Co., 1943), 52.

21. Cited in Strawson, *The Battle for North Africa,* 21.

22. Woollcombe, *The Campaigns of Wavell,* 24.

23. Ian Beckett, "Wavell," in John Keegan, ed., *Churchill's Generals* (London: Warner Books, 1997), 75-80.

24. Churchill, *Their Finest Hour,* 1950 second ed., 376.

25. *Ciano Diaries,* loc 2096 & 2106.

26. Ibid., loc 4912.

27. Ibid., loc 5759.

28. Ibid., loc 5792. Interestingly, on 2 January 1940, Ciano confided to his diary, "Graziani, on the other hand, favours war at the side of Germany and tries to persuade the *Duce* to hasten it. We must neutralize his influence." Four months later Graziani reversed himself and became "clearly hostile to any war action on our part." Ibid., loc 4159 & 5095. Mussolini concluded, "one should only give jobs to people who are looking for at least one promotion." Ibid., loc 5792.

29. Ibid., August 8, 1940, loc 5792.

30. Ibid., loc 5814.

31. War Cabinet, "General Directive for Commander-In-Chief, Middle East." NA, CAB-66-11-wp-40-330-10. The War Cabinet also gave instruction with regard to other regions of Wavell's command responsibility. Specifically, the War Cabinet directed:

> *The evacuation of Somaliland is enforced upon us by the enemy, but is none the less strategically convenient. All forces in or assigned to Somaliland should be sent to Aden, to the Sudan via Port Sudan, or to Egypt, as may*

be thought best. East Africans may go to Kenya, if desired. The defence of Kenya must rank after the defence of the Sudan. There should be time after the crisis in Egypt and the Sudan is passed to reinforce Kenya by sea and rail before any large Italian expedition can reach the Tana river. We can always reinforce Kenya faster than Italy can pass large forces thither from Abyssinia or Italian Somaliland. It is not necessary to hold the frontier and you may be able to achieve economy of force by surrendering the desert areas to the enemy and holding the line of the Tana river with a suitable extension to cover essential communications in the gap between Garissa and Lake Rudolph. It is hoped to send to Kenya in the near future some A.F.V.'s [Armoured Fighting Vehicles] and anti-tank guns in order to compel the enemy to advance with heavy infantry forces. Accordingly, if this can be done without endangering Nairobi and the railway, either the two West African Brigades or two Brigades of the K.A.R. should be moved forthwith to Khartoum. General Smuts is being asked to allow the Union Brigade, or a large part of it, to move to the Canal Zone and the Delta for internal security purposes. Arrangements should be made to continue their training. The Admiralty are being asked to report on shipping possibilities in the Indian Ocean and the Red Sea.

32. The War Cabinet directed:

The two Brigades, one of Regulars and the other Australian, which are held ready in Palestine, should now move into the Delta in order to clear the Palestine communications for the movement of further reserves as soon as they can be equipped for field service or organised for internal security duties. The rest of the Australians, numbering six battalions, in Palestine will thus be available at five days' notice to move into the Delta for internal security or other emergency employment. However, immediately three or four Regiments of British Cavalry, without their horses, should, it would seem, take over the necessary duties in the Canal Zone, liberating the three Regular battalions there for general reserve of the field army of the Delta. The Polish Brigade should move to the Delta from Palestine as may be convenient and join the general reserve, which already includes the French Volunteer unit. The movement of the Indian Division and the three Batteries of British Artillery, although horse-drawn, now embarking or in transit are being accelerated to the utmost. Most of the above movements should be completed before the 1st October, and on this basis the army of the Delta should comprise: (a) The British Armoured Force in Egypt. (&) The Five British battalions at Mersa Matruh, the two at Alexandria and the two in Cairo—total nine. (c) The three Battalions from the Canal zone. (d) The reserve British Brigade from Palestine—total fifteen British Regular Infantry Battalions. (e) The New Zealand Brigade. (f) The Australian

Brigade from Palestine. (g) The Polish Brigade and French Volunteer Unit. (h) Part of the Union Brigade from East Africa. (i) The Fourth Indian Division now in rear of Mersa Matruh (less one Brigade). (j) The new Indian Division, less one brigade, in transit. (k). The 11,000 men in drafts arriving almost at once at Suez, and additional 13,700 details arriving about the 15th September. (l) All the artillery (212 guns) (including from India) now in the Middle East or en route from India. (m) The Egyptian army so far as it can be used for field operations. Ibid.

33. War Cabinet, "General Directive for Commander-In-Chief, Middle East." NA, CAB-66-11-wp-40-330-10.

34. Ibid.

35. Ibid. The War Cabinet, stressed:

It must be expected that the enemy will advance in great force, limited only, but severely, by the supply of water and petrol. He will certainly have strong armoured forces, on his right hand to contain and drive back our weaker forces unless these can be reinforced in time by the armoured regiments from Great Britain. He may attempt to mask if he cannot storm Mersa Matruh. But, if the main line of the Delta is diligently fortified and resolutely held, he will be forced to deploy an army whose supply of water, petrol, food and ammunition will be difficult. Once the army is deployed and seriously engaged, the action against his communications by bombardment from the sea, by descent at Mersa Matruh, Sollum, or even much further west, would be a deadly blow to him. The campaign for the Defence of Egypt may, therefore, as a last resort, resolve itself into: strong defence with the left arm from Alexandria inland, and a reaching out with the right hand, using sea-power upon his communications... All trained or Regular units, whether fully equipped or not, must be used in defence of Egypt against invasion. All armed white men and also Indian or foreign units must be used for internal security. The Egyptian army must be made to play its part in support of the Delta front, thus leaving only riotous crowds to be dealt with in Egypt proper.

36. Strategicus, *From Dunkirk to Benghazi* (London: Faber & Faber Ltd., 1942), 148.

37. *The Ciano Diaries*, September 9, 1940, loc 5959.

38. D.W. Braddock, *The Campaigns in Egypt and Libya 1940-1942* (Aldershot: Gale & Polden Ltd., 1964), 7.

39. Ministry of Defence (MoD), *Destruction of an Army. The First Campaign in Libya. Sept. 1940- Feb. 1941* (London: Ministry of Information, 1941), 24.

40. *Ciano Diaries*, loc 5981 & 5993.

41. Ibid., September 30, 1940, loc 6059.

42. Churchill, *Their Finest Hour*, 1949 ed., 470.

43. Ibid., 416.

44. War Cabinet, "Weekly Resume (No. 55) of the Naval, Military and Air Situation From 12 Noon September 12th to 12 Noon September 19th, 1940. NA, CAB-66-12-wp-40-381-11. The War Cabinet noted "the strength of the Italian forces in Libya is estimated at 250,000 white troops and 25,000-30,000 natives, and of those in Italian East Africa of 111,000 white troops (including all potential reserves) and 195,600 native troops (including 44,000 irregulars).

45. On September 15, 1940, Ciano wrote in his diary, "I anticipate a bitter, hard, long very long conflict, which will end in victory for Great Britain." *Ciano Diaries*, loc 3397.

46. Strategicus, *From Dunkirk to Benghazi*, 149.

47. *Ciano Diaries*, October 2, 1940, loc 6077.

48. Ibid., October 16, 1940, loc 6132.

49. Playfair, *Vol 1, The Mediterranean and Middle East*, 257.

50. Cited in Robert Lyman, *The Longest Siege. Tobruk: The Battle that Saved North Africa* (London: Pan Books, 2009), 28.

51. Ibid., 28.

52. On October 22, 1941, Ciano wrote in his diary, "Naturally it [the ultimatum] is a document that allows no way out for Greece. Either she accepts occupation or she will be attacked." *The Ciano Diaries*, October 22, 1940, loc 6176.

53. Cited in John Connell, "Wavell's 30,000," *The History of the Second World War*, Part 12, 315.

54. Churchill, *Their Finest Hour,* 1949 ed., 483.

55. See Eliot A. Cohen, *Commandos and Politicians* (Cambridge: Center for International Affairs, Harvard University, 1978), 37-40; Maxwell Schoenfeld, *The War Ministry of Winston Churchill* (Ames: The Iowa State University Press, 1972), 124; and Patrick Cosgrove, *Churchill at War Alone 1939-1940* (London: William Collins Sons & Co. Ltd., 1974), 95.

56. David Jablonsky, *Churchill: The Making of a Grand Strategist* (Carlisle Barracks: Strategic Studies Institute, U.S. Army War College, 1990), 125.

57. Ibid., 92.

58. Fred Majdalany, *Cassino. Portrait of a Battle* (London: Cassell& Co. 1957, Kindle edition 2013), loc 1207.

59. Cited in Connell, "Wavell's 30,000," 315.

60. War Office, *Destruction of an Army*, 35.

61. Churchill, *Their Finest Hour,* 1949 ed., 542-543.

62. Woollcombe, *The Campaigns of Wavell,* 31.

63. Western Desert Force changed name to XIII Corps on 1 January 1941. Lyman, *The Longest Siege*, 69.

64. Churchill, *Their Finest Hour*, 1949 ed., 610.

65. Cited in Lyman, *The Longest Siege,* 38.

66. Playfair, *Vol 1, The Mediterranean and Middle East,* 273.

67. Churchill, *Their Finest Hour, 1949 ed.*, 544.

68. B.H. Liddell Hart, ed. *The Rommel Papers* (London: Collins, 1953), 93. (Henceforth, *The Rommel Papers*).

69. War Office, *Destruction of an Army*, 55; Woollcombe, *The Campaigns of Wavell* 41; Connell, "Wavell's 30,000," 327; Lyman, *The Longest Siege*, 75; and *The Rommel Papers*, 95.

70. Cited in Lyman, *The Longest Siege*, 75.

71. Cited in Woollcombe, *The Campaigns of Wavell*, 31.

72. War Office, *Destruction of an Army*, 55.

73. *The Ciano Diaries*, loc 6484.

74. *The Rommel Papers*, 91.

75. *The Ciano Diaries*, December 12, 1940, loc 6496.

76. Ibid., December 12, 1940, loc 6506.

77. Ibid., December 15, 1940, loc 6538.

78. Major-General I.S.O. Playfair, *The Mediterranean and Middle East. Volume II "The Germans come to the Help of their Ally (1941)* (London: Her Majesty's Stationery Office, 1956), 3.

79. Field Marshal The Lord Harding wrote, "At sea, [Admiral Andrew] Cunningham with weaker forces waged a relentless war against the Italian Navy, culminating in March 1941 with the great naval victory of Matapan. The virtual destruction of the Italian fleet in that encounter eliminated for the rest of the war any surface threat to our domination of Mediterranean waters. On land Wavell made the utmost use of his two winning cards, interior lines and a mobile, well-trained army. Striking first at the Italian army advancing on Cairo, then turning quickly to the south against the enemy forces in Eritrea and Abyssinia he eliminated the Italian threat on land." Field-Marshal The Lord Harding, *Mediterranean Strategy 1939-1945* (Cambridge: Cambridge University Press, 1960), 8.

80. Playfair, *Vol 1, The Mediterranean and Middle East*, 79.

81. *The Rommel Papers*, 104.

82. *War Cabinet Weekly Resume, (No. 71) of the Naval, Military and Air Situation from 12 noon January 2nd, to 12 noon January 9th, 1941*, 9 January 1941. NA, CAB/66/14/29, 6.

83. *The Rommel Papers*, 96. A British War Cabinet report noted, "If British armoured units even in small number appeared to threaten line of retreat, first Italian impulse was to hesitate and then assume defensive instead of trying to break through. Using different methods of surprise bold use of numerically inferior forces worked time after time." *War Cabinet Operations in Libya, Note by the Secretary of State for War.* 16 February 1941. NA, CAB/66/15/5, 1-2.

84. *The Rommel Papers*, 92.

85. *The Rommel Papers*, 97. A British War Cabinet weekly report that "three prominent Blackshirt Commanders made good their escape from Bardia by air or sea, probably during the night the 4th/5th January, deserting their troops

and leaving regular Commanders to fight on...Serious deterioration of morale, which has never been high, appears to have contributed to the Italian defeat. *War Cabinet Weekly Resume, (No. 76) of the Naval, Military and Air Situation from 12 noon February 6th, to 12 noon February 13th, 1941*, 13 February 1941. NA, CAB/66/15/4, 6.

86. *Ciano Diaries*, loc 8022.

CHAPTER 2

87. War Office, *Destruction of an Army. The First Campaign in Libya. Sept. 1940-Feb. 1941* (London: His Majesty's Stationery Office, 1941), 56.

88. Ibid., 56. The Senussi were a Muslim political and religious order that fought against the British in Egypt and the Sudan during World War I. In the interwar years they fought the Italian occupation in Libya and during World War II they supported the British in North Africa.

89. William Boyd Kennedy Shaw revealed that since 1927 he and other desert enthusiasts spent years and travelled by camel, car and aircraft at least forty-five thousand miles in the desert. During the war he served as the intelligence officer for the LRDG from July 1940 until February 1943. W.B. Kennedy Shaw, *Long Range Desert Group. The Story of its Work in Libya 1940-1943* (London: Collins, 1945), 5.

90. Lt.-Col. David Lloyd Owen, *The Desert My Dwelling Place* (London: Cassell and Company Ltd., 1957), 53.

91. John W. Gordon, *The Other Desert War. British Special Forces in North Africa, 1940-1943* (New York: Greenwood Press, 1987), 30.

92. Woollcombe, *The Campaigns of Wavell*, 20.

93. Lloyd Owen, *The Desert My Dwelling Place*, 54.

94. James Stejskal, *Masters of Mayhem. Lawrence of Arabia and the British Military Mission to the Hejaz* (Oxford: Casemate, 2018), 145.

95. Cited in Gordon, *The Other Desert War*, 37.

96. Although the LRDG was initially called the LRPU until November 1940, most memoirs and accounts simply call the unit LRDG from the beginning.

97. Lloyd Owen, *The Desert My Dwelling Place*, 55.

98. The term "cwt" referred to payload rating. It was the abbreviation for "hundred weight" or formerly, "centum weight."

99. Brigadier H.W. Wynter, "The History of the Long Range Desert Group, June 1940-March 1943," in National Archives, *Special Forces in the Desert War* (Kew, UK: National Archives, 2008), 18. Wynter's report was originally written for the Historical Section of the War Cabinet. It is also available at National Archives, CAB 44/151 and CAB 44/152. The first vehicles were 30 cwt. Chevrolet trucks, which were considered excellent. When these wore out and no more were available in March of 1941, they were replaced by 30 cwt. Ford models, which were assessed

as not as efficient or effective. Bagnold calculated 8-10 km per gallon meaning each vehicle had to carry over 350 gallons of petrol, not to mention food and water for the entire patrol. Owen, *Providence Their Guide*, 12.

100.   Cited in Major-General David Lloyd Owen, *Providence Their Guide* (Barnsley, UK: Leo Cooper, 2000), 5.

101.   Kennedy Shaw, *Long Range Desert Group*, 27.

102.   Cited in Gordon, *The Other Desert War*, 34.

103.   Letter, "Officer Commanding. Long Range Desert Group," 10 July 1941. NA, WO 218/89. War Diary of LRDG, July 1941, Appendix A2.

104.   "L.R.D.G.," circa 1942. Churchill Archives Centre, Churchill College, Cambridge, C 8-9.

105.   Kennedy Shaw, *Long Range Desert Group*, 18.

106.   Owen, *Providence Their Guide*, 25.

107.   Malcolm James, *Born of the Desert: With the SAS in North Africa* (London: Greenhill Books, 2001 ed.), 27.

108.   Cited in Sean Rayment, *Tales from the Special Forces Club* (London: Collins, 2016), 46. Major-General Owen asserted, "There was only one punishment and that was more effective than anything that King's Regulations laid down. It was to send the unsatisfactory man back to his unit." Owen, *The Desert My Dwelling Place*, 84.

109.   Rayment, *Tales from the Special Forces Club*, 46.

110.   Owen, *Providence Their Guide*, 12.

111.   Cited in Rayment, *Tales from the Special Forces Club*, 47.

112.   As impressive as the LRDG personnel were, one serving officer acknowledged the outer appearance of the desert warriors. He explained:

> *A stranger meeting a LRDG patrol returning from a month's trip in Libya would have been hard put to it to decide to what race or army, let alone to what unit, they belonged. In winter the use of battle dress made for some uniformity, but in summer, with a month-old beard thick with sand, with a month's dirt (for the water ration allowed no washing), skin burnt to the colour of coffee, and clad in nothing but a pair of torn shorts and chappies (the N[orth].W[est]. Frontier pattern sandals imported by Bagnold) a man looked like a creature from some other world.*

Shaw, *Long Range Desert Group*, 52. Another official report noted the unconventional dress. It recounted that GHQ dispatched an LRDG patrol to rescue a Free French pilot that had crashed and was reported hiding near a well in enemy territory. The LRDG patrol located the well but could not find the pilot. As they were about to leave, he showed himself. It turned out he was reluctant to reveal himself because "he thought that the party of bearded and dishevelled ruffians could not possibly be British troops." "L.R.D.G.," circa 1942. Churchill Archives Centre, Churchill College, Cambridge, C 8-9.

113. Stejskal, *Masters of Mayhem*, 147, 144.

114. Braddock, *The Campaigns in Egypt and Libya*, 6.

115. Kennedy Shaw, *Long Range Desert Group*, 30 & 37.

116. Wynter, "The History of the Long Range Desert Group," 18.

117. Ibid., 20.

118. Kennedy Shaw, *Long Range Desert Group*, 36.

119. War Office, *Destruction of an Army*, 58.

120. *War Cabinet Operations in Libya, Note by the Secretary of State for War.* 16 February 1941. NA, CAB/66/15/5, 1-2.

121. Cited in Gordon, *The Other Desert War*, 59.

122. Ibid., 53.

123. Wynter, "The History of the Long Range Desert Group," 23.

124. War Office, *Destruction of an Army*, 60.

125. Wynter, "The History of the Long Range Desert Group," 37.

126. "The Long-Range Desert Group," *The Fighting Forces,* Vol XIX, No. 3, August 1942, 146.

127. Cited in Kennedy Shaw, *Long Range Desert Group*, 18.

128. Lloyd Owen, *The Desert My Dwelling Place*, 85. Owen recalled, "at one point [we] had to select 12 men from 700 volunteers." Major-General David Lloyd Owen, *The Long Range Desert Group* (London: Leo Cooper, 2000), x.

129. Lloyd Owen, *The Long Range Desert Group* (2000 ed.), x.

130. One German General conceded, "apart from its [LRDG] intelligence and sabotage missions, carried out reconnaissance far behind the Italo-German fronts in Libya. The results obtained in this reconnaissance work formed the basis for the British maps on the Italian colony of Libya, which were incomparably better, so far as quality, accuracy, and detail were concerned, than the Italian maps. The British maps were considered a particularly valuable prize when captured." Major General Alfred Toppe, *Desert Warfare: German Experiences in World War II* (Fort Leavenworth, KA: US Army Command and General Staff College, 1991), 2.

131. Lloyd Owen, *The Desert My Dwelling Place,* 137-138.

132. W.B. Kennedy Shaw, *Long Range Desert Group* (London: Greenhill Books, reprint 1989), 165.

133. Translation of German document, "The British Commando," May 14, 1943. NA, DEFE 2/349.

134. Fitzroy Maclean, *Eastern Approaches* (London: Penguin, 1991), 206.

135. Cited in Lloyd Owen, *Providence Their Guide*, xii.

CHAPTER 3

136. Winston Churchill, *The Second World War. The Grand Alliance* (Toronto: Houghton Mifflin Coy, 1950), 5.

137. Ibid., 19.

138. Ibid., 63.

139. Ibid., 64.

140. Cited in B.H. Liddell Hart, *The German Generals Talk* (New York: Quill, 1979), 155. Von Thoma, after a visit to North Africa in October 1940, concluded that victory would only be possible if Italian troops were replaced by German troops. Both Badoglio and Graziani opposed such an idea as they still held visions of sweeping through Egypt.

141. Braddock, *The Campaigns in Egypt and Libya*, 26; and Strawson, *The Battle for North Africa*, 41.

142. Liddell Hart, *The German Generals Talk*, 47.

143. *Rommel Papers*, xviii.

144. Liddell Hart, *The German Generals Talk*, 497.

145. Churchill, *The Grand Alliance*, 200.

146. Albert Kesselring, *The Memoirs of Field-Marshal Kesselring* (London: Greenhill Books, 1997), 120.

147. Maj. Gen. F.W. Von Mellenthin, *Panzer Battles* (New York: Ballentine Books, 1956), 57.

148. Churchill, *The Grand Alliance*, 58.

149. Ibid., 198.

150. Toppe, *Desert Warfare*, 6. The original two-volume manuscript was written in 1952 by Toppe and nine German commanders who served in North Africa during the war.

151. *The Rommel Papers*, 98.

152. Colonel Ward A. Miller, The 9th *Australian Division Versus the Africa Corps: An Infantry Division Against Tanks – Tobruk, Libya*, 1941 (Fort Leavenworth, Kansas: Combat Institute Studies, 1986), 49.

153. Major-General I.S.O. Playfair, *History of the Second World War. The Mediterranean and Middle East. Volume II "The Germans come to the Help of their Ally (1941)* (London: Her Majesty's Stationery Office, 1956), 13.

154. Cited in Toppe, *Desert Warfare*, 1.

155. *The Rommel Papers*, 101.

156. Kesselring, *The Memoirs of Field-Marshal Kesselring*, 104.

157. *The Rommel Papers*, 100.

158. Lyman, *The Longest Siege*, 81.

159. Miller, *The 9th Australian*, 16.

160. Braddock, *The Campaigns in Egypt and Libya*, 30.

161. Toppe, *Desert Warfare*, 29-30.

162. Von Mellenthin, *Panzer Battles*, 56. Mellenthin also noted, however, that "His [Rommel] custom of 'leading from the front' occasionally told against him; decisions affecting the army as a whole were sometimes influenced unduly by purely local successes or failures." In addition, he conceded, "Rommel was not an easy man to serve; he spared those around him as little as he spared himself. An

iron constitution and nerves of steel were needed to work with Rommel." Ibid., 54.

163. Lyman, *The Longest Siege,* 82.

164. Ibid., 82.

165. Cited in Michael Archer, *Get Rommel. The Secret British Mission to Kill Hitler's Greatest General* (London: Cassell, 2004), 64.

166. Cited in David Fraser, *Knight's Cross. A Life of Field Marshal Erwin Rommel* (New York: HarperCollins Publishers, 1993), 163.

167. *The Rommel Papers,* 92.

168. *Ibid.,* 96. Rommel noted, "The gravest results of the Italian defeat were to their morale. The Italian troops had, with good reason, lost all confidence in their arms and acquired a very serious inferiority complex, which was to remain with them throughout the whole of the war." Ibid., 97.

169. Ibid., 96.

170. Ibid., 92.

171. Historian Robert Woollcombe explained the importance of El Agheila. He described it as "a formidable obstacle, specifically a bottle-neck, which was formed by the sea on one side and a daunting wadi combined with difficult sand terrain inland, which ran towards the sea from the east. The difficult inland travel was further exacerbated by salt marshes which extended from east to west around El Agheila ranging almost to the coast on its west side. El Agheila acted as a threshold to Tripolitania for those advancing West and the gateway to Cyrenaica for those advancing East. Some British commanders considered it 'the strongest position in Libya.'" Woollcombe, *The Campaigns of Wavell,* 79.

172. Churchill, *The Grand Alliance,* 202.

173. Kesselring, *The Memoirs of Field-Marshal Kesselring,* 120.

174. Lyman, *The Longest Siege,* 125.

175. Churchill, *The Grand Alliance,* 205.

176. *War Cabinet Weekly Resume, (No. 83) of the Naval, Military and Air Situation from 12 noon March 27th to* 12 noon April 3rd, 1941, 3 April 1941. NA, CAB/66/16/83, 6.

177. *The Rommel Papers,* 127.

178. Ibid., 130. Even Ciano conceded the failure of the Italian martial spirit and effectiveness. "In eight weeks," he lamented, "our losses amounted to two killed and four wounded out of four thousand men. Notwithstanding that, the surrender [at Debra Tabor, Ethiopia] took place with full honors." *Ciano Diaries,* 15 July 1941, loc 7482.

179. Kesselring, *The Memoirs of Field-Marshal Kesselring,* 106.

180. Toppe, *Desert Warfare,* 32.

181. *The Rommel Papers,* 111.

182. Playfair, *Volume II, The Germans come to the Help,* 20.

183. Churchill, *The Grand Alliance,* 216-217.

184. Ibid., 207.

185. Ibid., 208.

186. The Tobruk garrison consisted of 14,720 Australian, 9,000 British and 5,700 mixed troops of Commonwealth origin. Miller, *The 9ᵗʰ Australian Division*, 12.

187. *War Cabinet Weekly Resume, (No. 85) of the Naval, Military and Air Situation from 12 noon April 10th to 12 noon April 17th, 1941*, 3 April 1941. NA, CAB/66/16/10, 7.

188. Cited in Playfair, *Volume II, The Germans come to the Help*, 41.

189. Cited in ibid., 41.

190. Cited in ibid., 153.

191. Cited in Kenneth Macksey, *Afrika Korps* (New York: Ballantine Books, 1972), 26.

192. Churchill, *The Grand Alliance*, 213.

193. Ibid., 248.

194. Playfair, *Volume II, The Germans come to the Help*, 116.

195. Churchill, *The Grand Alliance*, 249.

196. Cited in Playfair, *Volume II, The Germans come to the Help*, 157.

197. Kesselring, *The Memoirs of Field-Marshal Kesselring*, 113.

198. *The Rommel Papers*, 139. One captured Panzer officer called Tobruk "a witch's cauldron." Cited in Miller, *The 9ᵗʰ Australian*, 43.

199. The Axis had more non-motorized troops than the British. These forces were always vulnerable to surprise Allied offensives. They could only be used to hold defensive positions (e.g., around Tobruk; holding the static Sollum-Sidi Omar line; and holding Bardia. In case of a wide flanking movement it was difficult to withdraw these forces prior to them being cut-off.

200. *The Rommel Papers*, 137.

CHAPTER 4

201. Churchill, *The Grand Alliance*, 338.

202. *The Rommel Papers*, 140.

203. Ibid., 141.

204. Cited Woollcombe, *The Campaigns of Wavell*, 138.

205. Fraser, *Knight's Cross*, 255.

206. Toppe, *Desert Warfare*, 32-33.

207. Cited in Lyman, *The Longest Siege*, 188.

208. Churchill, *The Grand Alliance*, 341.

209. Lyman, *The Longest Siege,* 190. Statistics are always hard to nail down as they differ from source to source. Often times the problem is how individuals categorize casualties and equipment. In any case, Major-General Playfair, (*Volume II "The Germans come to the Help of their Ally*, 171) gave the numbers as: WDF lost – 122 killed, 588 wounded and 259 missing. Four guns lost and of the ninety cruisers and roughly 100 I tanks which began the battle twenty-seven cruisers and sixty-four I

tanks were lost from enemy action or breakdown. RAF lost thirty-three fighters and three bombers. Germans lost ninety-three men killed, 350 wounded and 235 missing. Twelve tanks destroyed approximately fifty damaged. Woollcombe (*The Campaigns of Wavell*, 147) put the three-day battle costs at: British 1,000 casualties, ninety-one tanks totally lost (Rommel stated 220), fifty-nine damaged. Germans – 700 casualties, twelve tanks (Rommel stated twenty-five). Finally, Churchill gives the losses as approximately 1,000 casualties, 150 killed and 250 missing. He stated tank losses were twenty-nine cruiser tanks and fifty-eight "I" Tanks. He states that 100 enemy tanks were destroyed and 570 enemy prisoners taken. Churchill, *The Grand Alliance*, 342.

210. Von Mellenthin, *Panzer Battles*, 53.

211. Barrie Pitt, *The Crucible of War. Auchinleck's Command* (London, Cassell & Co., 1986), xiii.

212. Stephen Hastings, *The Drums of Memory* (South Yorkshire, UK: Leo Cooper, 2001), 32. The "I" or infantry (Matilda) tank was a heavily armoured, slow tank designed to accompany and support the infantry. The "cruiser" tank was an up-gunned, faster but lighter armoured tank designed as a highly mobile fighting platform. The "light" tank was fast but with very thin armour and normally a light gun and / or a machine gun, designed for reconnaissance.

213. Cited in Woollcombe, *The Campaigns of Wavell*, 147.

214. *The Rommel Papers*, 146.

215. War Office, *Destruction of an Army*, 44.

216. Toppe, *Desert Warfare*, 59.

217. Ibid., 76.

218. Cited in Liddell Hart, *The German Generals Talk*, 155.

219. Kesselring, *The Memoirs of Field-Marshal Kesselring*, 105.

220. Ibid., 109. The RN, as well as aircraft from Malta, were increasingly dominating the Mediterranean. At the Battle of Cape Matapan (27-29 March 1941) the British scored a victory but had not yet conclusively gained control of the Sea. Nonetheless, the Italian Navy lost three fast heavy cruisers, two large destroyers and 2,400 men. The British lost one aircraft and its crew. A decisive difference in the battle was the fact that the RN had practiced night fighting with all of its classes of ships for years. However, up to the battle, the Italians had considered night fighting with heavy ships as impractical. Axis convoys suffered heavily in the aftermath. For example, on 16 April 1941, the RN sank an entire convoy off Sfax, Tunisia. The Germans lost 350 men killed and 300 vehicles, as well as 3,500 tons of stores. Lyman, *The Longest Siege*, 85; and Playfair, *Volume II, The Germans come to the Help*, 69.

221. *Ciano Diaries*, 22 November 1941. Loc 8070. Ciano also revealed, "Since September 19 [1941] we had given up trying to get convoys through to Libya; every attempt had been paid for at a high price, and the losses suffered by our merchant marine had reached such proportions as to discourage any further

experiments." Ibid., Loc 7948.

222. Miller, *The 9ᵗʰ Australian Division*, 40; and Strawson, *The Battle for North Africa*, 57.

223. Toppe, *Desert Warfare*, 34.

224. Rowan-Robinson, *Auchinleck to Alexander*, 44.

225. Ibid., 44.

226. Playfair, *Volume II, The Germans come to the Help*, 244.

227. Churchill later wrote, "At home we had the feeling that Wavell was a tired man." Churchill, *The Grand Alliance*, 344.

228. Cited in Strawson, *The Battle for North Africa*, 67. Wavell magnanimously responded, "In think you are wise to make change and get new ideas and action on the many problems in Middle East and am sure Auchinleck will be successful choice." Ibid., 67.

229. Wavell replaced Auchinleck as C-in-C India. In September 1941, the War Office created East African Command, which was directly responsible to the War Office. This change relieved Auchinleck of a distraction with which his predecessor was saddled.

230. Cited in Woollcombe, *The Campaigns of Wavell*, 152.

231. Playfair, *Volume II, The Germans come to the Help*, 263.

232. A German armoured division consisted of one tank regiment of two battalions; one reconnaissance unit, which included an armoured car company; one machinegun battalion, one *Panzerjäger* (tank-hunter) unit; one engineer battalion; and one artillery regiment of three batteries. Major-General I.S.O. Playfair, *The Mediterranean And Middle East, Volume II (September 1941 to September 1942) British Fortunes reach their Lowest Ebb* (London: Her Majesty's Stationery Office, 1960), 29.

233. Cited in Macksey, *Afrika Korps*, 43.

234. Churchill, *The Grand Alliance*, 401.

235. Chester Wilmot, *The Struggle for Europe* (London: Fontana, 1952), 148.

236. Strawson, *The Battle for North Africa*, 79.

237. Auchinleck's demands tried Churchill's patience. The Prime Minister wrote, "Generals only enjoy such comforts in Heaven and those that demand them do not always get there." Cited in Pitt, The *Crucible of War*, 4.

238. For example, by the end of October 1941, 300 British cruiser tanks, 300 American Stuart light tanks, 170 "I" Tanks, 34,000 trucks, 600 field guns, 80 heavy and 160 light anti-aircraft guns, 200 anti-tank guns and 900 mortars arrived in theatre. Playfair, *Vol II, British Fortunes*, 3-4.

239. Strawson, *The Battle for North Africa*, 72. The German fuel shortage sparked concern. One young officer approached Rommel and stated, "Herr General, we need more fuel." Rommel snapped back, "Well, go and get it from the British." Cited in Ibid., 96.

240. Eighth Army consisted of two corps – XIII Corps (4th Indian Infantry

Division, 2nd New Zealand Division and 1st Army Tank Brigade) and XXX Corps (7th Armoured Division, 1st South African Infantry Division, 22nd Guards Brigade, 4th Armoured Brigade Group)

241. Wynter, "The History of the Long Range Desert Group, 87.

242. All elements were in place by November 9, 1941.

243. Letter, Auchinleck to Bagnold, September 29, 1941. Churchill Archives Centre, Churchill College, Cambridge.

244. Letter, "Appreciation of Services," CGS MEF to Bagnold, 25 October 1941. Churchill Archives Centre, Churchill College, Cambridge.

245. Braddock, *The Campaigns in Egypt and Libya*, 47. Exact numbers as mentioned earlier are always contentious depending on the exact date numbers are taken, the category / nomenclature of vehicles used, etc. For instance, Woollcombe places the numbers as: British armour – 700 tanks compared to 314 German tanks. Churchill gives the numbers as 724 British tanks (367 being Cruisers) with another 200 tanks in reserve. See Woollcombe, *The Campaigns of Wavell*, 156; and Churchill, *The Grand Alliance*, 558.

246. Playfair, *Vol II, British Fortunes*, 15. The numbers refer only to serviceable aircraft. In fact, the British had a total of 650 aircraft in Egypt and 74 in Malta, while the Germans had a total of 536 aircraft in the desert.

247. Cited in Pitt, The *Crucible of War*, 36.

248. The lost water was only part of the problem. In order to replenish the stockpile, at one-point fuel for the transport vehicles was consuming 180,000 gallons of gasoline a day. Playfair, *Volume II (September 1941 to September 1942) British Fortunes reach their Lowest Ebb*, 11.

249. Pitt, The *Crucible of War*, 36-37.

250. *The Rommel Papers*, 158.

251. "Intention of General Erwin von [sic] Rommel," October 8, 1941, 38. NA, WO 201/2254, "Appreciation of the Situation by Commander of TOBFORT & General Rommel October 1941.

252. "Appreciation of the situation by General Rommel on 7 October 1941," 41. NA, WO 201/2254, "Appreciation of the Situation by Commander of TOBFORT & General Rommel October 1941.

253. Ibid., 41. Rommel desired to advance first to Sidi Barrani to seize landing grounds to deprive British of forward air bases, and thus, force British bombers to operate from bases further east thereby protecting Tripoli, Benghazi and Derna from heavy air attacks. He anticipated being able to strike by October 21st, "but this is dependent upon no serious interruption of my line of supply by the British. The latter have been uncomfortably successful in interrupting my programme recently so I feel that the margin between 21 Oct and 1 Nov is very narrow."

254. "Appreciation of the situation by General Rommel on 7 October 1941," 41. NA, WO 201/2254, "Appreciation of the Situation by Commander of TOBFORT & General Rommel October 1941.

255. Ibid.

256. Ibid.

257. Ibid.

258. Ibid.

259. Ibid.

260. Ibid.

261. "Appreciation of the Situation by TOBFORT Commander at Tobruk onto Oct 1941," 2. NA, WO 201/2254, "Appreciation of the Situation by Commander of TOBFORT & General Rommel October 1941. Ciano himself questioned the quality of Italian fighting troops. "We receive particulars on the surrender of Debra Tabor [Ethiopia]. In eight-weeks our losses amounted to two killed and four wounded out of four thousand men. Notwithstanding that, the surrender took place with full honors." *Ciano Diaries*, July 16, 1941, loc 7486.

262. "Appreciation of the Situation by TOBFORT Commander at Tobruk onto Oct 1941," 8. NA, WO 201/2254, "Appreciation of the Situation by Commander of TOBFORT & General Rommel October 1941.

263. Churchill, *The Grand Alliance*, 558.

264. *War Cabinet Weekly Resume, (No. 117) of the Naval, Military and Air Situation from 0700 November 20th to 0700 November 27th, 1941*, 27 November 1941. NA, CAB/66/20/13, 5.

265. Ibid.

266. Message, "Eighth Army Operation Instruction No. 18," BGS Eighth Army to CO LRDG, November 11, 41. NA, WO 218/89. War Diary of LRDG, November 1941.

267. One LRDG officer recorded, "Road Watch – send a patrol up near enough to the coast road to take a census of all the traffic that passed along it. ...trial week in September 1941 – day in and day out, for twenty-four hours a day, four hundred miles behind the enemy's line, LRDG made a census of everything that passed along the road." Kennedy Shaw, *Long Range Desert Group* (1945), 209.

268. Lloyd Owen, *The Desert My Dwelling Place,* 208.

269. Kennedy Shaw, *Long Range Desert Group* (1945), 220.

CHAPTER 5

270. Hilary St. George Saunders, *The Green Beret. The Story of the Commandos* (London: Michael Joseph, 1956), 118.

271. Churchill, *Their Finest Hour*, 31-32.

272. Ibid., 32.

273. Ibid., 42.

274. See Christopher Hibbert, "Operation Dynamo," *History of the Second World War*, Part 6, 164; Cesare Salmaggi and Alfredo Pallavisini, *2194 Days of War* (New

York: Gallery Books, 1988), 4 June 1940; I.C.R. Dear, ed., *The Oxford Companion to World War II* (Oxford: Oxford University Press, 1995), 312-313; and A.J. Barker, *Dunkirk: The Great Escape* (London: J.M. Dent & Sons Ltd., 1977), 224. Exact numbers vary between these sources and others but they all reflect the general magnitude. A major problem with determining numbers is the actual categorization / description of weapons and equipment.

275. John Parker, *Commandos. The Inside Story of Britain's Most Elite Fighting Force* (London: Headline Book Publishing, 2000), 15.

276. Cecil Aspinall-Oglander, *Roger Keyes. Being the Biography of Admiral of the Fleet Lord Keyes of Zeebrugge and Dover* (London: Hogarth Press, 1951), 380.

277. Ibid., 380. Vice-Admiral Lord Louis Mountbatten put it in simpler terms. He declared, "We cannot win this war by bombing and blockade alone." Cited in in John Terraine, *The Life and Times of Lord Mountbatten* (London: Arrow Books, 1980), 83.

278. Churchill, *Their Finest Hour*, 243.

279. Ibid., 246-247. The Prime Minister also added the requirement for deep inland raids that left "a trail of German corpses behind." Churchill, *Their Finest Hour*, 246-247. See also Colonel J.W. Hackett, "The Employment of Special Forces," *Royal United Service Institute* (henceforth RUSI), Vol 97, No. 585, February 1952, 28.

280. Major-General Laycock wrote, "After the withdrawal of the British forces from France and Norway and the subsequent occupation by Germany of those and the intervening countries, it became evident that the enemy, by his acquisition of a coast-line stretching from Narvik to Biarritz, had laid himself open to attack by sea-borne raiders." Memorandum, "Memorandum on the Re-Organization of the Commandos," ND, 1. NA, WO 201/731.

281. Cited in Nassir Ghaemi, *A First-Rate Madness* (New York: Penguin Books, 2012), 61.

282. Lieutenant-General Bernard Montgomery, as the XII Corps Commander responsible for home defence of Britain, although not a supporter of special operations forces, realized the value of commando raids. "These raids," he wrote, "even though quite small, are going to give us the opportunity of training our commanders, and staffs in the planning and conduct of actual battle ventures, and our regimental officers and men will begin to smell the battle atmosphere." Lieutenant-General B.L. Montgomery, "Corps Commander's Personal Memoranda to Commanders," 1 November 1941. Department of National Defence (DND) Directorate of History and Heritage (DHH), File 145.3009 (D5), Org and admin correspondence, Jul 42/Dec 44.

283. Colonel D.W. Clarke, "The Start of the Commandos," 30 October 1942, 1. NA, DEFE 2/4, War Diary Combined Operations Command (COC).

284. Memorandum, "Memorandum on the Re-Organization of the Commandos," ND, 1. NA, WO 201/731.

285. Hugh McManners, *Commando. Winning the Green Beret* (London: Network Books, 1994), 7; and "Commandos," *Canadian Army Training Memorandum (CATM)*, No. 20, November 1942, 20.

286. Cited in William Stevenson, *A Man Called Intrepid* (Guilford, Connecticut: The Lyons Press, 2000), 131.

287. D.H. Horner, *SAS: Phantoms of the Jungle. A history of the Australian Special Air Service* (Nashville: The Battery Press, 1989), 22.

288. *Combined Operations. The Official Story of the Commandos* (New York: The Macmillan Company, 1943), 16.

289. Clarke, "The Start of the Commandos," 2.

290. "Early History - Interview with Colonel Dudley Clark," 30 October 1942. NA, DEFE 2/4, War Diary COC; Brigadier Peter Young, *Storm from the Sea* (London: Wrens Park, reprint 2002), 8; *Combined Operations*, 4; Parker, *Commandos,* 19-21; Brigadier John Durnford-Slater, *Commando* (Annapolis: Naval Institute Press, reprint 1991), 14.

291. Clarke, "The Start of the Commandos," 2.

292. *Combined Operations,* 5.

293. See Peter Wilkinson and Joan Bright Astley, *Gubbins and the SOE* (London: Leo Cooper, 1997), 50-68; and *Combined Operations*, 5.

294. Aspinall-Oglander, *Roger Keyes*, 381; Durnford-Slater, *Commando*, 14.

295. "Hand-out to Press Party Visiting The Commando Depot Achnacarry, 9-12 January 1943," 2. NA, DEFE 2/5, War Diary COC [henceforth "Hand-out"].

296. "Hand-out," 2; and Brigadier Peter Young, *Commando* (New York: Ballantine Books, 1969), 12.

297. Durnford-Slater, *Commando,* 15, 20.

298. "Hand-out," 2. Each Commando had a HQ (consisting of 36 all ranks) and ten troops each consisting of three officers and 47 other ranks (ORs).

299. Brigadier T.B.L. Churchill, "The Value of Commandos," *RUSI*, Vol 65, No. 577, February 1950, 85. Colonel William Darby echoed a similar sentiment. "Commanding the Rangers," he asserted, "was like driving a team of very high-spirited horses. No effort was needed to get them to go forward. The problem was to hold them in check." US Brigadier General Bill Yarborough, agreed. He observed, "They were gallant bloodletters. They were fighting machines. They were anything but diplomats, and rejected any suggestion that they ought to be. And they paid little attention to what we might call the more humane qualities, like compassion, pity, and mercy...They were there to cut a swath. Wherever you turned the Rangers and commandos loose, boy, there they would go. There wasn't any question about it." William O. Darby and William H. Baumer, *Darby's Rangers. We Led the Way* (Novato, CA: Presidio Press, reprint 1993), 184; and Tom Clancy with General Carl Stiner, *Shadow Warriors. Inside the Special Forces* (New York: Putnam, 2002), 87.

300. Messenger, *The Commandos*, 411.

301. *Combined Operations*, 7; and Durnford-Slater, *Commando,* 15.

302. Saunders, *The Green Beret*, 29.

303. Cited in Rayment, *Tales from the Special Forces Club*, 110-111.

304. Cited in Will Fowler, *The Commandos at Dieppe: Rehearsal for D-Day* (London: Harper Collins, 2002), 29.

305. Cited in Ibid., 29.

306. Parker, *Commandos*, 65.

307. "Role of the Special Service Brigade and Desirability of Reorganization," 2. NA, DEFE 2/1051, Special Service Brigade; "Organization and Training of British Commandos," Intelligence Training Bulletin No. 3, Headquarters First Special Service Force (FSSF), 11 November 1942, 5. DND DHH, file 145.3009 (D5), Organization and Instructions for the 1st Canadian Special Service Battalion.

308. "Role for the Special Service Brigade...," 3, 10; "Hand-out," 2; and "Commandos," *CATM,* 29.

309. "Notes on Commando Training," 1 November 1942, para 5. NA, DEFE 2/4, War Diary, COC.

310. "Notes on Commando Training," paras 1-18; "Organization and Training of British Commandos...," 4; *Combined Operations*, 6-8; "Role for the Special Service Brigade and Desirability of Reorganization," 10-11; and Saunders, *The Green Beret*, 36-38, 41-42.

311. "Notes on Commando Training," 1 November 1942, paras 1-18; *Combined Operations*, 6-8; and Saunders, *The Green Beret*, 36-38, 41-42.

312. Young, *Commando*, preface.

313. Thompson, *War Behind Enemy Lines*, 2.

314. Churchill, *Their Finest Hour*, 467.

315. "The Role of the Special Service Brigade...," 13.

316. Churchill, *Their Finest Hour*, 165-166; and see also Ronald Lewin, *Churchill as Warlord* (London: B.T. Batsford Ltd., 1973), 51.

317. Churchill, *Their Finest Hour*, 466.

318. Ibid., 467; and Robert W. Black, *Rangers in World War II* (New York: Ivy Books, 1992), 8.

319. "Early History - Interview with Colonel Dudley Clarke."

320. The raid was led by Major R.J.F. Todd and was conducted by No. 11 Commando which was a fictitious organization put together just for this raid. See "Interview with Colonel Dudley Clarke"; *Combined Operations*, 18-21; Saunders, *The Green Beret*, 24-29; Parker, *Commandos*, 22-24; Thompson, *War Behind Enemy Lines*, 3; and Christopher Buckley, *The Commandos. Dieppe* (London: His Majesty's Stationery Office, 1951), 167.

321. Saunders, *The Green Beret*, 30.

322. The raid was led by Lieutenant-Colonel Durnford-Slater and was conducted by elements of No. 3 Commando and No. 11 Independent Company (led by Major Todd). See Durnford-Slater, *Commando*, 22-33; "Interview with Colonel

Dudley Clarke"; *Combined Operations*, 20-21; Saunders, *The Green Beret*, 30-29; Parker, *Commandos*, 24-27; and Thompson, *War Behind Enemy Lines*, 3.

323. Durnford-Slater, *Commando*, 32.

324. Cited in Ibid., 32-33; and Aspinall-Oglander, *Roger Keyes*, 383.

325. "Draft Directive to Director Combined Operations," 12 October 1940. NA, DEFE 2/1, War Diary Independent Companies. See also Rear-Admiral J. Hughes-Hallett, "The Mounting of Raids," *RUSI*, Vol 65, No. 580, November 1950, 581-582.

326. Letter, Roger Keyes to Anthony Eden, 7 October 1940. NA, DEFE 2/1, War Diary Independent Companies.

327. *Combined Operations*, 26; and Young, *Commando*, 15.

328. Cited in Aspinall-Oglander, *Roger Keyes*, 407. See also Fowler, *The Commandos at Dieppe*, 25.

329. Memorandum, "Memorandum on the Re-Organization of the Commandos," ND, 2. NA, WO 201/731.

330. · "Organization and Training of British Commandos...," 2.

331. Memorandum, "Memorandum on the Re-Organization of the Commandos," ND, 2. NA, WO 201/731.

332. In order to accommodate the GLEN ships the Commando establishment was modified – the "new" Commando had a HQ and six troops, each of 65 all ranks instead of the original ten troops of 47 all ranks. This number allowed two troops to fit into two assault landing craft (ALC).

333. "GLEN ships" were infantry landing ships. The 10,000 ton, seventeen knot converted merchantmen GLEN ships had some serious issues according to HQ staff. They were described as "too slow and too vulnerable, their defensive and A/A armament is negligible and they have no offensive power. They present a large and distinctive silhouette and their lowering gear is noisy and can be heard four miles off shore. They cannot operate without escorting destroyers and it is not practical for them to remain within enemy bombing range during hours of daylight unless in company with an A/A cruiser or fighter escort. Their comparatively slow speed and inability to close the beaches seriously reduces the time which landing parties can remain ashore. Memorandum, "Memorandum on the Re-Organization of the Commandos," ND, 1. NA, WO 201/731.

334. 51 ME Commando (originally No. 1 Palestinian Auxiliary Military Pioneer Corps (AMPC) Coy) served with the BEF. It also served in the Sudan. It comprised of a mix of Arabs and Jews. Casualties and sickness and the requirement to dismiss twenty-five percent "as being unsuitable" left the commando undermanned. In addition, it was difficult to find replacements. The caliber of recruit was also questionable. One report noted, "OC the Depot Commando states that the men concerned are on the level of the ordinary Palestinian A.M.P.C. recruit, i.e. only too keen to avoid work and in particular to avoid being sent on operations." 52 ME Commando was formed in 1940 and consisted of soldiers serving in the Middle

East. It had an HQ and three troops with an establishment of 19 officers and 361 ORs. Memorandum, "Commando & Layforce," ADAG, MEF to 'A'G, 31 May 1941. NA, WO 201/716.

335. Brigadier H.W. Wynter (Historical Section of the War Cabinet), *The History of Commandos and Special Service Troops in the Middle East and North Africa January 1941 to April 1943* (Kew, Richmond: National Archives, 2008), 242-243.

336. Memorandum, "Memorandum on the Re-Organization of the Commandos," ND, 2. NA, WO 201/731.

337. Letter, Simpson (GHQ ME) to MacDonald (WO), 19 March 1941.NA, WO 193/405.

338. Minute Sheet, M.O. 1 to DDMO (H), dated 26 November 1941. NA, WO 193/405.

339. Pitt, The *Crucible of War,* 7-8. A subaltern is an officer in the British Army below the rank of captain.

340. Wynter, *The History of Commandos,* 252. Laycock himself faced acrimony for withdrawing on the last ship with his HQ rather than staying with his beleaguered rear-guard. He put his casualties in Crete at 70 percent. Telegram, C-in-C ME to WO, 18 June 1941. NA, WO 193/405.

341. Telegram, C-in-C ME to WO, 18 June 1941. NA, WO 193/405.

342. A staff assessment wrote, "A large number of sea-borne raids were planned, but the majority were postponed for Naval reasons, and only three were carried out. The Naval reasons were bad weather, and shortage of destroyers." "Formation Commandos for Combined Operations. "Note on Commandos," DDO to C-in-C, 11 September 1941, NA, WO 201/731.

343. Telegram, C-in-C ME to WO, 18 June 1941. NA, WO 193/405.

344. Ibid.

345. Message, from C-in-C Mediterranean, 2 July 1941. NA, WO 193/405.

346. Telegram, C-in-C ME to WO, 25 June 1941. NA, WO 193/405.

347. Minute, PM to General Ismay for COS Committee," 23 July 1941. NA, WO 193/405.

348. Minute, S.D.1. to M.O. 5., 23 July 1941. NA, WO 193/405.

349. "Formation Commandos for Combined Operations. Note on Commandos," DDO to C-in-C, 11 September 1941, NA, WO 201/731.

350. Chiefs of Staff Committee, Meeting to be held on 24th July 1941. Note on COS (41). 456, "Glen Ships and Commandos in the Middle East. NA, WO 193/405.

351. Ibid.

352. Minutes, War Cabinet. Chiefs of Staff Committee. Extract from the Minutes of the 267th Meeting, held 30 July, 1941, para 4. NA, WO 193/405.

353. Ibid.

354. Minutes, War Cabinet. Chiefs of Staff Committee. Extract from the Minutes of the 274th Meeting, held 2nd August, 1941, para 4. NA, WO 193/405.

355. Ibid.; and Telegram, WO to C-in-C ME, 18 August 1941. NA, WO 193/405.
356. Minutes, War Cabinet. Chiefs of Staff Committee. Extract from the Minutes of the 274th Meeting, held 2nd August, 1941, para 4. NA, WO 193/405.
357. Message, Sugden (MEF HQ) to Hollis (Offices of the War Cabinet), 25 August 1941. NA, WO 193/405.
358. Memorandum, "Formation ME Commandos," DAG, MEF to Distribution List, 31 August 1941. NA, WO 201/716.
359. Memorandum, "Memorandum on the Reorganization of the Commandos by Col. Laycock," D.O.L., 13 November 1941. NA, WO 201/731.
360. Letter, Laycock to C-inC, ND. NA, WO 201/731.
361. Ibid.

CHAPTER 6

362. Message, CIGS to C-in-C MEF, ND. NA, WO 201/731.
363. "Brief History of 'L' Det. S.A.S. Brigade & 1st S.A.S. Regiment." NA, WO 218/173.
364. Ibid.
365. Cited in John Strawson, *A History of the SAS Regiment* (London: Secker & Warburg, 1985), 14.
366. Cited in Ben MacIntyre, *Rogue Heroes. The History of the SAS, Britain's Secret Special Forces Unit That Sabotaged the Nazis and Changed the Nature of Warfare* (New York: Signal, 2016), 7.
367. Cited in A. Kemp, *The SAS at War* (London: John Murray, 1991), 6.
368. The entire narrative of Stirling's headquarters' escapade is based on Virginia Cowles, *The Phantom Major. The Story of David Stirling and the S.A.S Regiment* (London: St. James Place, 1958), 15.
369. Cited in Gavin Mortimer. *Stirling's Men. The inside history of the SAS in World War II* (London: Cassell, 2004), 13.
370. Colonel David Stirling, "Memorandum on the Origins of the Special Air Service," in Christopher Westhorp, ed., *The SAS Pocket Manual* (London: Conway, 2015), 48.
371. Ibid., 48-49.
372. Cited in Strawson, *A History of the SAS Regiment*, 19.
373. Will Fowler, *SAS Behind Enemy Lines. Covert Operations 1941-2005* (London: HarperCollins, 2005), 17.
374. Clarke went to the extent of dropping dummy parachutists to simulate training exercises near PoW cages and he parked dummy gliders in the desert hoping the German reconnaissance planes would pick up on the aircraft.
375. Stirling, "Memorandum on the Origins...," 51.
376. Major Bill Fraser, "Bill Fraser's War Diary," unpublished memoir, 36. Https://thequietmancunian.com/links/other-projects/bill-fraser---l-detachments.pdf,

accessed 24 May 2021.

377. James, *Born of the Desert*, 5.

378. Elizabeth Keyes, *Geoffrey Keyes* (London: George Newnes Ltd, 1956), 186.

379. Stirling was allowed to visit "C" Bn Layforce in Cyprus to "see if there are any volunteers for a special S.S. unit, which he is forming. Any officers or other ranks who volunteer and who can be spared by you, will be replaced provided 'C' Bn is not disbanded." Stirling was also given authority to interview all personnel from the disbanding Layforce battalions who requested to remain with a Command unit. Memorandum, "Volunteers for special S.S. Unit," DAG, MEF to OC 'C' Bn Layforce, August 8, 1941. NA, WO 201/716.

380. Hastings, *The Drums of Memory*, 46.

381. Stiirling, "Memorandum on the Origins...," 51. Stirling himself did not help his cause. He continually avoided following procedure and the chain-of-command and often deliberately used vagueness and deception to achieve his needs. For example, GHQ continually wasted time trying to sort through his schemes. One simple example demonstrated between the correspondence between ME GHQ and the Eighth Army demonstrate: "We have been in great difficulty during the last thirty-six hours over an alleged parachute operation which you have in view. Sterling [sic] appears to have told someone in RAF ops about it, but of course not the right man. Sterling never breathed a word of it to anybody on the Ops side here. Sterling's RAF confidant made arrangements for converting the aircraft but did nothing about telling any of his colleagues or about planning the operation. The result was that yesterday they turned on us for information as to the number of men to be dropped, the weight of stores, the mileage and so on, all of which was essential for them to know if they were to fit out the aircraft properly. We all know sterling's weakness for laying on his plans by the queerest methods. His ideas of organisation ae elementary to say the least of it. I have an idea moreover, that he is apt to think out his own operations, try to lay them on without any authority form your HQ and then come and offer it to us on a plate. He probably tells you that it is all arranged at this end, whereas, in point of fact nothing has been laid on except by verbal arrangement with him and then we have a frightful period much as is now going on. I fully realize the need for extreme secrecy in this type of operation, nevertheless, the present system cannot continue. I am therefore arranging with RAF that they will not deal with Sterling direct unless he is armed with a written request from G(Ops) GHQ." The Eighth Army reply attempted to placate the GHQ staff officers: "Stirling arranging things on his own outside normal procedures in this case attempting to acquire modified aircraft. Eighth Army HQ had to smooth things over with GHQ. 'I am sorry you had all this bother...I entirely agree with you that a repetition of these muddles must be prevented and I have sent for Sterling [sic] to report here on his return, when I shall make the new procedure clear to him. I hope it will work, but I have found that his natural impetuousness and importunity makes it difficult for him to stick

to any procedure!'" Letter, Lieutenant-Colonel Jennings, GHQ MEF to Colonel Thurburn HQ Eighth Army, 30 December 1941. NA, WO 201/2261; and Letter, Thurburn Eighth Army HQ to Jennings GHQ MEF, 31 December 1941. NA, WO 201/2261.

382. Hastings, *Drums of Memory*, 52.

383. Jon E. Lewis, *The Mammoth Book of Covert Ops* (Philadelphia: Running Press, 2014), 251.

384. Maclean, *Eastern Approaches*, 191.

385. "Brief History of 'L' Det. S.A.S. Brigade & 1st S.A.S. Regiment." NA, WO 218/173. The history also revealed, "Members of the unit have walked back many miles of desert on foot in order to rejoin the unit & carry on offensive operations. These walks meant possibly 100 or more miles without food or water & any slight error in navigation may have meant starvation or certain death through lack of water."

386. Maclean, *Eastern Approaches*, 195.

387. Major "Bill Fraser's War Diary," 38.

388. Stirling, "Memorandum on the Origins...," 50; and Cowles, *The Phantom Major*, 39.

389. McIntyre, *Rogue Heroes,* 48.

390. Cited in Cowles, *The Phantom Major*, 40.

391. Lloyd Owen, *Providence Their Guide*, 61.

392. Rayment, *Tales from the Special Forces Club*, 111.

393. Cited in Cowles, *The Phantom Major*, 15.

CHAPTER 7

394. Message, "Eighth Army Operation Instruction No. 18," BGS Eighth Army to CO LRDG, 11 Nov 41. NA, WO 218/89. War Diary of LRDG, November 1941.

395. Cited in Cowles, *The Phantom Major*, 40.

396. Cited in Gordon, *The Other Desert War*, 83.

397. Cited in Cowles, *The Phantom Major*, 41.

398. "Bill Fraser's War Diary," 39.

399. Gordon Gaskill, "Toughest Job in the War," *The American Magazine*, July 1942, reproduced in Christopher Westhorp, ed., *The SAS Pocket Manual* (London: Conway, 2015), 70.

400. Kennedy Shaw, *Long Range Desert Group* (1945), 121.

401. Cited in Mortimer, *Stirling's Men*, 23.

402. Cited in Strawson, *A History of the SAS Regiment*, 27.

403. Asher, *Get Rommel*, 215.

404. Stirling, "Memorandum on the Origins, 53.

405. Cited in James, *Born of the Desert*, 21-23.

406. Mortimer, *Stirling's Men*, 24.
407. Cited in Asher, *Get Rommel*, 218.
408. Stirling's account given to his biographer Virginia Cowles. Cowles, *The Phantom Major*, 40-41.
409. Cited in Mortimer, *Kill Rommel*, 73.
410. James, *Born of the Desert*, 21-23.
411. Cited in Mortimer, *Stirling's Men*, 24.
412. Cited in Ibid., 26.
413. Cited in Ibid., 26.
414. "Recce Report No. 20 (R1 Patrol), 26 November 1941." NA, WO 218/89. War Diary of LRDG, November 1941.
415. Maclean, *Eastern Approaches,* 191.
416. Stirling, "Memorandum on Origins," 53. A heavy bomber raid on Gazala and the Tmini area was conducted, including the dropping of numerous flares so that the parachute-dropping aircraft could establish a point on the coast line from which the navigators could determine a fixed line bearing for the drop zone (DZ). The high winds and subsequent sand storms negated this effort.
417. Cited in Asher, *Kill Rommel*, 302.
418. Maclean, *Eastern Approaches*, 193.
419. Cited in Asher, *Kill Rommel*, 304.

CHAPTER 8

420. Cited in Richard Mead, *Commando General. The Life of Major General Sir Robert Laycock KCMG, CB, DSO* (Barnsley, UK: Pen & Sword, 2016), 53.
421. Layforce was tasked with providing a rear guard to hold the Germans back while the Allied forces withdrew south to Sphakia for evacuation by sea. A controversy later erupted when Laycock and part of his headquarters decided to withdraw, leaving the better part of his force to fight on and eventually be captured by the Germans. Only approximately 200 of the 800 Layforce commandos that landed on Crete were eventually withdrawn. Allegations that Laycock abandoned his troops and withdrew against orders quickly surfaced and hounded Laycock for years after the war.
422. Laycock is described in different sources as both colonel and lieutenant-colonel. However, Laycock himself signed off his after-action reports on January 5, 1942 as lieutenant-colonel. By March of that year, he was promoted to brigadier.
423. In October 1941, MEF HQ placed the ME Commandos (six officers and fifty-three ORs) under operational command of the Eighth Army.
424. Keyes was replaced by Lord Louis Mountbatten in October 1941, who was given the title "Chief Advisor of Combined Operations" and the rank of acting Commodore. Approximately, six months later in April 1942, Churchill, desperate

for offensive action, appointed Mountbatten the Chief of Combined Operations and promoted him to the rank of Vice-Admiral, as well as the equivalent honorary rank of Lieutenant-General in the Army and Air Marshal in the Air Force. Churchill also made him a de facto member of the Chiefs of Staff Committee. As such, Mountbatten was the only individual other than the King to have rank in all three Services. "Commandos," *Canadian Army Training Memorandum* (*CATM*), No. 20, November 1942, 20.

425. Cited in Keyes, *Geoffrey Keyes*, 135.

426. The assault landing was originally set for 0400 hours on July 8th. However, reasons for delay have both been given for rough seas, and another account stated that the French Vichy Navy intercepted the British 15th Cruiser Squadron that comprised three cruisers, eight destroyers and the Glengyle. As a result, the landing was postponed until the Vichy Navy vessels were dispersed.

427. Captain Tommy MacPherson wrote on October 4, 1941, "A red letter day! Today Geoffrey found a great idea and we began to put it over – it will be a fight." He later wrote to Keyes' family and recounted, "[Geoffrey] burst radiantly into our orderly room after a promising visit to headquarters and said 'If we get this job, Tomm, it's one people will remember us by." Cited in Gavin Mortimer, *Kill Rommel! Operation Flipper 1941* (Oxford: Osprey, 2014), 14.

428. Cited in Asher, *Get Rommel*, 83.

429. Orders, "'Flipper,' Operation Order Number One, The Scottish Commando (8th Army Operation Instruction No. 12. Naval Operation Order 'Copper')" LRDG, 11 November 1941. NA, DEFE 2/349.

430. Ibid.

431. "Telephone Message from BGS 8 Army to DDO," October 18, 1941. NA, WO 201/731.

432. Orders, "'Flipper,' Operation Order Number One, The Scottish Commando (8th Army Operation Instruction No. 12. Naval Operation Order 'Copper')" LRDG, November 11, 1941. NA, DEFE 2/349. The submarines could only accommodate 28 raiders and their equipment per vessel.

433. The rubber boats used were Royal Engineer reconnaissance two-man dinghies. The submarines carried eighteen of these boats deflated in their bags. Fourteen were for the operation with four as spare. "Report on Operations 'Copper and 'Flipper' – 20 October -24 November, 1941," 12 March 1942. NA, DEFE 2/349.

434. Orders, "'Flipper,' Operation Order Number One, The Scottish Commando (8th Army Operation Instruction No. 12. Naval Operation Order 'Copper')" LRDG, November 11, 1941. NA, DEFE 2/349. Upon a successful landing, Mae Wests were to be fastened to rubber boats, which were to be tied to a grass-line and towed back out to the submarines.

435. Orders, "'Flipper,' Operation Order Number One, The Scottish Commando (8th Army Operation Instruction No. 12. Naval Operation Order 'Copper')" LRDG, November 11, 1941. NA, DEFE 2/349. See also, "Supplementary Report

on Operation Flipper," 5 January 1942. NA, WO 201/720, Lt. Col. Laycock's Report on Operation Flipper.

436. Orders, "'Flipper,' Operation Order Number One, The Scottish Commando (8th Army Operation Instruction No. 12. Naval Operation Order 'Copper')" LRDG, November 11, 1941. NA, DEFE 2/349.

437. Ibid.

438. Ibid.

439. Ibid.

440. Minute Sheet, "ME Commandos," DDMT to DDO, October 2, 41. NA, WO 201/731.

441. Wynter, "The History of the Long Range Desert Group, 419. Haselden was eventually promoted to the rank of lieutenant-colonel. He was subsequently killed during the raid on Tobruk on September 13/14, 1942.

442. The Admiralty planners deemed Ras-el- Hilal as the best location based on the protection it provided for a safe landing based on the weather, particularly the winds, at that time of year. It also had good exits from the beach and the surrounding country afforded cover for the raiders during the approach. "Report on Operations 'Copper and 'Flipper' – 20 October -24 November, 1941," 12 March 1942. NA, DEFE 2/349.

443. The other G(R) officers were Bob Melot, Bill Chapman and an officer under training named Westall.

444. One of the participants of the raid, Lieutenant Tommy Macpherson, revealed, "Laycock was in our eyes a 'society cavalryman,' with a close and exclusive interest in his own career: he was a bullshitter of the highest order. For him the Rommel Raid was a no-lose situation. If it was successful then by going along he would get the credit, and if it wasn't then by staying on the beach, he would almost certainly be in a position to get out." Cited in Asher, *Get Rommel*, 92.

445. Mead, *Commando General*, 111.

446. Cited in Keyes, *Geoffrey Keyes*, 204.

447. Cited in Ibid., 210. See also Asher, *Get Rommel*, 102 & 180. Miers had the unfortunate nickname "Crap Miers."

448. Cited Keyes, *Geoffrey Keyes*, 210.

449. Cited in Mortimer, *Kill Rommel!*, 27-28.

450. Lieutenant-Colonel Laycock later wrote in his official report, "Capt. Haselden's activities were invaluable and that his calculated daring and physical endurance are worthy of the highest praise." Lieutenant-Colonel Laycock, "Supplementary Report on Operation Flipper," January 5, 1942, 2. NA, WO 201/720, File: Lt. Col Laycock's Report on Operation Flipper.

451. Lieutenant-Colonel Laycock, "Supplementary Report on Operation Flipper," January 5, 1942, 2. NA, WO 201/720, File: Lt. Col Laycock's Report on Operation Flipper.

452. Cited in Asher, *Get Rommel*, 183.

453. "HMS Torbay Report of Seventh Mediterranean War Patrol," ND. NA, ADM 236/32.

454. Cited Keyes, *Geoffrey Keyes*, 214.

455. Cited in Asher, *Get Rommel*, 193.

456. "Report on Operations 'Copper and 'Flipper' – 20 October -24 November, 1941," March 12, 1942. NA, DEFE 2/349.

457. "HMS Talisman – Report of 4th Mediterranean War Patrol," ND. NA, ADM 236/32.

458. "Report on G(R) Activity in Cyrenaica Conducted by Capt. J.F. Haselden and Party," December 1941. NA, DEFE 2/349. Captain Haselden reported only four others making it to shore from the *Talisman*.

459. A grass-line is a "rope made of coir [coconut fibre], not particularly strong but which has the useful property of floating on the surface of the water. It had several uses at sea before synthetic rope superseded natural fibre, particularly in cases of rescue and salvage, when a grass-line floated down across the bows of a disabled ship in rough weather could be easily picked up and used to haul across a towing cable." Taken from http://oxfordindex.oup.com/view/10.1093/oi/authority.20110803095904347, accessed September 10, 2020.

460. Cited in Keyes, *Geoffrey Keyes*, 221.

461. Cited in Ibid., 217.

462. Lieutenant-Colonel Laycock, "Supplementary Report on Operation Flipper," January 5, 1942, 4. NA, WO 201/720, File: Lt. Col Laycock's Report on Operation Flipper.

463. Cited in Keyes, *Geoffrey Keyes,* 221.

464. Haselden, later promoted to lieutenant-colonel, died on 7 August 1942 while leading a raid on the German occupied port of Tobruk. He led a group of German-speaking Austrian Jews from the Middle East Commandos, as well as some members of the SAS. They entered the German lines in three trucks filled with "British prisoners-of-war." Once inside the German port they wreaked havoc until they were all killed or captured. Only four individuals escaped back to British lines in Egypt.

465. Cited in Keyes, *Geoffrey Keyes*, 222.

466.
 Ibid., 223.

467. Cited in Asher, *Kill Rommel*, 227.

CHAPTER 9

468. Cited in Asher, *Kill Rommel*, 235.

469. Cited in Keyes, *Geoffrey Keyes*, 227-228.

470. Ibid., 230.

471. Cited in Ibid., 230.

472. Accounts differ on the number of Germans in the room. A German report notes there were five. Allied accounts cite ten.

473. Pitt, The *Crucible of War*, 41. In the aftermath the German report on attack, as well as some scholarly work in the aftermath, points to the conclusion that both British officers were shot by their own men. For example, see Asher, *Kill Rommel*, 256, 258.

474. Cited Keyes, *Geoffrey Keyes*, 232-234.

475. Cited in Ibid., 234.

476. In his supplementary report Laycock stated, "While he was attending to him [Keyes] Capt. Campbell was hit by a stray bullet which broke his lower leg." It is not clear if Laycock was confused on the circumstances, or whether he chose to cover-up the friendly fire incident. Lieutenant-Colonel Laycock, "Supplementary Report on Operation Flipper," January 5, 1942, 5. NA, WO 201/720, File: Lt. Col Laycock's Report on Operation Flipper.

477. Cited in Asher, *Kill Rommel*, 279.

478. Cited in Keyes, *Geoffrey Keyes*, 241. Cooke was captured and sent to an Italian prisoner of war camp. He escaped, was shot in the leg and was recaptured. The Italian colonel commandant was so incensed by the escape that he shot Cooke and another escapee. Cooke, however, survived and testified against the Italian colonel after the war.

479. Cited in Ibid., 237-238. Awad complained in 1945, that as a result of his assistance he had to flee into the desert and the Italians confiscated all his cattle.

480. The Carabinieri are the national gendarmerie of Italy. Their primarily function is to conduct domestic policing duties. The Arma dei Carabinieri, also commonly known as "Carabinieri' are also Military Police for the Italian Armed Forces.

481. The term "folbot" was derived from the name of the company that manufactured the boat at the time.

482. A major problem Laycock later revealed was the fact that the raiding party had no engineers or signalers with them. When Layforce was disbanded the specialists were removed. When the ME Commando was established, from the remnants of Layforce, no specialists were attached. As such, the raiders had only rudimentary instruction in explosives. Also, Laycock was the only one capable of sending Morse Code but he had to use a flashlight and use the on / off button to send the messages so he was unsure how readable they were.

483. Miers later indirectly criticized Laycock's decision. He stated, "the failure to re-embark was unfortunate but could have been avoided if the officer in charge on the beach had been prepared to let the men abandon their arms and equipment and swim a distance of fifty yards." "HMS Torbay Report of Seventh Mediterranean War Patrol," ND. NA, ADM 236/32.

484. "Report on G(R) Activity in Cyrenaica Conducted by Capt. J.F. Haselden and Party," December 1941. NA, DEFE 2/349.

485. Cited in Keyes, *Geoffrey Keyes*, 245.

486. Cited in Ibid., 245.

487. Cited in Mortimer, *Kill Rommel*, 58.

488. Cited in Asher, *Kill Rommel*, 297.

489. Pryor later learned that the commando who accompanied him was shot point blank by an Arab when he tried to surrender.

490. Lieutenant-Colonel Laycock, "Supplementary Report on Operation Flipper," 5 January 1942, 9-11. NA, WO 201/720, File: Lt. Col Laycock's Report on Operation Flipper. Laycock's account differs significantly from that of others with regard to the presence of Germans, the numbers of Italians or the force in total, as well as the amount of rifle fire. Elizabeth Keyes in her account explains the difference due to Laycock having binoculars which gave him a better view of the battlefield. Another explanation could be that he exaggerated the amount of enemy force and action to avoid more criticism as he was disparaged for his escape from the besieged battle of Crete, when he was ordered to fight the rearguard but instead left part of his force behind and joined the evacuation.

491. Cited in Keyes, *Geoffrey Keyes*, 247.

492. Cited in Ibid., 254.

493. Cited in Ibid., 254.

494. The submarine skippers demonstrated commendable perseverance. They were under strict orders to ensure that "the safety of their submarine is in any way prejudiced." In fact, the Admiralty stressed, "The decision of the Commanding Officer of a submarine is final in this respect and overrides any military consideration." NA, ADM 236/32, "Operation Copper," November 9, 1941.

495. Admiral A.B. Cunningham, the Commander-in-Chief Mediterranean Station, assessed, "This difficult operation [Operation Flipper] was hampered throughout by unfavourable weather. It was, nevertheless, carried out with most commendable determination by all concerned, and might well have had far-reaching results. The good co-operation of the Naval and Military units concerned was most satisfactory." *Torbay* returned to Alexandria on November 24th. "Report on Operations 'Copper and 'Flipper' – 20 October -24 November, 1941," 12 March 1942. NA, DEFE 2/349.

496. "HMS Torbay Report of Seventh Mediterranean War Patrol," ND. NA, ADM 236/32.

497. Apparently, one of the Italian aligned Arabs told Drori that they were about to withdraw when they saw the raiders break and run. Cited in Keyes, *Geoffrey Keyes*, 248.

498. Cited in Ibid., 248.

499. Cited in Ibid., 268.

500. Extract from the *War Diary of the Panzer Gruppe Afrika O.Q. Department*, dated 18 November 1941, cited in Keyes, *Geoffrey Keyes*, 268. A German circular on Commandos provided an example of a raid (albeit very inaccurate). It stated,

"November 15th 1941, three days after the British offensive in Libya, a 'Commando' composed of 310 men disembarked 350 kilometers from the interior of the Italo-German lines. Its task was to kill or capture General Rommel. On the night of the 17th and 18th, it approached the known point (P.C.) making use of a river-bed. It penetrated into Headquarters and did not find the General who was away for the day. The whole Headquarters was aroused, the British had to retreat under the protective fire of some automatic arms. The survivors re-assembled at the point arranged beforehand then in two they sought refuge in the Djebel Akhdar before rejoining the British lines." Translation of German document, "Commando," 14 May 1943. NA, DEFE 2/349.

501. Cited in Keyes, *Geoffrey Keyes*, 270.

502. Cited in Ibid., 270.

503. Cited in Mortimer, *Kill Rommel*, 65.

504. *The Rommel Papers*, 156.

505. Ibid., 67.

506. Cited in Wynter, "The History of the Long Range Desert Group," 424.

507. Mortimer, *Kill Rommel*, 69.

508. Many point to an intelligence failure. Because of the Allied ULTRA capability, intercepted German messages using their Enigma coding machines clearly revealed on 2 November that Rommel had left for Rome. On 14 November, the last day the raiders had contact with GHQ there was still no word that Rommel had returned to North Africa. As such, regardless of location, there was no chance of capturing or killing Rommel. See Asher, *Kill Rommel*, 274.

509. Two German officers and two German soldiers were also killed.

510. See Appendix 1 for Lieutenant-Colonel Keyes' VC citation.

511. Cited in Asher, *Kill Rommel*, 321.

512. Mead, *Commando General*, 114. Rommel was known to have spent a night or two at the villa according to German sources. Mortimer, *Kill Rommel*, 43.

513. In fact, Laycock wrote in his official report, "It is however particularly unfortunate that General Rommel himself was absent attending a birthday party in Rome." Lieutenant-Colonel Laycock, "Supplementary Report on Operation Flipper," 5 January 1942, 5. NA, WO 201/720, File: Lt. Col Laycock's Report on Operation Flipper.

514. Rowan-Robinson, *Auchinleck to Alexander*, 36.

515. Playfair, *Vol II, British Fortunes*, 22.

516. Cited in Asher, *Get Rommel*, 171. She also wrote "But Geoffrey was far too realistic to suppose that a man of General Rommel's type could be captured and marched across country to be embarked in a submarine. He... told his men they were going to 'get Rommel' – a very different story ... He can have been under no illusions as to the possibility of taking prisoners under such conditions. He himself never expected to get back."

CHAPTER 10

517. Cited in Pitt, *The Crucible of War*, 44.

518. "War Cabinet Weekly Résumé (No. 117) of the Naval, Military and Air Situation from 0700 November 20th, to 0700 November 27th, 1941.NA, CAB 66/20/13.

519. Pitt, *The Crucible of War*, 43. Each brigade required 1,000 vehicles to carry personnel, equipment, weapons and munitions. With tactical spacing this created a tail 160 km long and took six and a half hours to pass any given point.

520. *The Rommel Papers*, 158. Liddell Hart's editorial comment. There is a substantial difference in numbers between sources. The *Rommel Papers* put the British at 724 tanks with 200 in reserve and Rommel with 414 (which included 154 Italian tanks) no reserve but fifty in repair at the start of the offensive.

521. Rowan-Robinson, *Auchinleck to Alexander*, 39.

522. Churchill, *The Grand Alliance*, 560.

523. "War Cabinet Weekly Résumé (No. 117) of the Naval, Military and Air Situation from 0700 November 20th, to 0700 November 27th, 1941.NA, CAB 66/20/13.

524. Pitt, *The Crucible of War*, 44.

525. "War Cabinet Weekly Résumé (No. 116) of the Naval, Military and Air Situation from 0700 November 13th, to 0700 November 20th, 1941.NA, CAB 66/19/49.

526. "War Cabinet Weekly Résumé (No. 117) of the Naval, Military and Air Situation from 0700 November 20th, to 0700 November 27th, 1941.NA, CAB 66/20/13.

527. Ibid.

528. Ibid.

529. Ibid.

530. Ibid.

531. Von Mellenthin, *Panzer Battles*, 63.

532. *The Rommel Papers*, 156. Determining definitive numbers is always difficult as sources always vary. Part of the problem is the numbers represent a snapshot in time and depending when that "snapshot" is taken the numbers will vary due to breakdowns, losses and simple reporting error. In addition, numbers provided by the opponent are quite often exaggerated (both enemy strength and enemy losses).

533. "War Cabinet Weekly Résumé (No. 117) of the Naval, Military and Air Situation from 0700 November 20th, to 0700 November 27th, 1941.NA, CAB 66/20/13.

534. Ibid.

535. "War Cabinet Weekly Résumé (No. 120) of the Naval, Military and Air Situation from 0700 December 11th, to 0700 December 18th, 1941.NA, CAB 66/20/24.

536. Ibid.

537. Ibid.

538. Pitt, *The Crucible of War*, 64.

539. Lloyd Owen, *The Desert My Dwelling Place*, 109.

540. "War Cabinet Weekly Résumé (No. 117) of the Naval, Military and Air Situation from 0700 November 20th, to 0700 November 27th, 1941.NA, CAB 66/20/13.

541. The Tobruk Garrison, which had been ordered to make a sortie at dawn, was making slow progress towards Sidi Rezegh. Their push had been preceded by a successful feint attack by British and Polish infantry on the western sector, intended to cover the real point of exit on the eastern perimeter. However, strong opposition from German infantry as well as extensive minefields on the eastern flank slowed down the advance. Nonetheless, the Allies captured 1,100 prisoners, half of them German. "War Cabinet Weekly Résumé (No. 117) of the Naval, Military and Air Situation from 0700 November 20th, to 0700 November 27th, 1941.NA, CAB 66/20/13.

542. Cited in Pitt, *The Crucible of War*, 90.

543. Ibid., 37.

544. Ibid., 37, 41.

545. Von Mellenthin, *Panzer Battles*, 88.

546. Cited in ibid., 88.

547. Fraser, *Knight's Cross*, 287.

548. *The Rommel Papers*, 163.

549. German Major General Alfred Toppe later provided an analysis of why Rommel was so successful in the desert. He explained, "In desert warfare a unit commanded from a rear HQ runs the risk of being encircles and annihilated. To a large extent, Rommel's victories were based on the fact that he realized these tactical necessities of desert warfare and consistently acted accordingly, while the British adhered strictly to orders that they had received a long time previously and were no longer applicable to the existing situation." Toppe, *Desert Warfare,* 72.

550. Cited in Pitt, *The Crucible of War*, 118.

551. Lloyd Owen, *Providence Their Guide*, 61. At the time, Captain Owen commanded the Yeomanry Patrol of the LRDG.

552. Ibid., 62.

553. Churchill, *The Grand Alliance*, 569.

554. Cunningham flew back to Cairo on the same aircraft that brought Richie. Subsequently, he was admitted to the hospital for severe exhaustion.

555. Von Mellenthin, *Panzer Battles*, 90.

556. Lloyd Owen, *The Desert My Dwelling Place*, 89.

557. "LRDG. Mid-November Operations in Cyrenaica. Operation Instruction No. 22, 24 November 1941." NA, WO 218/89. War Diary of LRDG, November 1941.

558. Ibid.

559. Lloyd Owen, *The Desert My Dwelling Place*, 110.

560. Kennedy Shaw, *Long Range Desert* Group (1945), 113; and "Some Account of the Part Played by LRDG in the operations of 8 Army in Cyrenaica in November – December 1941. Period Nov. 1 – Dec. 6." NA, WO 218/89. War Diary of LRDG, November 1941.

561. Churchill, *The Grand Alliance*, 568.

562. Von Mellenthin, *Panzer Battles*, 66.

563. Ibid., 96.

564. Ibid., 97.

565. Ibid., 98.

566. Ibid., 68.

567. Cited in Pitt, *The Crucible of War*, 146.

568. *The Rommel Papers*, 170.

569. Cited in Pitt, *The Crucible of War*, 142.

570. *The Rommel Papers*, 171.

571. Cited in Fraser, *Knight's Cross,* 300.

572. The Sollum front / Halfaya Sector was still holding out, although it was 192 km from the main force of the Afrika Korps. The last vestiges of the German position in the Halfaya Sector held out until January 17, 1942. Cut-off, starving, with exhausted supplies of water and stores, they were forced to surrender. The main German disposition to the West, in its main defensive position now extended from Gazala for some forty km to the south. The main position around Gazala was defended with a tank detachment astride the Trigh El Abd trail. The remaining Axis armoured forces, estimated by the British to be only approximately fifty tanks and wheel-borne infantry were positioned in the centre of the defensive position approximately 19 km south of Gazala. "War Cabinet Weekly Résumé (No. 120) of the Naval, Military and Air Situation from 0700 December 11th, to 0700 December 18th, 1941.NA, CAB 66/20/24.

573. Playfair, Vol II, *British Fortunes*, 91.

574. *The Rommel Papers*, 175.

575. Ciano confided to his diary on December 17th, "Things are not going well in Libya. Even Mussolini is beginning to admit it, and blames Rommel, who he believes, spoiled the situation with his recklessness." *Ciano Diaries*, December 17, 1941, loc 8250.

576. On January 5th, a resupply convoy arrived in Tripoli carrying fifty-five tanks, twenty armoured cars, anti-tank guns and other supplies. Not surprisingly, Rommel immediately began to think of a new offensive.

577. Strawson, *The Battle for North Africa*, 77.

578. Cited in Pitt, *The Crucible of War*, 152.

579. Churchill, *The Grand Alliance*, 575. Historian David Wilson Braddock concluded, "Statistically, the British also appear to have come out of Operation

Crusader as the victors. Between November 1941 and January 1942, the 8th Army lost 17,700 men, approximately 15 percent of the number engaged. Conversely, the Germans suffered 38,300 casualties or 32 percent of their total strength." Braddock, *The Campaigns in Egypt and Libya*, 71.

580. Wynter, "The History of the Long Range Desert Group, 119.

581. Wynter, *The History of Commandos...*, 311-315; and Mortimer, *Stirling's Men*, 30-35.

582. The outcome of the North African campaign took almost another eighteen months. The German U-boat campaign in the Mediterranean became very effective. Combined with Italian frogmen in human torpedoes planting time-bombs on battleships in Alexandria harbour and minefields, the Axis badly damaged the Mediterranean fleet. Churchill lamented to the House of Commons "in a few weeks we lost, or had put out of action for a long time, seven great ships, or more than a third of our battleships and battle-cruisers." He explained, "Up to the end of November our combined efforts by land, sea and air had prevailed in the Mediterranean. We had now suffered fearful naval losses." On December 5th, Hitler had ordered the transfer of a whole air corps from Russia to Sicily and North Africa. The Luftwaffe now held mastery of sea routes to Tripoli, allowing Rommel to refit his army. In addition, on the same day, Rommel received additional tanks and fuel. He then pre-empted General Auchinleck's plan to attack Tripolitania by launching another offensive on January 21st. Although this attack ran out of steam, he again took the offensive on June 20th and seized Tobruk the following day. The garrison of 25,000 men, as well as enormous stocks of supplies fell into German hands. Three days later Rommel crossed the border and continued the advance arriving in front of the British El Alamein defensive positions on June 28th. His troops were now exhausted and he had only fifty serviceable tanks. Moreover, the El Alamein positions were better fortified than any previous defensive lines the Germans had faced. The El Alamein battle commenced at 2300 hours on October 23, 1942. The Eighth Army had 1,200 tanks against 200 German and 250 Italian (which were of little value) tanks. Allied air superiority was ten to one and the Allies had overwhelming superiority in artillery and ammunition. The Eighth Army held at El Alamein and then launched a counter-attack which drove Rommel out of Cyrenaica. On November 8, 1942, as part of Operation Torch, the Allies landed 65,000 troops at Casablanca, Oran and Algiers. On November 28, 1942, Rommel flew to Hitler's HQ and unsuccessfully argued that the African theatre of operations should be abandoned. Under continuing pressure Rommel abandoned Tripoli on January 23, 1943 and withdrew to Tunisia. Rommel launched his final offensive in Africa on March, 6, 1943. Three days later, Rommel, who was extremely ill returned to Germany. He never returned to Africa. With an ever-tightening naval blockade and a massive superiority on ground and land, the Allies drove the Axis forces into the Cap Bon Peninsula in Tunisia. All resistance ended May 13th, 1943. Churchill, *The Grand Alliance*, 577; and Toppe, *Desert*

Warfare, 45-56.

CHAPTER 11

583. Cohen, *Commandos and Politicians*, 95.

584. Damien Lewis, *The Ministry of Ungentlemanly Warfare* (New York: Quercus, 2016), 347.

585. Churchill, *Their Finest Hour*, 413-414.

586. Ibid., 413-414 and 467. See also Saunders, *The Green Beret*, 29-30.

587. Churchill, *Their Finest Hour*, 467; and Black, *Rangers in World War II*, 8.

588. "Role of the Special Service Brigade and Desirability of Reorganization," 2. NA, DEFE 2/1051, Special Service Brigade, role, re-organization, 1943-1944.

589. Kemp, *The SAS at War*, 10.

590. Lewis, *The Ministry of Ungentlemanly Warfare*, 347.

591. Field Marshal Sir William Slim, *Defeat into Victory* (London: Cassell and Company Ltd., 1956), 548. Slim concluded that "British special operations had become a cult, whose doctrinal proponents in mass persuasion evangelized their tactics as the path to strategic salvation, when in fact their modest achievements were bought at great cost to the rest of the army." Ibid., 546-549; and cited in Douglas Porch, *Counterinsurgency. Exposing the Myths of the New Way of War* (Cambridge: University of Cambridge Press, 2013), 143.

592. See Messenger, *The Commandos*, 408; Eric Morris, *Churchill's Private Armies* (London: Hutchinson, 1986), 172 & 243 and T.B.L. Churchill, "The Value of Commandos," 85-86.

593. Slim, *Defeat into Victory*, 446.

594. Quoted in James Kiras, *Special Operations and Strategy* (London: Routledge, 2006), 90.

595. "Precis of a Memorandum by Commander 1 Airborne Corps on the Value and Future Use of SAS Regiment," 3. NA, WO 193/705, "Future of SAS Regiment."

596. Ibid., 6. Admiral Hugh Sinclair, Chief of the British Security Intelligence Service (SIS) and the officer responsible for creating Section D, responsible for sabotage and subversion, lamented that the Foreign Office "seemed to fear Section D as much as the Nazis – going to great lengths to contain, delay and thwart its plans." He warned his subordinate commander for the section that "Everything you do is going to be disliked by a lot of people in Whitehall – some in this building. The more you succeed, the more they will dislike you and what you are trying to do." An internal SIS report in 1946 noted, "It was painfully evident that Commanders-in-Chief in the early years of the War without exception regarded the clandestine effort not only as a nuisance but also as a serious handicap." Malcolm Atkin, *Section D for Destruction. Forerunner of SOE* (Barnsley, UK: Pen & Sword, 2017), 3, 8 & 32.

597. "Precis of a Memorandum by Commander 1 Airborne Corps on the Value and

Future Use of SAS Regiment," 4. NA, WO 193/705, "Future of SAS Regiment." Famous journalist and writer Evelyn Waugh who joined the Royal Marines in December 1939 at the outbreak of the war in 1939. An unpopular officer, he eventually transferred to the Commandos and became a member of Layforce under Colonel Robert Laycock in November 1940 and served in the rearguard action in Crete. He transferred to the Royal Horse Guards on 10 June 1942. Waugh used his experience to capture the sentiment of the mainstream military to the Commandos in his book, *Officers and Gentlemen*. One of his Regular Force officer characters explained, "There's no place here for private armies. We've got to get these fellows, whoever they are, reorganized as a standard infantry brigade." Another noted, "As we see it sir, either the Commandos become a corps d'elite, in which case they seriously weaken the other arms of the service, or they become a sort of Foreign Legion of throw-outs, in which case we can hardly see them making very much contributions to the war effort." Evelyn Waugh, *Officers and Gentlemen* (London: Chapman and Hall, 1955, Kindle Edition 2019), loc 1821 & 1861.

598. "Precis of a Memorandum by Commander 1 Airborne Corps on the Value and Future Use of SAS Regiment," 4. NA, WO 193/705, "Future of SAS Regiment."

599. Park Yunnie, *Fighting with Popski's Private Army* (Barnsley, S. Yorkshire: Greenhill Book, Kindle Ed., 2011), 102. Harry Verlander, a SOE operative, noted, "As far as the generals were concerned, we were not real soldiers. They said, 'That's not how you fight a war, that's not cricket.' Well, I say we weren't bloody playing cricket." Rayment, *Tales from the Special Forces Club*, 284.

600. Thomas K. Adams, *US Special Operations Forces in Action. The Challenge of Unconventional Warfare* (London: Frank Cass, 1997), 40; and Troy J. Sacquety, *Burma. Jungle War against the Japanese* (Lawrence, Kansas: University of Kansas, 2013), 15.

601. Gray, *Explorations in Strategy,* 223.

602. Cited in Sacquety, *Burma. Jungle War...*, 21.

603. Kennedy Shaw, *Long Range Desert Group*, 165.

604. "The Long-Range Desert Group," *The Fighting Forces*, Vol 19, No. 3, August 1942, 147-148.

605. Maclean, *Eastern Approaches,* 191.

606. Stirling, "Memorandum on the Origins...", 54.

607. Lloyd Owen met Stirling in the desert November 20, 1941 after the terrible drop. Lloyd Owen suggested to Stirling that the LRDG could deliver his raiding teams to his objectives, by dropping them eight kilometres out and then picking them up after the raid. Stirling pondered the idea and then questioned, "can you guarantee to get us anywhere without being seen on the way?" Lloyd Owen replied, "yes, very nearly." Stirling then queried, "What about extra load of men and explosives which we'll want to carry? Will your vehicles take it?" Lloyd Owen later revealed, "David was still a bit sceptical Lloyd Owen, *The Desert My Dwelling Place*, 113-114.

608. Maclean, *Eastern Approaches*, 194.

609. Ibid., 193.

610. Stirling, "Memorandum on the Origins...", 55. The SAS used ¼ ton 4x4 Jeeps (Willys-Overland model M and Ford Model GPW).

611. "Brief History of 'L' Det. S.A.S. Brigade & 1ˢᵗ S.A.S. Regiment." NA, WO 218/173. Despite the SAS success, the LRDG CO lamented, "the 'Stirlings' would dash in and destroy enemy aircraft on their landing-grounds, or some other equally tempting target, and wake the whole area up. When they had gone – usually leaving the desert strewn with what they had jettisoned – the enemy's patrols would come out in strength in an energetic search for them, sometimes to find and flush out instead the beautifully sited and carefully concealed observation posts of the LRDG." Cited in Lloyd Owen, *Providence Their Guide*, xii.

612. Tony Geraghty, *Inside the SAS* (Toronto: Methuen, 1980), 11; and Philip Warner, *The Special Forces of World War II* (London: Granada, 1985), 21. The number of enemy aircraft destroyed varies. Most accounts place the number at 400, however, a War Office brief stated, "Throughout the whole North African campaign, no less than 350 confirmed enemy aircraft were totally destroyed together with petrol dumps, ammo & bomb dumps, torpedo dumps, stores wrecked & countless vehicles of all types including A.F.W.'s etc." "Brief History of 'L' Det. S.A.S. Brigade & 1ˢᵗ S.A.S. Regiment." NA, WO 218/173. The SAS in France accounted for six times their own numbers in enemy casualties. Kemp, *SAS at War*, 141.

613. Gordon Gaskill, "Toughest Job in the War," *The American Magazine*, July 1942, reproduced in Christopher Westhorp, ed., *The SAS Pocket Manual* (London: Conway, 2015), 65.

614. D.I. Harrison, *These Men are Dangerous. The Special Air Service at War* (London: Cassell & Company Ltd., 1957), v.

615. Gavin Mortimer. *Stirling's Men*, 8; and MacIntyre, *Rogue Heroes*, 12.

616. MacIntyre, *Rogue Heroes*, 166.

617. Gaskill, "Toughest Job in the War," 67.

618. Rayment, *Tales from the Special Forces Club*, 118.

619. Cited in Gordon, *The Other Desert War*, 115; and *Rommel Papers*, 292.

620. *The Rommel Papers*, 393.

621. Harrison, *These Men are Dangerous*, 15.

622. In April 1942, Stirling took on new recruits to bring them back up to strength. He accepted a unit of 60 Free French parachutists who were trained at Ringway. He also took on Captain Herbert Cecil Buck with approximately a dozen German-speaking ex-regular soldiers who had escaped Germany before the war for political or other reasons.

623. Lewis, *The Ministry of Ungentlemanly Warfare*, 343.

624. Letter Eisenhower to Brigadier McLeod, SAS Brigade, 8 October 1944, reproduced in Harrison, *These Men are Dangerous*, 234, Appendix B.

625. Morris, *Churchill's Private Armies*, 163; and Adrian Weale, *Secret Warfare* (London: Coronet Books, 1997), 63-64. For a detailed account of Operation Colossus see Bernd Horn, *The Wrecking Crew: Operation Colossus 10 February 1941* (Toronto: Dundurn, 2019).

626. James Dunning, *When Shall their Glory Fade?* (London: Frontline Books, 2011, 26; and Nicholas Rankin, *Ian Fleming's Commandos: The Story of 30 Assault Unit in WWII* (London: Faber & Faber, 2011), 120-121.

627. Dunning, *When Shall their Glory Fade?*, 32.

628. Warner, *The Special Forces of World War II*, 78; and Parker, *Commandos*, 42.

629. For a detailed account of the Bruneval Raid see Ken Ford, *The Bruneval Raid. Operation Biting 1942* (Oxford: Osprey, 2010).

630. Major-General John Frost, *A Drop Too Many* (Yorkshire: Leo Cooper, 2002), 58-59; *Combined Operations*, 65-70; Thompson, 293-295; A Wing Commander, "The Bruneval Raid," *Royal Air Force Journal*, Vol 2, No. 5, May 1944, 159-160; and "The Bruneval Raid," *War*, No. 32, 28 November 1942, 6-10.

631. *Combined Operations*, 71-100; Denis and Shelagh Whitaker, *Dieppe. Tragedy to Triumph* (Toronto: McGraw Hill Ryerson, 1992), 48; and Hughes-Hallett, "The Mounting of Raids," 583-584.

632. See "Amphibious Warfare Headquarters Small Scale Raids in Europe." PRO, DEFE 2/ 694. There were only 4 raids conducted in 1944.

633. Cited in Mead, *Commando General*, 130.

634. Lewis, *The Ministry of Ungentlemanly Warfare*, 226.

635. Reproduced in Parker, *Commandos*, 2-3.

636. These accomplishments do not even take into account the achievements of German and Italian Special Forces that similarly were used to seize vital infrastructure such as bridges, tunnels and airfields in the invasion of Poland, the Low Countries, Western Europe and Russia; the capture of the "impregnable" Fortress of Eben Emael, the rescue of Mussolini, which kept a pro-German regime in place in Northern Italy, the control of Hungary when it attempted to capitulate to the Allies, the massive confusion behind Allied lines during the "Battle of the Bulge" and the destruction of Allied warships. See James Lucas, *Kommando. German Special Forces of World War Two* (Toronto: Stoddart, 1985); Alex Swanston, *The Atlas of Special Operations of World War II* (New York: Skyhorse Publishing, 2014), 10; Otto Skorzeny, *Skorzeny's Special Missions. The Memoirs of "the Most Dangerous Man in Europe"* (London: Greenhill Books, 1997); and William H. McRaven, *Spec Ops. Case Studies in Special Operations Warfare: Theory and Practice* (New York: Presidio, 1996).

637. Elizabeth Keyes in her biography of her brother noted, "Such men as Stirling, Lewis, Mayne and Jellicoe dropped the name Commando, it is true, but bobbed up again in a variety of new disguises. Wherever they went they specialised in causing consternation and dismay, and nothing daunted their offensive spirit." Keyes, *Geoffrey Keyes*, 185.

638. Wynter, "The History of the Long Range Desert Group, 212; and Kennedy Shaw, *Long Range Desert Group,* 238.

639. Wynter, *The History of Commandos,* 240.

640. "Report on G(R) Operations in Cyrenaica, 11 December 1941. NA, DEFE 2/349.

641. Kennedy Shaw, *Long Range Desert Group,* 165.

642. *The Rommel Papers,* 292. He added, "They tried again and again to incite the Arabs against us – fortunately, with little success, for there is nothing so unpleasant as partisan warfare."

643. Memorandum to Prime Minister, "SOE Activities - Summary for the Prime Minister - Quarter: Mar-Jun 1942." NA, REM 3/409/5.

644. "F Section," no date, 7. NA, HS 7/121. File - SOE History 86.

645. Ibid., 13-14.

646. "SOE Activities in Greece," 8 April 1943. NA, HS 5/578, File - Greece No. 578.

647. Memorandum to Prime Minister, "SOE Activities - Summary for the Prime Minister - Quarter: Apr-Jun 1943." NA, REM 3/409/5; and "Situation in Yugoslavia," Appendix A. NA, HS5/151, File - SOE Balkans, No. 7.

648. "S-2 Report, No. 136, Enemy Situation," 27 April 1944. Library Archives Canada (LAC), RG 24, War Diary 1 CSS Bn, Vol 15,302.

649. M.R.D. Foot, "What use was SOE?" Royal United Services Institute (RUSI), February 2003, 80.

650. Memorandum to Prime Minister, "SOE Activities - Summary for the Prime Minister - Quarter: July-Sep 1943." NA, REM 3/409/5.

651. Ibid.

652. "F Section," no date, 11. NA, HS 7/121. File - SOE History 86.

653. Ibid., 12.

654. There were also numerous individual acts that have not captured that added to the cumulative effect. For instance, the "Salesman" network sunk a 900-ton minesweeper that was overhauled and repaired in Rouen. After its trials were complete and twelve million francs of ASDIC (a sonar system for locating submarines) equipment, twenty tons of ammunition, and supplies for three months had been loaded, the ship was sunk by saboteurs. Another network destroyed a foundry in Leroy and a number of factories in their area of operation; disabled locomotive turntables and engines, derailed troop trains, destroyed the telephone exchange, destroyed warehouses full of German equipment and supplies, loading cranes and a steel railway bridge. By the Allied seizure of France, SOE had fifty networks operating in France. Ian Dear, *Sabotage and Subversion. The SOE and OSS at War* (London: Cassell, 1996), 145 & 149.

655. Foot, "What use was SOE?" 80. FFI was the formal name given to French Resistance fighters by General Charles De Gaulle during the later stages of the war. The name change was intended to reflect the changing nature of French resistance

from an occupied country to one in the process of liberating itself. During the liberation of France, FFI units were more formally organized into light infantry units that served the Allied cause along with Free French Forces. By October 1944, FFI units were amalgamated into the French regular army.

656. "Chiefs of Staff Committee Value of SOE Operations," COS (45) 146, July 18, 1945. NA. The SOE network "Hugh" reported 500 rail cuts in its area between June 6th and July 6, 1944. Nonetheless, it must also be pointed out that it has been shown that a major cause of delay to enemy troop movements was due Allied strategic and tactical air forces.

657. Dear, *Sabotage and Subversion*, 152.

658. Ibid., 188. For detailed accounts of the Jedburgh teams see: Colin Beaven, *Operation Jedburgh. D-Day and America's First Shadow War* (London: Penguin Books, 2006); Roger Ford, *Steel From the Sky. The Jedburgh Raiders, France 1944* (London: Weidenfeld & Nicolson), 2004; Will Irwin, *The Jedburghs. The Secret History of the Allied Special Forces, France 1944* (New York: Public Affairs, 2005).

659. "F Section," no date, 74. NA, HS 7/121. File - SOE History 86.

660. "Chiefs of Staff Committee Value of SOE Operations," COS (45) 146, 18 July 1945. NA.

661. "F Section," no date, 15. NA, HS 7/121. File - SOE History 86.

662. "Chiefs of Staff Committee Value of SOE Operations," COS (45) 146, July 18, 1945. NA. The Committee also noted that SOE actions "successfully attacked targets which had been unsuccessfully attempted in the aerial interdiction programme."

663. Cited in E.H. Cookridge, *They Came From the Sky* (New York: Thomas Y. Crowell Company, 1965), 107.

664. Ibid., 108.

665. "Chiefs of Staff Committee Value of SOE Operations," COS (45) 146, 18 July 1945. NA.

666. Ibid.

667. Lt. Col. (ret) Will Irwin, *The Jedburghs. The Secret History of the Allied Special Forces, France 1944* (New York: Public Affairs, 2005), 238 & 338.

668. Ibid., 239.

669. Ibid., 237.

670. Dear, *Sabotage and Subversion*, 17.

671. "Chiefs of Staff Committee Value of SOE Operations," November 21, 1945, 2. NA, AIR 20/7958.

672. "Annex - The Value of SOE Operations in the Supreme Commander's Sphere," 1. NA, AIR 20/7958.

673. "Chiefs of Staff Committee Value of SOE Operations," November 21, 1945, 3. NA, AIR 20/7958.

674. Cited in Foot, "What use was SOE?" 83.

675. "Annex - The Value of SOE Operations in the Supreme Commander's

Sphere," 2-7. NA, AIR 20/7958.

676. Ibid., 7.

677. Dwight D. Eisenhower, *Crusade in Europe* (Garden City, NY: Doubleday, 1948), 296.

678. Quoted in Irwin, *The Jedburghs*, 241-241.

679. Cookridge, *They Came From the Sky*, vi.

680. Irwin, *The Jedburghs*, 237.

681. Ibid.

682. Kermit Roosevelt, *War Report of the OSS* (New York: Walker and Company, 1976), v.

683. "Precis of a Memorandum by Commander 1 Airborne Corps on the Value and Future Use of SAS Regiment," 1. NA, WO 193/705, "Future of SAS Regiment."

684. Ibid.

685. Emphasis of underlining is in the original report.

686. "Precis of a Memorandum by Commander 1 Airborne Corps on the Value and Future Use of SAS Regiment," 2. NA, WO 193/705, "Future of SAS Regiment."

687. Ibid. The report also observed, "The ordinary private soldier is not necessarily the type required for this form of warfare. He most successful parties have been led by men who have great individualism and who have experience in foreign countries."

688. Cited in Colin S. Gray, "Handfuls of Heroes on Desperate Ventures: When do Special Operations Succeed?" Parameters, Vol 29, No. 1, Spring 1999, https://press.armywarcollege.edu/parameters/vol29/iss1/4, accessed November 19, 2021.

APPENDIX 1

689. Complete citation is taken from: https://www.thegazette.co.uk/London/issue/35600/supplement/2699; "KEYES, Lt Col. Geoffrey Charles Tasker, VC," http://www.commandoveterans.org/KeyesVC; and http://www.vconline.org.uk/geoffrey-c-t-keyes-vc/4587307857 accessed October 24, 2020.

APPENDIX 2

690. "The German Watch on the Sahara," October 20, 1942. NA, HW 13/52.

691. "German Intentions South of Caucasus," September 21, 1942, 3-4. NA, HW 13/52.

692. German commanders responsible for the special Secret Service network in the Mediterranean theatre requested that "all lone desert-patrollers with special tasks" be subordinated to Operation Dora (Special Detachment D). This request was duly actioned.

693. Interestingly, Rommel initially limited the Brandenburgers in their ability to use enemy uniforms and equipment to conduct operations. He, like many

conventional military commanders, had a strong aversion to "the war in the dark." Rommel demanded confirmation the British LRDG and SAS were using such tactics. He received the necessary proof in September of 1942, when German troops had located six "lost" German officers in Tobruk. A German Afrika Korps officer, Lieutenant Zeller, while walking down a side street of Tobruk, had recognized a German officer, Lieutenant Großmann, as being a former schoolmate from Berlin. But, it then also quickly occurred to Zeller that his friend had emigrated to the UK in 1938 because of his Jewish heritage. A small scuffle ensued, and Großmann was apprehended, along with five other "German" soldiers, whose origins were questionable and quickly identified as being British. As a result of further interrogation efforts, Rommel was advised that these six "British" Germans were actually a diversion of Operation "Springtime" (all six British commando team members were actually Germans who had departed Germany before the war because of their Jewish backgrounds). Further German investigation efforts uncovered numerous time-bombs at key German harbor and supply facilities in Tobruk. These were all defused by the Germans. In the process, a number of additional British commando team members were also uncovered.

694. The LRDG in cooperation with Général de brigade Philippe Leclerc, the Commander of the Free French, launched a raid against the Italian garrison of Murzuk on December 21, 1941. The raid was repulsed and the Allied forces returned to Chad.

695. British archives provide a different account of the raids. An official report noted, "Three sabotage missions were attempted by the Arab speaking Germans or Arab allies. Two attempts on 30 December 1942 – groups landed by DFS 230 gliders to blow up railways. The first in the Kasserine area – 7 ORS from 3 Coy / Parachute Engineer Bn and a Tunisian Arab landed at 0500 hrs and took cover in hills. Slept most of the day. In the evening after they had eaten most of their rations, the Oberfeldwebel [staff sergeant] in charge decide that the opportunity had passed and their mission should be abandoned. The Arab sent to buy food caused suspicion by his Tunisian accent and the party was arrested. The other in the Meskiana area – officer / Sr NCO and 7 ORs. Captured after blowing up a minor bridge." "The German-Arab Lehrabteilung and other recent Abwehr Activity in N. Africa," February 22, 1943, 3. NA, HW 13/52.

696. Popski's Private Army refers to the smallest independent unit in the British Army in World War II. It was a special forces unit commanded by Major Vladimir Peniakoff, nicknamed "Popski" by the LRDG with whom he initially worked. His unit was officially designated No. 1 Long Range Demolition Squadron. It was operated in armed jeeps behind enemy lines during the Western Desert, North African and Italian campaigns. Prior to this appointment he commanded the Libyan Arab Force Commando, which was responsible for taking control of the friendly Arab tribes in the Jebel Akhdar and destroying enemy petrol dumps. See Lt. Col Vladimir Peniakoff, *Popski's Private Army* (Pickle Partners Publishing,

2016 Kindle Ed).

697. There exists much contradictory information on German covert operations which makes research quite difficult. Sources used in this appendix include: Adrian Denis Warren O'Sullivan, "German Covert Initiatives and British Intelligence in Persia (Iran), 1939-1945," unpublished PhD dissertation, University of South Africa, June 2012. https://www.academia.edu/24675794/German_Covert_Initiatives_and_British_Intelligence_in_Persia_Iran_1939_1945, accessed 11 December 2021; Mike Haught, *Unternnehmen Dora. Official Briefing.* https://UnternehmenDora-WWII.pdf/, accessed 11 December 2021; Avro Vercamer, "Brandenburg During North African Campaign 1941-1943." https:/Carte Sonderkommando Dora | I Misteri del Sahara | Sahara.it, accessed 11 December 2021; and "First Deployments of Brandenburgers in Africa," https://first deployments of the Brandenburgers in Africa (balsi.de), accessed 11 December 2021.

698. "German Intentions South of Caucasus," September 21, 1942, 1. NA, HW 13/52.

699. Ibid.

700. Ibid.

701. "The German-Arab Lehrabteilung and other recent Abwehr Activity in N. Africa," February 22, 1943, 1. NA, HW 13/52.

INDEX

Eden, Anthony, 22-23, 67, 89,179

Egypt, 2, 4-8, 10-11, 13-15, 17, 21-24, 25-28, 30-31, 36-39, 44, 51, 54, 56-57, 59-60, 63, 71, 73, 75, 94, 96, 99, 127-128, 162,166, 169-171, 204-206, 210n-212n, 215n, 218n, 223n

Eighth Army, 70-71, 77, 113, 123, 126-127, 129, 154, 162, 167-168,170-173176-177, 182, 222n, 231n, 233n

Eisenhower, General Dwight, 187, 200

El Alamein, 36, 192, 207, 243n

El Gatrun, 205-206

Ellis, Bombardier Ray, 53

England, 1-2, 4, 7, 9, 14, 29, 67, 81, 84, 92, 97, 125, 181, 189

Ethiopia, 4, 9, 219n, 224n

Europe, 2, 5, 7, 79, 82, 84, 93,95, 181, 183, 187, 190, 195, 199-200, 247n

Farrar-Hockley, Brigadier Anthony, 88

Feebery, Corporal Cyril, 154

Felmy, General der Flieger, 208

Fliegerkorps X, 46, 49, 58, 204

Folbot, 132

Fowler, Private Robert, 146

France, 6, 9, 44, 68, 80, 92, 94, 181, 188, 193-195, 197-200225n, 248n-249n

French Forces of the Interior (FFI), 195, 197, 200

Freyberg Major-General Bernard, 39

Frost, Major-General John, 189

Fuller, Major-General J.F.C., 7, 30, 209

Gambut, 126, 157, 167

Gariboldi, Marshal Italo, 25, 47-48, 50, 52, 55, 68

Gazala, 36, 110, 113, 116, 118, 122, 126, 155, 166, 168,175-176, 233n, 242n

Geisler, General Hans Ferdinand, 49

General Headquarters (GHQ), 11, 28, 32, 34, 37-38, 39-41, 94, 96, 98-100, 103, 108, 113-114, 123, 158, 182, 186, 231n, 239n

German and Italian Forces

    2nd SS Panzer Division, 195

    3rd Reconnaissance Battalion, 49

    5th Light Motorized Division, 49, 55, 60, 68

    5th Panzer Regiment , 52

    7th Panzer Division, 44

    15th Panzer Division, 60-61, 63, 164, 168-169, 173

    20th Motorized Corps, 68

    21st Corps, 68

    21st Panzer Division, 68, 164, 169,

142, 144, 146, 149, 155, 157-159, 202-203, 234n, 238n, 247n
Khartoum, 26, 211n
Koenen, First Lieutenant Friedrich von, 207
Kufra, 26, 37, 71

L Detachment, 108-110, 113-114, 128, 181, 183, 186
Langton, Lieutenant Tommy, 131, 155
Lassen, Captain Anders, 187
Lawrence, T.E., 29
Laycock, Major-General Robert, 93-97, 99-101, 124-127, 130, 134-135,
    147-150, 152, 154, 158-159, 229n, 233n, 235n, 237n-239n, 245n
Layforce, 94-96, 100, 106, 109, 114, 125, 128, 231n, 233n, 237n, 245n
    A Battalion (see also 7 Commando), 94-95
    B Battalion (see also 8 Commando), 94
    C Battalion (see also 11 Commando), 94-96, 128, 231n
    D Battalion (see also 50 and 52 ME Commando), 95
Lebanon, 125, 182
Leipzig, First Lieutenant Helmut von, 205-206
Leros, 182
Lewes Bomb, 111-112, 118
Lewes, Lieutenant Jock, 101-103, 110, 112, 120-123
Libya, 2, 4, 6-7, 10-15, 17, 21-23, 26, 28, 36-38, 40, 43-44, 56, 71, 75, 114,
    129-130, 167, 170, 174, 204-206, 213n, 215n-217n, 221n, 239n
Litani River, 96-97, 125
Lock, Corporal Charles, 133
Lofoten Raids, 187
Long Rane Desert Group (LRDG), 11, 17, 27, 31-32, 34, 38-42, 70-71,
    77-78, 95, 108, 110, 113-114, 119-123, 128-130, 136, 146, 153-154,
    171-172, 177, 181-184, 191-192, 205, 207, 215n-217n, 224n
Long Range Patrol Unit (LRPU), 11, 30-32, 37, 71

MacArthur, General Douglas, 181
Macedonia, 23
Maclean, Fitzroy, 41, 110, 122
Macpherson, Lieutenant Tommy 129, 234n-235n
Maddalena, 11, 76, 170
Malta, 5, 8, 69, 72, 221n, 223n
Matapan, Battle of, 23, 214n, 221n
Mayne, Paddy, 121-122, 186
Mclean, Fitzroy, 183
Mechili, 55-56, 61, 172, 176
Mediterranean Sea, 2, 6, 14, 23, 46, 58, 66, 69, 94, 98, 114, 174, 190, 197-
    198, 207n, 214n, 221n
Mellenthin, Major-General Friedrich von, 45, 50, 64, 165, 168, 171-172,

Oran, 243n
Owen, Major-General Lloyd, 27,31, 34, 40-41, 78, 112, 122, 167, 171-172, 217n, 245n

Palestine, 4-5, 73, 204, 211-212
Panzer Gruppe Afrika, 68, 126, 155-156, 174
Patton, General George, 200
Paulus, Lieutenant-General Friedrich, 58-59
Pedder, Lieutenant-Colonel Richard, 96, 125
Persian Gulf, 5, 73
Pitt, Barrie, 95, 177
Polish Brigade, 56, 212n
Port Said, 17
Prefettura, 137, 140, 156
Prendergast, Lieutenant-Colonel Guy Lenox 27, 70, 77, 113-114
Pryde, Lance-Corporal Bill, 152
Pryor, Lieutenant John, 132, 134, 149-151, 158, 238n

Qattara Depression, 6, 36

Rew, Major Henry, 20
Rhodesia, 5, 39
Ritchie, Major-General Neil, 105, 108, 123, 171
Ritter, Major Nicolaus, 204
Road Watch, 78, 181, 224n
Rome, 15, 47, 55, 175, 239n
Rommel, General Erwin, 2-3, 21-22, 24-25, 44-65, 67-68, 73-75,77, 101, 112, 125-126, 130, 135-136, 147, 155-159, 161-165,167, 169-177, 186, 192, 202, 205-207, 218n, 221n-222n, 223n-224n, 239n, 241n-243n, 251n
Roosevelt, President Franklin Delano, 82
Rowan-Robinson, Major-General H., 11, 67
Royal Air Force (RAF), 17-18, 20, 37-38, 56,67, 72, 78, 81, 90-91, 101-102, 113-115, 123, 165, 190
Royal Marine Commandos, 190
Royal Navy (RN), 18, 23, 60, 66, 80-81, 191, 221n

Sadler, Mike, 185
Sahara Desert, 6, 204, 207
Sand Sea, 26-28, 30, 36
Schilling, Ernst, 155
Schleusener, Colonel, 157-158
Scots Guards, 105, 109, 168
Senussi, 26, 126,135, 137, 148, 152, 154, 215n

262 | UNLEASH THE DOGS OF WAR

Toppe, Major-General Alfred, , 50, 63, 67, 218n
Torbay, His Majesty's Submarine, 126-128, 130-134, 136, 148, 154-155, 159, 238n
Tragino Aqueduct (see also Operation Colossus), 187
Trento Motorized Division, 46
Trieste Division, 68
Tripoli, 6-7, 20, 23-24, 44, 46-49, 53, 59, 67, 78, 182, 207, 223n, 243n
Tripolitania, 2, 7, 9, 15, 24, 44, 47, 76, 78, 176, 219n, 243n
Tunisia, 184, 186, 206-207, 221n
Turkey, 4, 44, 69

Vaagos Raid, 188
Varney, Private Frank, 152
Vichy French , 4, 68, 95-96, 125

War Cabinet, 4, 7, 13-14, 16, 23-24, 38, 53, 57, 76, 81, 99, 161, 210n-215n
War Office (WO), 26, 28, 37-38, 83, 89, 93-94, 96, 98, 125, 179-181, 183, 187, 201
Wavell, Lieutenant-General Sir Archibald, 5-12, 14-15, 17-24, 26, 28-30, 32, 37-39, 42-44, 46, 51-54, 56-58, 60-65, 67-69, 71, 79, 209n-210n, 214n, 222n
West, Warrant Officer Charles, 115
Western Desert Force (WDF), 7, 21, 23, 58, 213n, 220n
Willmot, Lieutenant-Commander M., 132-133
Wilson, Lieutenant-General Henry, 56, 198
Wingate, Major-General Orde, 180
World War I (WWI), 29, 44, 215n
Würtzburg radar, 188-190
Wynter Brigadier H.W., 191, 215n

Yasotay, 201
Yates, Sergeant, 118
Yugoslavia, 56, 183, 194

PRAXIS
TACTICUM

THE ART, SCIENCE AND
PRACTICE OF MILITARY TACTICS

COLONEL CHARLES S. OLIVIERO

PRAXIS TACTICUM
The Art, Science and Practice of Military Tactics

"Praxis Tacticum" will help young leaders learn and master modern combat team tactics...It's a fascinating series of intellectual and practical exercises which will help those leading fast moving and hard-hitting troops in combat, a unique blend of both the science and art of war.

Lieutenant-General (ret'd) The Hon. Andrew Leslie, PC, CMM, MSC, MSM, CD, MA, PhD

Chuck brings the discussion on tactics to the 'centre of gravity' between operational and theoretical perspectives. Praxis Tacticum is for professionals, people interested in tactics and the general reader of history.

Major-General (ret'd) David Fraser, CMM, MSC, MSM, CD

Pundits the world over have long predicted the end of conventional warfare but for the foreseeable future, it is here to stay. Counter insurgency, guerrilla warfare, terrorism, peace enforcement, policing duties. All of these forms, like conventional warfare, are as old as mankind. Modern militaries claim that they are professional bodies, responsible to teach, control and discipline their members. But at least one aspect of this claim is poorly executed: tactics are not taught to junior leaders, which is why this practical guide is essential reading for all junior leaders, officers and NCOs alike.

There is an old military adage that there is no teacher like the enemy. True; but the wise commander will prepare to meet that enemy and become the teacher and not the student.

STRATEGIA

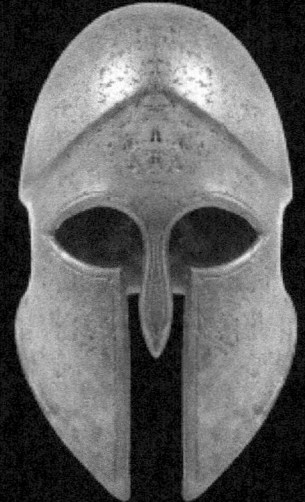

A PRIMER ON PHILOSOPHY THEORY AND
STRATEGY FOR MILITARY
PROFESSIONALS

COLONEL CHARLES S. OLIVIERO

STRATEGIA
A PRIMER ON THEORY AND STRATEGY FOR STUDENTS OF WAR

A must read for practitioners and students of the art of war.
LCol Professor David Kilcullen, PHD

These days we fight wars but we do not win them...Colonel Oliviero shows us the way to go at it. The colonel knows the deal.
Daniel P. Bolger, Lieutenant General, US Army, Retired

...a much needed guide to becoming [a] well-informed and deeply versed strategist...free from the curse of parroting bromides they learned at staff college as a substitute for serious and rigorous thought.
Dr. John Grenier, author of The First Way of War

War fascinates us, but what do we really know about its nature?

Strategia is the product of Colonel Oliviero's decades-long intellectual quest to address this fundamental query. His work offers both the serious student and the casual reader a foundation stone upon which to build a deeper understanding of military thought and theory, and thereby a richer appreciation of mankind's deadliest pursuit.

Strategia introduces many of the major contributors to military thought and theory as well as some of their most profound impacts on the conduct of war, from Sun-Tzu to the modern day, encompassing warfare on land, at sea and in the air, as well as in the cyber-realm.

While not an all-encompassing deep dive, Strategia is an essential primer and a point of departure. With this foundation stone in place, the student of war can proceed to follow Clausewitz's admonition to develop a "fine and penetrating mind."

DOUBLE‡DAGGER
— www.doubledagger.ca —

Double Dagger Books is Canada's newest military-focused publisher. Conflict and warfare have shaped human history since before we began to record it. The earliest stories that we know of, passed on as oral tradition, speak of war, and more importantly, the essential elements of the human condition that are revealed under its pressure. We are dedicated to publishing material that, while rooted in conflict, transcends the idea of "war" as merely a genre. Fiction, non- fiction, and stuff that defies categorization, we want to read it all.

Because if you want peace, study war.

ABOUT THE AUTHOR

Colonel (Retired) Bernd Horn, OMM, MSM, CD, PhD is a former infantry officer who has held key command and staff appointments in the Canadian Armed Forces, including Deputy Commander of Canadian Special Operations Forces Command (CANSOFCOM), Commanding Officer of 1st Battalion, The Royal Canadian Regiment and Officer Commanding 3 Commando, the Canadian Airborne Regiment. He is currently the CANSOFCOM Command Historian, an appointment he fills as a civilian. Dr. Horn is also an adjunct professor of history at the Royal Military College of Canada and a senior non-resident fellow at the Joint Special Operations University in Tampa. He has authored, co-authored, edited or co-edited more than 50 books and numerous monographs / chapters / articles on military history, Special Operations Forces, leadership and military affairs.

www.ingramcontent.com/pod-product-compliance
Lightning Source LLC
Chambersburg PA
CBHW061140120626
46546CB00005B/1863